Praise for Peter Winnington's biographies

On *Love in the Revolution,* Christoph Irmscher (Provost Professor
of English at Indiana University) wrote, 'I really like your com-
panionable voice – it draws you in and helps you make sense of
the individual stories without being judgmental or overbearing.
You wear your learning and the considerable research that has
gone into the book lightly. It's really a sort of backdoor approach
to early 20th century history that works marvelously well and
proves, once again, the old adage that the personal is the political.'

Reviewing *Vast Alchemies,* his life of Mervyn Peake, the TLS
declared, 'Peter Winnington is good not only as a biographer
but as a critic' too, and the *Birmingham Post* declared,
'Few books uncover the creative processes as well as this one . . .
Indispensable.'

Martin Ceadel, the Professor of Politics at the University of
Oxford, described *Walter Fuller: The Man Who Had Ideas*
as 'highly readable and carefully researched'.

Other biographies by the same author
Vast Alchemies (2000); reissued,
revised and expanded, with illustrations, as
Mervyn Peake's Vast Alchemies (2009).
Walter Fuller: The Man Who Had Ideas (2014)
Harriet Martineau, Miss J and Ellen McKee (2019)

Books edited
Mervyn Peake: the Man and His Art (2006)
Miracle Enough: Papers on the Works of Mervyn Peake (2013)
Kissing the Joy: The Autobiography of Rosalinde Fuller OBE (2015)
A History of Music in the British Isles
(two volumes) by Laurence Bristow-Smith (2017)

Author information
https://gpeterwinnington.com/

Love in the Revolution

True Stories of Russians and Anglo-Saxons

G. Peter Winnington

The Letterworth Press

Published in Switzerland by the Letterworth Press
https://TheLetterworthPress.org
Third edition

Whilst every care has been taken to ensure the accuracy
of the information in this book, the publisher cannot accept
responsibility for any mistakes that may have been included.
Persons wishing to supply corrections or additional information,
of any kind, are invited to contact the author.

ISBN 978-2-9701307-1-0

3579864

Contents

Illustrations

Preface

I WANT TO TELL YOU some (historically) true love stories, of one
kind and another, from around the time of the Bolshevik
Revolution of 1917. They are all memorable stories, worth repeating.
They all involve Russians and Anglo-Saxons; in most cases, the love
affair enabled a Russian woman to leave Soviet Russia, thereby
saving her from persecution, a slow death in the gulag, or simply
execution. (The name *gulag* for the Soviet slave labour camps
derived from the acronym of the Main Administration of
Corrective-Labour Camps and Colonies.) I have chosen these
stories, among the thousands from this time that might be told,
because I am interested in the people involved, both those who are,
or used to be, very well known, and the less familiar faces. Then,
long after choosing the stories, I started to find extraordinary connections between them.

Although most of these stories have been told before, often in
fragments and in different places, there is also a great deal in this
book that is quite new. Nowhere will you find so much about the
Krylenko family as in Chapter 2. Hugh Brogan's biography of
Arthur Ransome does not mention Lola Kinel, who is the heroine
of Chapter 4; as her autobiography ends with the mid-1930s, what
I tell of her subsequent years is quite new. No one has ever told the
story of Natasha Duddington before, nor has anyone placed Lev
Karsavin's great love affair in the context of his sister Tamara's life.
And so on.

Some of the leading Bolsheviks are also involved in these stories.
This turns them into real people rather than cardboard symbols of
oppression and torture. The kindest of all the big-name Bolsheviks

turns out to have been Maxim Litvinov; he figures in the first and
last of my stories. Of all Stalin's pre-Revolutionary comrades and
post-Revolutionary colleagues, he was the only one to escape the
purges of the 1930s. That he was married to an English woman cannot be taken as the sole cause of his preservation, for he was not
unique in this: Yakov Peters – Bruce Lockhart's respectful jailor in
1918 – had also married an English woman, and he was executed in
the late 1930s just like all the other old Bolsheviks.

As I said, my interest is in the people rather than the politics of
this time. I want to know how the couples met and fell in love and
how they managed their bi-cultural partnership. The women all
became exiles, and enriched the culture of their adoptive country at
the very moment when the cultural values of Tsarist Russia were
being almost totally extinguished by Marxist materialism. I find it
striking how much literature played a part in their stories. It was
often through literature, mainly novels, that they learned of their
partners' culture. My second and last stories are about women who
were active in translating books, making the riches of one culture
available to readers in another. And then, these were educated
people and several of them wrote their own account of this time.

That some of these stories have been recorded in writing by the
persons involved accounts for differences in the way I tell them.
With the benefit of a first-hand narrative, I can offer – with luck –
more insight into their experience. On the other hand, I have
invented nothing. Whenever possible, I have drawn on multiple
sources, combining several versions into the one that seems to me
to be the closest to the truth, insofar as we can know it.

The great disadvantage of this approach is that, unlike invented
stories, which come with a plot, a clear beginning, a middle and an
end, real life stories are plotless and have no clear boundaries at all.
There's nothing one can do about this: that's life.

To appreciate these stories, we need to know the context. So my
first chapter sets the scene, with relevant episodes from the time of
the Revolution. (Since there were three revolutions in Russia at the

beginning of the twentieth century – in 1905, in March 1917, and in November 1917 – I have reserved the capitalized form for the last of them, and lower cased, usually with a qualifying date, the previous ones.) I speak of 'episodes' in the Revolution because it requires a massive tome, such as Richard Pipes produced, to detail the Revolution and its aftermath. Pipes ended his narrative with the assassination of the Tsar and his family. For the purposes of my stories, I have included the civil wars up to 1923, when the Union of Soviet Socialist Republics was formed.

A word about terminology: throughout this book, I have called the Party that seized power in the Revolution 'the Bolsheviks', although I am aware that on 6 March 1918 Lenin decreed that they were henceforth to be known as the Communist Party. The reason for my choice is quite simple: the change of name was a highly successful attempt at whitewashing. Communism was an admirable ideal, dissociated in the eyes of the world from the violence of the Bolsheviks and the state capitalism that they practised. The name stuck; the violence continued, and the capitalism that it masked continued unabated.

The conventions for transliterating Cyrillic to English have evolved steadily over the years. Maxim Litvinov, for instance, was still called Maksim Litvinoff in the 1940s. I have used the forms most commonly found today.

This choice causes some oddities: for Russian speakers, the name of Princess Marie Gagarin should be written *Gagarina*, but her printed memoir is signed *Gagarin*, and I have left it that way. Similarly, Tatiana Tchernavina signed herself *Tchernavin* in English.

The Russian pronunciation of the first name *Elena* causes some sources to transcribe it *Yelena*, and I have followed them. Max Eastman always referred to his wife as *Eliena*; I have retained his spelling for her name.

Even English (or in this case, Scottish) names can be problematic: Robert Bruce Lockhart, whose famous love affair features in Chapter 6, is frequently referred to as 'Lockhart', even though his surname was actually 'Bruce Lockhart' (unhyphenated). When convenient, I have called him just 'Lockhart' too.

At the time of the Bolshevik Revolution, the Latvians were called *Letts* and their soldiers *Lettish* troops. I have used *Latvian* without regard for the old names. Place names have also changed a good deal since the beginning of the twentieth century. Saint Petersburg was renamed *Petrograd* in 1914 (to avoid the Germanic *-burg* suffix), and then it became *Leningrad* after Lenin's death in 1924. It reverted to *Saint Petersburg* in 1991. For the sake of simplicity, I have used that name throughout (abbreviating the *Saint* to *St*), irrespective of the date. All other proper names are in the form most commonly found today.

Tsarist Russia used the Julian calendar, which was thirteen days behind the Gregorian calendar used in western Europe. The Bolsheviks brought their country into line by dropping the first thirteen days of February in 1918. (Russia still celebrates major feasts like Christmas according to the Julian Calendar.) I have used New Style dates throughout, while continuing to call the 'October' Revolution by its traditional name, even though it took place in November by the New Style calendar.

I have listed my sources at the end of each chapter – immediately before the reference notes – which strikes me as most convenient for the reader. And I name only the sources I refer to or quote from. A list of all the books, articles and websites I consulted would have taken far too many pages. All the books listed were published in London unless otherwise indicated.

I have done my best to find suitable photographs of these people. Good ones, of a size and quality to print in a book, are hard to find. So there are relatively few illustrations in this book, except in the chapter about Tamara Karsavina, of whom a great many pictures were made.

Here then are my stories, written for your pleasure and mine, each reflecting different expressions of love. They are dedicated to the faceless multitude of those who did not survive the Bolsheviks.

Acknowledgments

A number of kind people have helped me with this book. I am particularly grateful to Sebastian Garrett; he not only provided information about his grandmother, Natasha Duddington, but also offered most useful corrections to all the chapters. His cousin Katya Aron supplied the pictures of Natasha for me, and his son Tim scanned letters by Gordon Craig in his possession, which he kindly permitted me to quote from. Philippa Parker generously shared information she had found on Jack Duddington's divorce case. John Duddington, Katya Aron, and Barbara Thacker also provided information, as did Dr Anil Gomes, Fellow and Tutor in Philosophy at Trinity College, Oxford, and Associate Professor at the University of Oxford.

Finding anything about Ursula Cox proved disproportionately time-consuming compared to the tiny role she plays in the book. Of those who offered help, Jane Norwich, with her skill in genealogical searches, was the most successful; and Sarah Watling put me in touch with a descendant of Ursula's Olivier cousins. Jason Nargis, Special Collections Librarian at the University Libraries of Northwestern University, copied several of Ursula's letters for me.

Helen Rappaport told me of Michael Welch's interest in Anglo-Russian marriages, and he was most generous with his time. He put me in contact with Yuri Totrov, who very kindly shared with me some documents relating to William Hicks.

Andrew Foster, the great authority on Tamara Karsavina's life and career, generously allowed me to read his transcriptions of the letters that she and Benjie Bruce wrote to Valerian Svetlov during her separation from her husband. While they helped me to understand Tamara, I opted not to make any direct quotations from them.

Christoph Irmscher, Provost Professor of English at Indiana University, and author of a biography of Max Eastman, kindly allowed me to quote Eliena Eastman's 'Will' from his website.

Lesley Chamberlain, author of *The Philosophy Steamer: Lenin and the Exile of the Intelligentsia*, answered questions about her book. Ekaterina Shatalova patiently fielded my questions about Russian language and culture, and helped with my research by directing me to Russian websites that I would not have found for myself.

Laurence Bristow-Smith obligingly read a draft of the book and sent me his comments.

Finally, though, the mistakes and defects you may find are mine alone.

I am grateful to Oliver Garnett for permission to quote from the books by David Garnett and Richard Garnett.

ꝛ

The third edition incorporates information that arrived only after the book had been published, in particular the portraits of Natasha and Jack Duddington, and the group photograph with Ursula Cox, Lenochka Goncharova and Elena Ertel (aka Lola). I have taken this opportunity to make some minor revisions.

Our weak intelligentsia souls are simply incapable of con-
ceiving abominations and horrors on such a Biblical scale
and can only fall into a numbed and unconscious state.
— Semyon Frank on the Russian Revolution[*]

[*] Quoted by Chamberlain in *The Philosophy Steamer* (p.45) from Philip Boobbyer, *S. L. Frank: The Life and Work of a Russian Philosopher*, p.116.

1 The Revolution

IN TIMES OF WAR and great social upheaval, people desperately feel the need for love (if only the physical comfort of love-making), and the context of violence tends to make their love affairs more truly heartfelt. Tania Alexander (whose mother is the subject of Chapter 6) refers to 'the feeling that war and revolution inevitably create: that you should get out of life what you can today, because there may be no tomorrow.'[1] *Carpe diem.* The Russian Revolution was the greatest social upheaval of the twentieth century – its death toll defies belief – and the love stories I shall be telling you here were proportionally powerful.

Let me attempt to put the scale of the loss of human life during the Revolution and its protracted aftermath into perspective. When the *Titanic* collided with an iceberg and sank on its maiden voyage in April 1912, 1,517 passengers and crew were drowned, and Britain reeled in horror. When it declared war on Germany in August 1914 and before anyone had died on the battlefield, Walter Fuller (later to edit the BBC's *Radio Times*) recorded, 'I have not felt such depression of spirits since the *Titanic* went down. Now a thousand *Titanics* seem to be sinking – and I feel myself drowning.'[2] He was chillingly clear sighted: the overall death toll of the First World War amounted to 8,500,000 lives. That's like three-and-a-half *Titanics* every day. The Russian Empire lost 1,700,000 men in that conflict. It was not yet over when the Bolsheviks seized power; the civil wars that ensued between 1918 and 1923 caused the deaths of another 7 to 12 million people, up to seven times as many as in the War.

The killing did not end there. Over the next thirty years, Soviet Russia and the Soviet Union that followed it wiped out another

50,000,000 lives, through civil war, class cleansing, deliberate starvation, torture (including overwork in the gulag), and 'plain' execution, *not* including those killed in the Second World War.[3] That's
like a line of *Titanics* 10,000 kilometres long. And the victims
were invariably ordinary citizens. It stands beside the Great Leap
Forward and the Cultural Revolution in China as one of the largest
mass exterminations in recorded history.

When the Romanov imperial ship of state collided with the
Bolshevik iceberg in 1917, all its passengers were left desperately
swimming for their lives. Only survivors can tell their tales; these
are the stories of a few of those who, through love, found a life-ring
to cling to.

To understand the violence of the Revolution and its lengthy aftermath, we need to know something of the national character of the
Russians. The way they look at their own history is revealing – just
as it is with any other country. Here's what the ballerina Lydia
Kyasht – the least violent of young women – wrote in her autobiography:

> When Ivan the Great abolished the system of Independent
> Principalities and became the first Tsar in 1462, he adopted the
> policy of suppression that was to be such a feature of future
> Imperial Rulers. He imprisoned and beheaded his unfortunate
> nobles upon the most paltry excuses.... His grandson, Ivan the
> Terrible ... when still only a boy of thirteen, asserted his authority
> by accusing some of the nobles of robbing the Treasury, and
> ordered the leader, Prince Shuiski, to be torn to pieces by a pack of
> hounds as a warning to his followers....
>
> Tsar Alexander II added a fresh terror ... by creating a force of
> mounted policemen... to patrol the country districts and to arrest
> summarily anyone who aroused their suspicions.[4]

She calmly accepts the use of gratuitous cruelty and random arrest
to terrorize a people into submission.

By contrast, when we (the British) recall violent episodes in our national history, we do so with a sense of shame, for we believe that there are better ways of resolving political conflict. 'The Princes in the Tower', the Civil Wars of the seventeenth century, and the Peterloo Massacre in 1819, for instance, are felt to be stains on our 'naturally' tolerant and peace-loving character. We absorb these attitudes, along with clichés like 'the Dunkirk spirit', quite unconsciously as we grow up; they are reinforced by the teaching of national history in schools. Thus they become part of our personal identity, of who we feel ourselves to be. Because they are largely unconscious, they are not easily changed; it usually takes more than one generation for emigrés to fully embrace a new nationality.

In this context, it is striking to notice that the first time English 'bobbies' were seen shooting in public was during the Siege of Sidney Street, in London, in January 1911. They were responding to gunfire from so-called anarchists or nihilists who had been surprised committing a burglary and taken refuge in a nearby house. They were actually Russian communists, trying to rob a jeweller's to fund their Party. Here the clash of cultures began in bloodshed.

Russians continue to grow up inculcated with the belief that only a really strong man like Ivan the Great can rule their country. Just look at how often President Putin has himself photographed doing manly things (often shirtless to show off his physique). He does this not just out of vanity, but in a deliberate attempt to match his people's image of the successful ruler. Along with this image comes the acceptance of violence: taking their lesson from their own history, Russians believe that only violence can make their unruly peoples toe the line.

In 1917, it was only twelve years since the Tsar had used the Army and his secret police (the dreaded *Okhrana*, the successors of Tsar Alexander II's mounted police) to violently suppress a revolution. For all their admirable ideals of social equality, the Bolsheviks shared these beliefs about how to rule (and they wanted revenge for years of violent repression), so when they got hold of the whip handle, they acted in accordance with them. Their violence sent

Russia back to a level of uncivilization not seen in Europe since the Middle Ages.

ف

Romanov Russia of the early twentieth-century was barely known in Western Europe. The ballerina Tamara Karsavina (who is the subject of Chapter 7) offered an explanation for this in her autobiography:

> To the average occidental mind, the whole of our vast country still remained a land of barbarians. I often wondered if our history had ever been a subject of school study abroad, as that of other countries had been for us. An exception was China: of China we knew little, but probably hardly less than Europe knew of us. Russia, crude and refined, primitive and sophisticated, the country of great learning and appalling ignorance; Russia of immense scale – no wonder that Europe would not attempt to understand.[5]

In Britain, from where Russia seemed forbiddingly dark, remote, and vast, it was perceived as a threat to some of the borders of the Empire. So it was with some surprise that, in the last years of the nineteenth century, people discovered that although Russia had known no Renaissance or Reformation, it nonetheless boasted writers to place beside the giants of western Europe. Hardly had they finished reading the first translations of Dostoevsky, Tolstoy, and Chekhov than they discovered Russian ballet in 1910; its dancers swept aside the popular image of a barbarian civilization. Britain began a brief love affair with Russian culture, and the feeling was reciprocated.

At the end of the nineteenth century and up to 1917, many educated Russians were Anglophile; some even affected an English accent when speaking their native language and wore English clothes and shoes (or rather boots). On the eve of the First World War, Arthur Ransome noticed how 'the jaunty cock of Admiral Beatty's hat' was being copied by young Russian naval officers.[6] As Denis Garstin put it in *Friendly Russia*, referring to this time,

> Ask an Englishman if he is a Russian, and you insult him. Ask a

Russian if he is English, and you lift him to the seventh heaven of complacency. He would not be English au fond, but he has achieved the English appearance, and he is, in his own way of saying it, 'quite orright'.[7]

These positive feelings were reinforced by the fact that Tsar Nicholas II had married one of Queen Victoria's granddaughters; moreover, during the First World War, Britain and Russia were allied against the Central Powers. At the outbreak of the March revolution in 1917, Ransome recorded how a mounted Cossack had flourished his revolver in his face and demanded, 'For the people or against the people?'

'I am English,' Ransome replied.

'Long live England!' returned the Cossack and galloped off.[8]

It was the barbarity of the Bolsheviks that blew this romance to smithereens.

༄

The overthrow of the harshly repressive Romanov dynasty was welcomed by democrats and socialists around the world. The United States was the first country to recognize the Bolshevik Revolution; after all, a hundred years before, the Americans had refused to be subjected to a monarch and fought to place the control of their country in the hands of its people. In addition, the Socialist Party of America was a significant political force in 1917, with two Representatives, dozens of state legislators, more than a hundred mayors, and countless lesser officials. It fielded a candidate at every Presidential election up to 1939. The Bolsheviks gave socialism a bad name and caused its decline in the US.

To ensure a complete takeover of the country by the proletariat (called 'the workers' by Marxists, as though the other classes did not work), the Bolsheviks acted in accordance with Marx's 'class warfare'. They assumed that the rest of the population – aristocrats, landowners, bourgeois, employers, professional people, scientists and teachers, writers, painters, and composers: in short, everyone with the potential to earn more money than the proletariat – were de facto against them, and had to be eliminated, even before they voiced an opinion. This pre-emptive extermination continued for the next thirty-five years; in the early 1950s, for instance, Stalin had large numbers of doctors arrested; most them were saved by his death, which also halted his plan to deport all Russia's Jews to Siberia.

The great break-up of Russian society began with the abdication of the Tsar, on 15 March 1917. The Romanovs had been ruling over many other nationalities, from the Poles in the west to the peoples of Siberia and the Kamchatka Peninsula beyond it in the far east, and from Norway to the peoples living between the Black Sea and the Caspian. Many of them had long resented Russian domination and they took this opportunity to proclaim their independence. The Bolsheviks' chief Commissar for Nationalities, Joseph Stalin, spent the best part of the next five years organizing branches of the Bolshevik party in each of the newly independent republics, help-ing them to revolt against their new national governments. This is the main reason why he was barely heard of before he brought them together again to form the Union of Soviet Socialist Republics (the USSR) on 30 December 1922. Thus he restored not just Russia's old Imperial borders, but also its national pride along with access to much greater supplies of food, natural resources (including oil), and manufacturing facilities (antiquated and badly damaged though they were by civil war).

The abdication of the Tsar caused all the mechanisms of Imperial government to be closed down. Suddenly, there was no Depart-ment of Police, no corps of Gendarmes, no secret police, no auth-ority but the Army to suppress demonstrations in the streets – and many soldiers joined the demonstrators. The administrative struc-ture that the Bolsheviks introduced was based on freely elected councils, or *soviets*. (Although the term had already been used in the 1905 revolution, in 1917 it was still new to almost everyone out-side Russia.) In the *soviets*, the Russian people were to be repre-sented in a notional pyramid, all the way from the Supreme Soviet down to the level of the street and apartment blocks occupied by several families; every workshop and factory was to have its *soviet*. But the Bolsheviks introduced this idea in a power vacuum. Like the surrounding republics, Russian society had already collapsed into total disorder, aided by the revolutionaries' practice of liberating the inmates of all the prisons; they hastened to raid the police stations, the Palace of Justice, and the court buildings and destroy their records. So when in October 1917 Lenin announced that the Bolsheviks had taken over, there was no authority left to contradict him – least of all the Army.

The original idea was that the principle of *soviets* should apply in the Army as well – but this is where the theory broke down. Countless soldiers had joined the demonstrators in the streets of St Petersburg during the March revolution. Realizing that they would be heavily punished when they returned to their barracks, Lenin issued 'Soviet Order No 1' on 14 March in the name of the St Petersburg Soviet of Workers' and Soldiers' Deputies, intending it to apply only to soldiers who were not on duty. For lack of clarity, however, it was interpreted to apply generally, which effectively destroyed the Imperial Army. First, the Order required soldiers and sailors to obey their officers and the Provisional Government *only* if their orders did not contradict the decrees of the St Petersburg Soviet. As there were as yet no decrees to consult, the soldiers chose to disobey. Secondly, it called upon each unit to elect a *soviet* to run the unit and to elect representatives to send to the next higher *soviet*. Thirdly, all arms were to be handed over to these *soviets* 'and shall by no means be issued to the officers, not even at their insistence.' This was intended to ensure that officers did not attempt to use their weapons against their own men, or to suppress the Bolshevik revolution, but in effect it armed the soldiers who wished to support the revolution. Furthermore, the Order allowed soldiers to dispense with standing to attention and saluting when off duty; on the other hand, strict military discipline was to be maintained while on duty. Soldiers were no longer obliged to address their officers as 'Your Excellency' but rather as 'Sir' (*Gospodin*, in Russian). And finally, soldiers of all ranks were to be addressed with the respectful 'you', *vy*, rather than the condescending *ty* form, which officers had previously used for their men, just as they would for children and menial servants. These rules undermined military discipline: once soldiers were linguistically on an equal footing with their officers, which made them feel like ordinary citizens, they saw no good reason why things should be different when they were on duty.

Most importantly, Order No 1 did *not* tell soldiers to elect their officers, for Lenin feared that Army officers could too easily be manipulated in favour of a counter-revolution. However, the release of the Order coincided with a joint proclamation issued by the Russian Socialist Democratic Labour Party and the St Petersburg Committee of Socialist Revolutionaries (the SRs) calling on 'Comrade Soldiers' to elect their own platoon, company and regimental commanders. This gave rise to the popular belief that Order No 1 called for soldiers to elect everyone over them in the Army. Discipline rapidly evaporated and conscripts began returning home from the front (sometimes shooting their officers before they left). Although the election of *soviets* did take place in the new Red Army formed by Trotsky, the higher up the pyramid, the greater was the number of non-elected members. The man at the top appointed his staff in decisions that were not democratically arrived at. By 1924, when Lenin died, Stalin had used this means to place his henchmen in all the top *soviets*, and soon this was the way the whole country was run: decisions were taken by trusted Party members, and the *soviets* became just echo chambers. The Marxist dream of a dictatorship of the proletariat had become a dictatorship *tout court*.

For Marxists, it was a basic tenet that communism was what the people really wanted (and that copycat revolutions would shortly break out across Europe), so it was a shock for them to discover that a large proportion of the proletariat did *not* want them in power. Their first response to this was to abolish freedom of speech by silencing the press, except for their own organ, *Pravda* – its title, *Truth*, being a prize example of their doublespeak. Russians love to discuss politics and current affairs, and their press was full of their opinions. By closing down practically every newspaper but their own, and forbidding street meetings, the Bolsheviks reduced Russia's citizens to talking at home, or in small clubs. But soon even the walls had ears, for in December 1917 the Bolsheviks replaced the *Okhrana* with the *Cheka*, an acronym for the All-Russian Extraordinary Commission, masterminded by the ruthless Felix Dzerzhinsky. The Cheka adopted and exaggerated all the cruel practices of the Okhrana, and made denunciation a virtue. Without an independent press to supply correct information, Bolshevik 'truth' became true in people's minds, for no one knew otherwise. A hundred years later, Putin is doing much the same: by setting up a Russian intranet, he is making it possible to isolate his people from the world wide web – and other opinions.

Brought up in an empire founded on cruelty and violence, the Bolsheviks perpetuated this way of life. Their violence was all the greater for the fact that they were a tiny minority, opposed by vast numbers of people all the way across the political spectrum and throughout Imperial Russia. The complete breakdown of the Russian economy reinforced this rejection: having destroyed Russia's free market, the Bolsheviks floundered when it came to controlling the economy. (Admittedly, the West is not much better at it today, with the result that the world economy lurches from boom to bust with monotonous regularity.) After nationalizing practically everything, and eliminating the class that had owned and run all the firms and businesses, they promoted poorly educated men to replace them, leaving the country with neither the know-how nor the manpower to make the economy work. (At the outbreak of the First World War, six out of ten Russians over the age of nine were illiterate; when the Cheka was created, few of the rank and file could read.) When machines broke down through

lack of maintenance, or when not enough food or goods were produced, the Bolshevik philosophy required that *someone* be blamed.
So *someone* (and a few others for good measure) was arrested and
tortured until they confessed to *wrecking*,* and either shot or sent
to the gulag. This was the State sabotaging itself, and Aleksandr
Solzhenitsyn bitterly denounced it in his *Gulag Archipelago*. In
1930–31, the scientist Vladimir Tchernavin, who specialized in the
study of fish, was serving his time in the gulag by advising the fishing industry; he tells us that

> out of the scientists and highly qualified specialists whom I knew
> personally or of whose fate I have been definitely informed,
> twenty-six were shot and thirty-four deported to concentration
> camps. Many more whom I did not know were either killed or
> deported at this same time.... This wholesale destruction of
> specialists could not fail to have fatal results for the fishing busi-
> ness.... For the second time the Bolsheviks were leading a rich and
> prosperous country into terrible poverty and dreadful famine.'[9]

This example could be multiplied ten thousand times.

꙰

After February 1917, the citizens who could read the writing on the
wall began to flee, creating Russian diaspora throughout the world.
Few returned; of those that did, few were allowed to survive long,
for they had seen what life was like elsewhere, and could disillusion
others at home. The Soviet Union indoctrinated its citizens with
the belief that Russia was the best place, and that other countries
were deserts of inequality and poverty for the proletariat. This was
why, in 1946–47, more than a million of the Russian prisoners taken
during the war – and refugees who had found themselves on the

* Tchernavin comments bitterly: '"Wrecking" did indeed exist, but it was
wrecking of unbelievable proportions, preplanned by the organization
headed by Stalin, the Political Bureau and the GPU' [Tchernavin, p.88].

wrong side of a battle front – were executed, or consigned to the gulag, as soon as they arrived home. For the same reason, Soviet girls who had gone out with foreign men during the war were rounded up as 'Socially Dangerous Elements' and sentenced under Article 7-35 (SOE) to be 're-educated'.[10] Few survived the ordeal.

Russia already had problems with the food chain before 1917; in fact, the March and October revolutions were fuelled by the shortage of bread. The Bolsheviks blamed this on the peasants, believing that they were withholding produce – particularly grain – from the market. To feed the towns, they sent raiding parties into the countryside to requisition foodstuff. The money they offered in compensation was worthless, and peasants who complained or resisted were shot. Worse, the raiding parties sometimes carried away grain that the peasants had set aside for their own consumption and for sowing the following year. Inevitably, the area of land under cultivation began to shrink and produce less; this led to more raids, more summary executions, and of course fewer peasants producing even less. Without sufficient food in the towns, large numbers of people fled into the countryside, where they began to starve alongside the peasants. Hence the terrible famines of 1921 and 1922. No wonder the peasants rose to join in the civil war against the Bolsheviks. They lost and the Bolsheviks persevered in their obtuseness. Seventy years after the Revolution, most of the citizens of the USSR were poorer than people in many Third World countries.

The traditional image of the October Revolution is of street fighting in St Petersburg. Nothing could be more misleading. A truer picture would be a vast panorama of running battles, skirmishes, and guerilla warfare all the way from the borders of Poland to Vladivostok, for five years, accompanied by immense loss of life, for all the forces involved committed atrocities. The Bolsheviks' hastily assembled Red Army, manned largely by soldiers from the disbanded Imperial Army, was faced by numerous smaller armies, known collectively as the White Army. Fighting against them both were so-called Green Armies, representing the local interests of both socialists and non-ideological groups. The conflict was prolonged and exacerbated by the support given to the Whites by the Allies, who sent in not only troops with their arms and ammunition but also heavier weapons, including tanks. In the East, the Japanese joined in too. Amazingly, the Red Army prevailed in the end, and the war ended in 1923 with the newly formed USSR under Bolshevik control, although it took them until 1934 to suppress pockets of armed resistance in Central Asia.

There was also violent resistance in St Petersburg itself. At the 5th All-Russia Congress of Soviets of 4 July 1918, delegates of the Left Socialist Revolutionary Party (the Left SRs for short), were outnumbered two to one by the Bolsheviks (745 to 352). They were opposed to the Brest-Litovsk peace treaty that the Bolsheviks had signed with the Central Powers, ending the war on the Eastern Front. They decided to sabotage it by assassinating the German ambassador, Count Mirbach, in his Embassy on 6 July. (Embassies are considered extra-territorial, so this was a doubly offensive act, tantamount – in diplomatic terms – to a killing on German soil.) It was a ham-fisted job, but Count Mirbach died. Although the assassins got away, they left behind the note they had presented at the door of the Embassy. It bore the signature of the head of the Cheka, Felix Dzerzhinsky. He stormed round to the headquarters of the Left SRs, intending to arrest one of the assassins who taken refuge there, and was himself taken hostage. The Left SRs occupied the Cheka headquarters in Moscow, seized the telephone exchange and telegraph office, and issued manifestos, bulletins, and telegrams declaring that they had taken power and that their action had been welcomed by the whole people. It was a miniature copy of the Bolshevik Revolution of the year before.

Lenin ordered the Latvian commander Jukums Vācietis to suppress it. By two o'clock the following day, the Left SRs' headquarters had been taken by Latvian riflemen (with some light artillery). The Left SRs took flight and were never again a significant political force. (The Constitutional crisis of 1993, exactly seventy-five years later, which ended with tanks shelling the Russian White House, seems almost like a re-run of this episode, except that the official death toll in 1993, with a mere 187 people killed and 437 wounded, pales in comparison with the 1918 figures: the Cheka admitted to shooting 937 Left SRs in July and August. The figures for the re-taking of the Left SRs' HQ are not known.) Dzerzhinsky resigned and his deputy Yakov Peters took over. In August the Cheka was authorized to shoot Left SRs without trial, along with all those guilty of counter-revolutionary agitation, such as inciting Red Army soldiers to disobey, aiding the Whites, engaging in espionage or sabotage, committing theft, banditry or corruption. It began by purging its own ranks with the result that, by October, Peters could boast that the 'best Party forces' were to be found in the Cheka. While only 4–6% of all Red Army soldiers and 5–6% of all government employees were Communists, 65% of all Chekists were card-carrying Communists. On 22 August, Dzerzhinsky was re-instated; Peters, who had lived in England, was not ruthless enough.

The revolt of the Left SRs, followed by the attempt on Lenin's life at the end of August, inspired the Bolsheviks to launch the Red Terror in September 1918. In the style of Tsar Alexander II, they aimed to terrorize the population into submission by mass executions, often of people who had been rounded up at random. Although the Red Terror was officially of short duration, the practice of intimidation continues to this day: in 2019, a young Moscow couple who took their child with them to a peaceful demonstration in favour of free elections was threatened with the loss of their parental rights. Extrajudicial executions continue, generally by means that can pass as fatal accidents, or easily escape detection; in 2018, an attempt was made to assassinate Sergei Skripal and his daughter in England, using a lethal nerve agent, Novichok.

Martin Latsis, who had been taken hostage alongside Felix Dzerzhinsky by the Left SRs, instructed his colleagues in the Cheka's new approach:

> Do not ask for incriminating evidence to prove that the prisoner
> opposed the Soviets either by arms or by words. Your first duty is
> to ask him to what class he belongs, what were his origins, educa-
> tion, and occupation. These questions should decide the fate of the
> prisoner. This is the meaning and essence of Red Terror.[11]

It was a pivotal moment: from now on, it was the Cheka that controlled the citizens of Soviet Russia. The Cheka's successors (the
GPU, the OGPU, the NKVD, the GUGB, the MGB, the MVD, and
the KGB) have gone from strength to strength. Since 1991, the KGB
has been split into the Foreign Intelligence Service (SVR), the
Federal Security Service of the Russian Federation (FSB), and
the Federal Protective Service (FSO). Nor should we forget the
military intelligence service and special forces, the GRU, founded
in October 1918 on the initiative of Leon Trotsky and now almost
ten times larger than the other three combined.

Not everyone was cowed by the Red Terror. In March 1921, the
sailors from the Kronstadt naval base just north of St Petersburg,
whose support had been crucial to the Bolsheviks in the early
months of the Revolution, turned on them and denounced all their
shortcomings: 'By carrying out the October Revolution the working class had hoped to achieve its emancipation,' declared the
sailors' manifesto.

> But the result has been an even greater enslavement of human
> beings. The power of the monarchy, with its police and gendarme-
> rie, has passed into the hands of the Communist usurpers, who
> have given the people not freedom but the constant fear of torture
> by the Cheka, the horrors of which far exceed the rule of the gen-
> darmerie under tsarism.

In terms that pulled no punches, and would be echoed by democrats and defenders of civil liberties for the next seventy years, they
denounced

> the moral servitude which the Communists have also introduced.
> They have laid their hands on the inner world of the toiling people,
> forcing them to think in the way that *they* want. Through the state

> control of the trade unions they have chained the workers to their machines, so that labour is no longer a source of joy but a new form of slavery. To the protests of the peasants, expressed in spontaneous uprisings, and those of the workers, whose living conditions have compelled them to strike, they have answered with mass executions and a bloodletting that exceeds even that inflicted by the tsarist generals. The Russia of the toilers, the first to raise the red banner of liberation, is drenched in blood.[12]

This uprising, whose basic demand was for free elections – which the Bolsheviks had initially promised – was instantly repressed with the utmost severity, for the truth hurt. Artillery shelled the Kronstadt fortress from both the north and the south; Cheka forces, with military support, crossed the ice surrounding the island and stormed it. Official figures suggest that 527 people were killed and 4,127 were wounded, but they do not account for all those who were drowned when shells punched holes in the ice, or the injured who were abandoned out on the frozen sea. Of the sailors, at least five hundred were subsequently executed, while an estimated eight thousand sailors and civilians managed to flee to Finland.

The suppression of the Kronstadt mutiny marks the beginning of the undisputed state terror and dictatorial rule that characterized Soviet Russia for the next thirty years and, to a lesser extent, the thirty years after that as well. It also marks the point at which Russia lost the support of a great many Socialists and Communists throughout the world. As the famous American anarchist, Emma Goldman, put it in *My Disillusionment with Russia* (1923),

> Kronstadt broke the last thread that held me to the Bolsheviki. The wanton slaughter they had instigated spoke more eloquently against them than aught else. Whatever their pretences in the past, the Bolsheviki now proved themselves to be the most pernicious enemies of the Revolution. I could have nothing further to do with them.

Most people agreed with her.

Not all the victims of the Bolsheviks were chosen at random or killed simply because of their social class; in 1922 Lenin personally drew up a list of some one hundred and sixty 'undesirable' intellectuals, particularly those with a Christian stance: 'We're going to cleanse Russia once and for all,' he told Stalin. They were arrested on trumped-up charges by the Cheka. To preserve the image of his regime abroad, Lenin chose to have them expelled from the country rather than exiled to Siberia or executed. The first group of undesirables, along with their families, was put on two steamships (now referred to as 'the Philosophers' ships'), which left St Petersburg in September and November 1922. Counted on arrival at Stettin in Germany (modern-day Szczecin in Poland), they numbered 228 people. Soon afterwards, more intellectuals and their families were expelled by train to Riga in Latvia and by ship from Odessa to Istanbul; their numbers do not appear to have been recorded.

These intellectuals were liberal-minded, and some were socialists; they were at a loss to understand the reason for their expulsion. What possible danger could they pose to the new Soviet Russia, they wondered. What they had failed to grasp was that for the materialist philosophy of Lenin and especially Stalin, nothing – be it poetry or creative literature, any inward reflection, exploration of the soul or metaphysical speculation – *nothing* that failed to further the functioning of the State by exalting it, had any right to exist. Spiritual values were irrelevant. A person who *thought*, or wrote of beauty or human feelings, was a drain on the economy, a body that it was pointless to feed. Under Stalin, such people were called *parasites*. In short, if they were not actively supporting the State, the State had no use for them. (This is why most of the doctors arrested along with the philosophers were sent to the Eastern provinces 'where their specialities can be of use.'[13])

This then was the Soviet Russia that was taking shape in 1917, the grim background to bear in mind as I tell these love stories. For in the midst of all this cruelty and violence, there was still love to be found.

Sources

Adelman, Jonathan R., and Walter Bacon. *Terror and Communist Politics: The Role of the Secret Police in Communist States.* Routledge, 2019.

Alexander, Tania. *A Little of All These. An Estonian Childhood.* Jonathan Cape, 1987.

Chamberlain, Lesley. *The Philosophy Steamer: Lenin and the Exile of the Intelligentsia.* Atlantic Books, 2007. Published in the USA as *Lenin's Private War: The Voyage of the Philosophy Steamer and the Exile of the Intelligentsia* by St Martin's Press.

Davies, Norman. *Europe: a History.* OUP, 1996.

Deacon, Richard. *A History of the Russian Secret Service* (1972). Revised and updated edition. Grafton, 1987.

Eastman, Max. *Love and Revolution. My Journey through an Epoch.* Random House, 1964.

Gagarin, Princess Marie. *Reminiscences of Old Russia.* Privately printed, 1951.

Garstin, Denis. *Friendly Russia.* Fisher Unwin, 1915.

Harrison, Mark, and Andrei Markevich, 'Russia's Home Front, 1914–1922: The Economy.' https://warwick.ac.uk/fac/soc/economics/staff/mharrison/public/rgwr_postprint.pdf

Hart-Davis, Rupert (ed.). *The Autobiography of Arthur Ransome.* Cape, 1976.

Hill, George. *Go Spy the Land.* Cassell, 1932.

Karsavina, Tamara. *Theatre Street.* Heinemann, 1930.

Kyasht, Lydia. *Romantic Recollections.* Brentano, 1929. (Facsimile reprint by Noverre Press, 2010.)

Pipes, Richard. *The Russian Revolution.* New York: Knopf, 1990.

Ransome, Arthur. *Dispatches from Russia. 1917–1924.* Vol. 1. Ed. J. M. Gallanar. Lulu.com, 2017.

Sixsmith, Martin. *Russia: A 1000-year Chronicle of the Wild East.* New York: Random House, 1911.

Solzhenitsyn, Aleksandr. *The Gulag Archipelago, 1918–1956: An Experiment in Literary Investigation.* New York: Harper & Row [1974–78].

Tchernavin, Vladimir. *I Speak for the Silent: Prisoners of the Soviets.* Trans. Nicolas Oushakoff. Boston & New York: Hale, Cushman & Flint, 1935.

Winnington, G. Peter. *Walter Fuller: The Man Who Had Ideas.* Letterworth, 2014.

Notes

1.   Alexander, p.43.
2.   Winnington, p.107.
3.   These figures are from Davies, pp.1328–9.
4.   Kyasht, pp.29–31.
5.   Karsavina, p.229.
6.   Hart-Davis, p.165.
7.   Garstin, pp.153–4.
8.   Adapted from Ransome, dated 18 March 1917. Also in Hart-Davis, p.214.
9.   Tchernavin, pp.87–88.
10.   Information from Solzhenitsyn.
11.   Adelman, among many others.
12.   Sixsmith, p.242.
13.   Chamberlain, p.102.

2 Eliena and Max

THE FIRST MAN to be placed in charge of Trotsky's new Red Army by the Bolsheviks was Nikolai Krylenko (1885–1938), a mere ensign or *praporshchik*. As he was to play a central role in Soviet Russia for twenty years, and was a major influence in my first love story, I need to tell you something of the Krylenko family.

Vasili and Olga Krylenko were born in the early 1860s; they were Russian, but they moved to Poland before 1900 after Vasili's social-ist sympathies cost him his job teaching natural science in a Russian university. Having six children, two boys and four girls, he needed a decent income and ended up as a tax collector in Lublin, a most unpopular job (for the Poles deeply resented their Russian overlords) in which he nevertheless managed to make everyone love him. He lined his home with books of science and literature, especially poetry, in three or four languages. His daughter Eliena recalled that 'kindness and tolerance, sympathy with one's fellow men, a love of beauty, a love of life, [and] a thirst for knowledge' were the values that he tried to instil in his children. His wife Olga was equally idealistic, but completely 'absorbed in the one divine, all-encompassing, ultimate event – *the revolution*.'[1]

Their elder son, Nikolai, took after his mother, as did their eldest daughter Sophia; both were active in the 1905 revolution in St Petersburg, where Nikolai – studying history and literature at the University – was already a member of the Bolshevik faction of the Russian Social Democratic Labour Party. The other children were more like their father: the second son, Volodia, became an engineer, and the second daughter, Vera, studied music and became a pianist.

In the crackdown that followed the 1905 revolution, the third and fourth daughters, Eliena and Olga, aged eleven and nine, could only look on aghast as their world collapsed about them. Because of Nikolai's political activities (and probably Sophia's too), their home was ransacked by the Okhrana, the Tsar's security police, and all their precious books were destroyed. Their vehemently non-political sister Vera was jailed in Lublin. Although their father had taken no part in the revolution, he was sent to a small rural town, eighty miles from the nearest railway station, where he rapidly became depressed and committed suicide. In St Petersburg, Nikolai and Sophia managed to escape arrest. Having made her own way home, Sophia travelled on as far as Paris and then to Liège, in Belgium, where her brother Volodia was studying at a mining and engineering school.

As the repression eased, Nikolai came out of hiding and returned to St Petersburg. For the next twelve years or so, his life was a dangerous game of snakes and ladders: he would be arrested for his political activity, imprisoned or exiled, and then climb again for another round. He managed to complete his arts degree at St Petersburg in 1909, and immediately began to study law. Conscripted in 1912, he was discharged (for political activism, of course) the following year. After working very briefly as an assistant editor on *Pravda* while liaising with the Bolshevist faction in the Duma, he was again arrested – still in 1913 – and exiled to Kharkiv; he later claimed to hold a degree in law from there. Early in 1914, he fled to Austria to escape re-arrest. When the First World War broke out in August that year, he was obliged to move on to Switzerland, where he got to know Lenin and became his favourite chess partner. Lenin sent him back to Russia to help rebuild the underground Bolshevik organization. In November 1915, he was arrested in Moscow as a draft dodger; the following April, after a few months in prison, he was sent to the South West Front.

A year later, after Order No 1 was issued, Nikolai (with the lowest commissioned rank of ensign) was elected chairman of the *soviet* of his regiment and then up, step by step, until he was chairman of the *soviet* of the 11th Army. The key to his success was the skill with which he addressed his fellow soldiers. Arthur Ransome declared:

> I have never heard any orator listened to by a Russian audience with such absolute attention as by this elderly ensign Krylenko.... He is a finished artist as an orator, this little genius, for he could hold an audience of simple Russian soldiers breathlessly interested for an hour and a half while he put before them the whole complex political situation.[2]

But he was obliged to resign almost immediately, for there were not enough other Bolsheviks in the *soviet* at that level to support his opposition to the Provisional Government. So in June 1917, he became a member of the Bolshevik Military Organization and was elected to the First All-Russian Congress of Soviets, at which he was elected to the permanent All-Russian Central Executive Committee. Arriving at the High Command HQ in Mogilev, he was arrested by forces of the Provisional government and imprisoned in Petrograd, where he remained until mid-September.

In another throw of the dice, Nikolai then helped the leading Bolsheviks prepare the October Revolution. At the Second All Russian Congress of Soviets, held the day after the coup, he was made a People's Commissar (minister) and member of the triumvirate responsible for military affairs. His oratorical gifts had carried him through.

After the fall of the Provisional Government, Kerensky fled and Nikolai Dukhonin stepped in as acting Supreme Commander-in-Chief of the Imperial Army. Within days, the Bolshevik leaders ordered him to stop the fighting and open negotiations with the Central Powers. Dukhonin flatly refused, maintaining that such an order could only be issued by 'a government sustained by the army and the country'. Lenin's response was typical: he took everyone short by going to the nearest radio station and announcing that Dukhonin had been dismissed and that Nikolai Krylenko was now

Commander-in-Chief of the Army. It was Nikolai who arrested his predecessor. Unfortunately, he then stood by and allowed his men to bayonet and shoot Dukhonin in a horrific scene fortuitously witnessed by Captain George Hill and described in his book, *Go Spy the Land*.[3]

There was one more turn to go – for the moment, at any rate – in this game of snakes and ladders. Lenin and Trotsky soon realized that an army with a chain of command elected by enlisted men (of which Nikolai was – understandably – a keen supporter) was not effective; in March 1918, acting on a suggestion by Trotsky, Lenin and the Bolshevik Central Committee agreed to create a Supreme Military Council. The entire Bolshevik leadership of the Red Army, including Nikolai Krylenko, protested vigorously and eventually resigned. The office of the 'Commander in Chief' was formally abolished by the Central Committee on March 13 and Nikolai was reassigned to the Collegium of the Commissariat for Justice. From May 1918, he was Chairman of the Revolutionary Tribunal of the All-Russian Central Executive Committee. In 1922 he became Deputy Commissar of Justice and assistant Procurator General of the USSR, serving as the chief Procurator at the show trials of the 1920s and as the Commissar for Justice in the 1930s. (Although the Russian title 'procurator' is often translated as 'prosecutor', it was a post in the Russian legal system with no equivalent in Anglo-Saxon countries. The procurator's primary role was to supervise state organs and ensure that they properly applied state measures within the prescribed legal limits.)

In Russia, trial by jury had been introduced by Tsar Alexander II in 1864 as part of his democratic reforms that had included the emancipation of the serfs three years earlier. Nikolai quickly put an end to this system, which was not re-introduced for more than seventy years. He argued that the needs of the Party took precedence over any question of guilt or innocence; people should be tried in accordance with the Party's political guidelines, and he wrote a number of books expounding this thoroughly Marxist notion. He was an enthusiastic exponent of the Red Terror, exclaiming, 'We must execute not only the guilty. Execution of the innocent will impress the masses even more.'[4]

Nikolai became notorious the world over for his specious arguments. On 23 June 1918, he famously explained that there had been no discrepancy between the execution of Admiral Alexei Schastny and the prior abolition of the death penalty by the Bolsheviks in October 1917 since the admiral had not been condemned 'to death' but 'to be shot'. Nikolai is of course the principal villain of Aleksandr Solzhenitsyn's *Gulag Archipelago*. He is quoted on the first page: 'In the period of dictatorship, surrounded on all sides by enemies, we sometimes manifested unnecessary leniency and unnecessary soft-heartedness.'

So where, in this abysmal system, is the love story that I promised you? For that, we must come back to Nikolai's sisters. We left Sophia in Belgium; after numerous adventures, she ended up in Moscow, running the office that supervised the tribunals on behalf of the All-Russia Central Executive Committee. (Nepotism was common among the Bolsheviks: they trusted family first.) I don't know what became of Vera, the pianist. Olga, the youngest (and prettiest) of the sisters, became the secretary to Lev Kamenev in the Politburo. (He was married to Trotsky's sister.) And Eliena worked as Maxim Litvinov's secretary in the Commissariat for Foreign Affairs. She had studied law at St Petersburg University, graduating at the very moment when the Bolsheviks – with her own brother foremost among them – abolished the legal system she had spent years studying. Although she dearly loved – and admired – Nikolai, she was never a member of the Communist Party. On the contrary, she dreamed – inspired by the stories of Huckleberry Finn and Tom Sawyer that her father had read to her when she was a little girl – of living in America. And at the Genoa Conference in 1922, to which she had accompanied Litvinov, she met the American who made her dream come true.

They actually met a little way along the Ligurian coast from

Genoa, at Santa Margherita. The Conference, convened at the insti-
gation of Lloyd George with the aim of solving all the world's problems, had opened on 10 April. Both the Russians and the Germans
were feeling badly treated by the victorious Allies, who were insisting that the Bolsheviks should honour the debts incurred by
Imperial Russia (which they refused to do) and preventing the
Germans from acquiring the natural resources they so badly
needed to rebuild their country. At the suggestion of Litvinov,
diplomats from those two countries met secretly in the Imperial
Palace Hotel in Santa Margherita. Within a week they had signed
the Rapallo treaty that facilitated trade between Germany and
Russia. So while Chicherin (the Soviet Minister for Foreign Affairs)
was at loggerheads in Genoa, his deputy in Rapallo achieved the
breakthrough that Lenin and Trotsky had been seeking for over a
year. It was quite a coup for Litvinov.

One evening, Max Eastman, waiting in the lobby of the hotel to
go up and interview Chicherin, whom he naively thought of as 'a
minister from Utopia,'

> saw one of the secretaries come downstairs with a skipping step,
> her hand sliding lightly along the banister. She was not exactly
> pretty, but looked so jolly, with her short nose, twinkling grey eyes
> and tiny front teeth, that I watched her with a feeling of reminis-
> cent mirth. She seemed like the girls back home – not too awfully
> foreign. (Maybe I was a little homesick.)[5]

The following day, he ran into the girl in the hotel garden.

> She was standing all alone under a kumquat tree, weeping and
> eating kumquats. Before I could find an expression for my feelings,
> or quite decide what they were, she exclaimed:
>
> 'These tears are not for you!'
>
> I couldn't help smiling, but managed to answer: 'I never
> dreamed they were.'
>
> An embarrassed silence followed, which I broke finally by say-
> ing: 'Even if I can't dry your tears, I might help you eat the
> kumquats.'

> She laughed without ceasing to cry, and reached up with a
> graceful gesture to pick one for me.[6]

It was not exactly Adam and Eve and the apple, and they did not make love … yet.

Max Eastman was an American writer (of two dozen books, in various genres) and poet, a socialist who had edited the progressive, literary and political periodical called *The Masses* during the nineteen-teens. After America's entry into the First World War, the magazine's anti-war stance caused Max to be accused of obstructing the draft; he was tried twice under the Sedition Act, and acquitted both occasions, but *The Masses* had to close. Well known as a humorist, he complained that under the Wilson administration, 'you can't even collect your thoughts without getting arrested for unlawful assembly.' Max and his sister Crystal, the leading socialist feminist of the day, responded to this intimidation by launching a fresh magazine, *The Liberator,* with many of *The Masses'* contributors and the same socialist stance. It printed reports from Jack Reed (*Ten Days that Shook the World*) and Lincoln Steffens ('I have seen the future and it works') on the Russian Revolution. H. L. Mencken called it 'the best magazine in America', and it sold 60,000 copies a month. In the end, Max felt he had to go and see for himself the new society that was emerging in Russia, and left *The Liberator* in the hands of faithful contributors. Although he had said, long before, that when the revolution came, there would be 'great evils and wastefulness and graft and scandal and vituperation – and something to kick about all the time, just as there is today',[7] he was deeply romantic at heart and 'expected to find a band of social engineers rationally employing the scientific principles of Marxism,' in accordance with the *Communist Manifesto* of 1848.[8] It took him many years to realize how completely mistaken he had been. By the 1950s he had became deeply conservative, although still thoroughly independent in his opinions: he roundly condemned the war in Vietnam, and was a lifelong atheist.

There was another reason why Max went to Russia: he was

broken-hearted. In 1911, six months after his mother's death, he had got married in haste to an old friend. Instantly regretting his loss of freedom, he left her very quickly, but they actually divorced only in 1922, shortly before he left for Russia. In the interval, he enjoyed short-term relationships; then he met the actress Florence Deshon and fell deeply in love. But Florence went to Hollywood and began an affair with Charlie Chaplin. Six months later, feeling terribly unwell, she came back to see Max. He at once called a doctor who realized that Florence was carrying a dead foetus. An immediate operation saved her life, but not her state of mind: she became deeply depressed and one night six months later she went to bed leaving the gas tap open. She was rushed to hospital by a neighbour who had been alerted by the smell; Max came with equal haste and the doctors tried live-transfusing her with his blood, to no avail. He was devastated.

Going to Soviet Russia would make a clean break with the past. The Genoa Conference was his first port of call. Meeting Eliena there seemed like a trump card falling into his hands: here was a girl he liked, who clearly liked him, and who not only worked for a Deputy Minister but was the sister of the Public Procurator! Four months later, having visited France and then Germany, Max arrived in Moscow to find the population looking cheerful and well fed. They were enjoying the effect of Lenin's short-lived New Economic Programme (NEP), introduced eighteen months before. The War Communism of the Revolution had ruined Russia's industrial capacity and left the people starving; the NEP maintained state-ownership of banks and major industries, but reintroduced private enterprise in smaller businesses and permitted the peasants to sell their grain on the open market. The effects were immediate: there was food in the shops and smiles on people's faces. Stalin repealed the NEP after Lenin's death, shortly after Max left Moscow; so his favourable impressions of the country belonged to a brief and quite atypical period in the history of Soviet Russia.

Until he arrived in Moscow, Max could only speak in French

with Eliena, for she knew little English; meeting up with her again, he was hoping that she would teach him Russian. He soon discovered that she was 'the most quick-witted, kind, and blithesome teacher imaginable,' but she was far too busy to give him lessons with any regularity; those she did give him were punctuated by gales of laughter, for she was 'the gayest person I have ever known' with 'an instinctive joy in the mere fact of living.'[9] She also knew the way to a man's heart: every evening she would bring him a bowl of warm rice, with raisins in it, tucked under her coat. They were soon lovers. For all the growing attractions of Eliena, Max left her for six or seven weeks to immerse himself in Russian. He wanted to learn it as quickly as possible.

Max had his own method for learning a language: it involved a love affair, and Soviet Russia happened to be perfectly suited to it.

> Only weeks after seizing power ... the Bolsheviks began to institute new laws and codes that reshaped the meaning and function of the family. Church weddings were no longer recognized. Divorce could be quickly granted to one party without explanation. Entering into or ending a marriage meant simply a reshuffling of paper.... The goal was to give women equal status in marriage and to protect them if a union was dissolved; to ensure that no one was trapped in a union that had gone wrong.... Sex was to be recognized in terms of both procreation and pleasure, and it was to be treated openly.[10]

This openness – which did not outlive the 1920s – suited Max down to the ground: women found him extremely attractive, and up to this point in his life the only obstacle to mutual enjoyment had been American puritanism.

The Russians he had met at Santa Margherita had assured him that the Black Sea coast at Yalta far outclassed the Ligurian coast, so Max – who loved swimming and diving – went to Yalta, found it Edenesque, and applied his method. He flirted with a young woman called Nina 'who was beautifully formed, brown-haired, her features keenly chiselled, her eyes almost too alertly bright. She was twenty-seven years old, the wife of an engineer in Kharkov, and was taking a holiday at the seaside during his absence on a long construction job.'[11] Knowing no English or French, which was ideal for Max's purposes, she agreed to help him learn Russian, and in the process they became lovers. 'Although married for nine years, Nina had not had the baby she longed for, and the answer seemed to flow from the mere logic of the beauty of our love when she asked me if I would give her one.'[12] He was happy to oblige. They would take long walks down the coast, talking all the way, find some quiet beach and make love in the sunshine. His Russian progressed in leaps and bounds; on his return journey to Moscow he even composed a poem for Nina in Russian. 'No poem was ever more sincere in its love for an experience and a language, the twin loves out of which all poetry is born.' He called on her a year later and learned that, unlike the language lessons, their love-making had not had the desired happy outcome: she had had a miscarriage as a result of a fall.

Back in Moscow, Max astonished Eliena with his new-found fluency, and explained how he had acquired it. Her response almost took his breath away.

'Tell me all about Nina,' she said, 'and you can tell me about all the other girls you have loved, and those you may love in the future – or not tell me, just as you wish. I won't be jealous in either case. I don't want to possess you. All my love asks is to see you happy.'[13]
She was true to her word.

In this respect, Eliena was exceptionally unselfish, deriving great satisfaction from other people's enjoyment. At the time when she met Max, she had

a cat named Seashell whom she loved, and who would come and sit by her at breakfast. [Max] remarked once, when she herself came to the table hungry, that she seemed more interested in feeding Seashell than in satisfying her own hunger. She was ready with an answer that tells how extrovert her love was:

'It's because I can see her enjoy it – I can't see myself enjoy it.'[14]

As Max suggests by qualifying it as 'extrovert', Eliena's enjoyment, which for most people is internal and subjective, was unusually vicarious, dependent on seeing another's enjoyment. Max will have been particularly attentive to this aspect of her personality: his first book (in 1913) was titled, *Enjoyment of Poetry.* It is surely not by chance that he went on to write *Enjoyment of Laughter* (1936), and then *Enjoyment of Living* (1948).

Thanks to introductions supplied by Eliena, his own initiatives, and his budding fluency in the language, Max was enabled to meet and talk with many of the big names of the day; most of them were subsequently purged by Stalin, including Trotsky. Max took to the latter at once and asked if he might write his biography. Hesitantly, Trotsky agreed, warning Max that they would not have many opportunities to talk together. He was right, and in the end Max had to settle for a short study, *Leon Trotsky: The Portrait of a Youth,* which was published in 1925. It's a perceptive book, though, for Max had understood the man and accounts convincingly for his downfall at the Thirteenth Congress of the Russian Communist Party. Five years later, he got to translate Trotsky's *History of the Russian Revolution* into English.

The love affair between Eliena and Max was not all plain sailing, by any means. Max had an existential horror of entrapment and there were times when he had to rush off elsewhere to put a distance between himself and Eliena. And even then, if he felt that she was trying to keep tabs on him, he could have all kinds of psychosomatic illnesses, accompanied by nightmares. On one of these escapes from Eliena, Trotsky called him to Kislovodsk, in the Causasus between the Black and the Caspian Seas. When Max arrived there, Trotsky was too busy to see him and then left for Moscow without mentioning that if Max went with him, they could talk on the train. Instead of interviewing Trotsky, Max bumped into – of all people – the world-famous dancer Isadora Duncan; I mention this not only because two or three years earlier, when Florence Deshon was in Hollywood, Max had fallen desperately in love with one of Duncan's six German-born pupils – 'the Isadorables' as they were known as – but also because Isadora Duncan has an uncanny propensity for popping up in my love stories, as you will see.

On another occasion, when Max was writing a novel down in Sochi, he encouraged Eliena to come and join him – Maxim Litvinov was the most understanding of bosses, for he gave her as much time off as she needed – only to find that he had awakened his old 'demon' and could not write a word, feeling *'I do not want her here. She is alien to me. My sublime joy in her companionship is gone.'*[15] When she arrived, Eliena showed infinite understanding by renting a room of her own; she would come each day to cook him meals, make his bed, and swim with him in the sea, returning to sleep in her own room at night. 'My needs were so in conflict with themselves,' observed Max, 'that she must have known I was sick – too sick to be left completely alone. I had to have her with me, although the cause of my sickness was that she was there.'[16]

To spare him, she went to stay with an aunt for a few weeks, 720 kilometres away in Yalta. When she came back to him, Max had not improved; she proposed to return to Moscow. He confessed, 'I accepted her offer with feelings of hope, fright, shame, reluctance, eagerness, gratitude – amazement. So much goodness of heart, such gallant goodness of heart, I had never imagined.'[17] With Eliena in Moscow, it was for Max to crawl back to her in shame, and seek the help of a psychologist. He recovered to the extent of being able to write when he was with Eliena, but he never lost the need to leave her for fresh adventures at the same time as admitting that her unwavering love was essential to him. Some people would call him a nutcase; others a cad.

There was a collateral advantage in these escapes: they enabled Max to travel extensively in Russia. (The galloping inflation in Soviet Russia, which reached 88% *per month* in February 1924, made Max a rich man: he could buy himself a full meal for a few American cents, and travel cost him almost nothing.) During the two years he spent there, he saw more of the country than most other visitors ever do, and learned a good deal about it and its people. 'Russia as I saw it from the Volga,' he wrote,

> was a nation of poor people.... All the human dwellings were one-storey squares, dull gray or wet-straw brown, drabber than the earth they clustered on, and the dwellers were dressed in that dusty, yellow flour-bag type of cloth that made Russian poorness look poorer than any other.[18]

He spent one day in Tsaritsyn, which had been the site of an eighteen-month-long battle in the civil war. Equipped with an introduction from Trotsky to the President of the local *soviet*, he asked to see the all the fine points of the town. 'We haven't any fine points,' replied his host. 'We can show you graves, and we can show you factories wrecked and destroyed by the civil war – that is about all. The town is a ruin.'[19]

Talking with a group of workmen one day, Max began to learn the truth about Soviet Russia. He asked if they felt that the Bolsheviks truly represented them.

> 'Self-appointed representatives!' said a ragged worker. 'You see,' he continued – and this was the first time I had heard it explicitly stated – 'all the important offices in our trade union are occupied by Communists, and they are decided upon from above. For instance, I think that I can say that I represent the workers in this shop, but they can't elect me to an important post because I'm not a Communist. I have no power. I can't decide anything.'[20]

This was far from the theory of Communism that Max had learned, and began the process of weaning him off his romantic illusions.

On returning to Moscow from his Russian lessons with Nina, Max arrived in time for the fifth anniversary of the Revolution and the Fourth Congress of the Communist International. He also attended the Twelfth Congress of the Russian Communist Party the following year. These occasions afforded him his only glimpses of Lenin, who almost immediately afterwards was incapacitated by a series of strokes (called 'brain haemorrhages' at the time) and died sixteen months into Max's stay.

Thanks to Eliena, Max had one of the best seats at the momentous Twelfth Congress: sitting beside Nikolai Krylenko, directly in front of the rostrum. Following Lenin's death, everyone expected Trotsky to be named his successor – everyone that is except Trotsky himself and the delegates, for the congress was 'packed with men who owed their jobs and prestige to Stalin.'[21] 'They were awaiting a battle … rather as the Greeks watched a tragedy or the Spanish a bull fight.'[22] Trotsky had realized that the Communist Party was about to become Stalin's puppet and that the 'dictatorship of the proletariat' was about to become a dictatorship by Stalin, who was the Chairman of the Council of People's Commissars and at the same time the only person to be a member of both the Politburo (which set policy) and the Secretariat (which managed personnel). Trotsky had attempted to avert the disaster, but at the Congress he was accused of 'forming a faction' and verbally trampled upon. As Max observed, Trotsky

> could command men; he could inspire them to action with great oratory; he could expound the grounds and principles of their action; but he could not manage them. He could not lead them. Leadership … requires a certain craftiness which Trotsky lacked altogether.[23]

It was the death of his career, and he was gradually eased out of power and then the country, so that from 1930 onwards Stalin was alone at the helm of the enormous USSR. The show trials and summary executions of the 1930s, the organized starvation (particularly in the Ukraine), and the proliferation of the gulag, were all his work.

On the principle that if you want to rewrite history, you must first eliminate the witnesses, Stalin killed off everyone associated with the early years of Bolshevism and the Revolution: all his erstwhile fellow revolutionaries, colleagues, and ministers, along with their families, friends and colleagues. In August 1940, Trotsky himself was assassinated in Mexico, where he had fled for safety.

Having seen the man he admired humiliated and scorned, Max was ready to leave Russia, and Eliena was ready to come with him.

But leaving Soviet Russia was never easy, and they both had difficulty obtaining their travel papers. Having been tried twice for
sedition, Max was refused an American passport in 1922 before he
even left for Russia; only after a struggle and some string-pulling
was he given one, valid for two years only and stamped 'Not to be
renewed without the Express Authorization of the Department of
State.' Now it had expired, and America had no diplomatic representation in Russia. Max could not leave without a passport, and he
could not obtain a passport without leaving. Once again Eliena
came to his rescue: Soviet Russia had no diplomatic relations with
Britain, but there was a British trade representative in Moscow,

> and Eliena persuaded him, as a favour to the Foreign Office[!], to
> give [Max] a piece of brown paper with permission to 'land at
> Folkestone on 7 June 1924 on condition that the holder does not
> remain in the United Kingdom longer than one month.'[24]

There yet remained the problem of crossing five countries, all of
which required a visa, before Max could set foot in Folkestone.
'Here again Eliena came to [his] help with a brilliant idea.' Her boss,
Maxim Litvinov, was due to attend an international conference in
London in June-July that year. Max tells us that she suggested that

> I should go along with Litvinov as first assistant to his secretary.
> Litvinov's feelings towards his secretary were not such as to make
> the company of a first assistant seem absolutely necessary, but he
> was kindly in his brusque and tight-lipped way. He took me along
> with my brown-paper passport, and moreover enriched my
> understanding by telling me the whole story of his political life on
> the way.

So that was how Eliena enabled Max to leave Russia. It is unfortunate that he did not record Litvinov's story, by the way; I shall
attempt to tell it in the final chapter of this book. Suffice to say that
Litvinov 'was at that time, in [Max's] opinion and Eliena's, disillusioned to the point of cynicism about the outcome of the revolution.'[25]

Then came a hitch for Eliena too: when she applied for her diplomatic passport to attend the conference as Litvinov's secretary, it was refused, with no explanation. She appealed to her brother Nikolai, who was informed that the GPU (as the Cheka had been renamed in February 1922) would explain things to her if she came to the Lubianka. It was not without good reason that, in the popular imagination, the words 'Abandon hope all ye who enter here!' were inscribed above the entrance to the headquarters of the secret police (with its notorious prison in the basement). In some trepidation, then, she duly presented herself. 'A sly creature with flabby lips and soft hands … a smutty worm' explained how she had fallen foul of the GPU: as she was preparing to return to Moscow from the conference at Genoa, two years before, someone gave her a letter for her sister Sophia, and she innocently popped it into the diplomatic bag along with everything else. The GPU found it – they find everything – and now she had to explain how she had come to use the diplomatic pouch for a message to her sister from an anarchist anti-Bolshevik organization in Germany.

Fortunately, according to Eliena, whenever Sophia felt that 'her rather fantastic conspiratorial activities' were close to being detected, she had 'a protective habit of going actually crazy and getting committed.' Even better, 'she was at that moment in an insane asylum.' So Eliena spoke freely and hid nothing. After four hours, her inquisitor began to relent. He told her that she might have a passport if she would accept any letters that might be handed to her while she was abroad and pass them straight on to the GPU. 'I *can't* do that,' she cried. 'There are certain moral standards that one has to live up to, otherwise life isn't worth living.' The 'smutty worm' reminded her that she was applying bourgeois standards when she was living in – and employed by – a proletarian state.

'In the course of a brief lecture on ethics and the Marxian philosophy,' her inquisitor 'managed to make it clear that my receiving a passport to London depended on my coming over to the morals of the proletariat.'[26] She was given until the next day to make up her mind. (Had her name not been Krylenko, she would probably have never been allowed to leave the building, except in a prison truck en route for the gulag.)

She returned home 'pale and tear-stained, feverish, and shaking her hands as though she had reached into some loathsome substance and could not get it off her skin.' She had barely recovered by the time she went back to work the following morning.

'What on earth has happened to you!' Litvinov exclaimed....

'Why do you get so excited about a little thing like that? Bourgeois or proletarian, what does it matter? It amounts to nothing. Go over immediately and sign the paper.'

Pausing – but not long enough for her to answer – he added in a lowered voice:

'You don't *have* to do it, you know.'

So Eliena left Russia enrolled as a spy and an agent provocateur for the GPU.[27]

Needless to say, she never passed anything back to Moscow. Nor did she ever return to Russia.

But they were not out of the country yet. Rather belatedly – on the very day their train was due to leave at two-fifteen in the afternoon – Eliena and Max realized that her diplomatic passport would of course be withdrawn the moment she announced to the Russian delegation that she would not be returning to Moscow with them. It was no use taking a Soviet citizen's passport with her: they were not accepted in Western Europe at that time. She would be stranded – a stateless person – and unable to live with Max as they intended. The solution they found was for her to marry Max and have her name on his passport – once he managed to get one in London. As we have seen, marriage was a formality in Soviet Russia. They hurried to the registry office, paid one rouble, signed the papers and prepared to leave. 'Wait!' cried the woman in charge. 'You can't be married without two witnesses to confirm your identity.' They telephoned to Olga's partner; he promised to come at once. As the minutes passed, Eliena made a snap decision: 'Stay here and get the signatures of the witnesses,' she told Max, 'while I

A late portrait of Eliena, by Richard L. Simon

go and get the bags.' So Max was married without his bride being present. It was really rather appropriate for a man with a phobia of matrimony.

They caught their train, passed through five countries without a hitch, and reached Folkestone, where the Home Office took hours to honour the promise made by the trade delegate in Moscow and allow Max not only to land but also to remain in England ... for two weeks. Once safely in London, he hastened to get an American passport and put Eliena's name on it too. On that shaky foundation, they spent the next thirty-four years together. Eliena tolerated Max's many affairs; she had a few of her own too, which he could find very hard to take. His love for her being 'more realistic than sensual',[28] he got the passion he needed through his affairs.

In America, Eliena painted and wrote poetry, but above all she kept house for Max and provided him with the love and trust that were so necessary to him; in short, she enabled him and his writing, and that seems to have satisfied her. She expressed this most eloquently in the Will that she wrote on a scrap of paper, a month before she died, aged only 61:

> I will you all my strength,
> Still so complete, unused,
> To keep your spirit firm, foot sure, and head high.

She was unselfish to the last. Below, Max responded in three lines, adding a promise:

> I have received, dear love,
> Your priceless bequest.
> My spirit firm, my foot sure, and my head high.
> I promise.[29]

As she lay dying in Max's arms, he told her that he still loved her, 'very much', and she answered, 'I am so very glad you do.'[30] They were her last words.

Two years later, Max married Yvette Szkely, who was born in Budapest in 1912.

⁊

Leaving Russia with Max undoubtedly saved Eliena's life; of her immediate family, only her mother seems to have died in her bed. Until Lenin was incapacitated by his strokes, Nikolai continued to play the occasional game of chess with him, and it was Nikolai, as chairman of the chess section of the All-Union Council for Physical Recreation, who decided to improve on the Imperial tradition of an all-Russian masters tournament by persuading the Soviet leaders to sponsor chess-playing in the USSR and to organize the great Moscow tournaments of 1925, 1935 and 1936. His aim was to enhance the international image of the country by producing world masters – which was achieved with considerable success: in the FIDE world championships between 1948 and 1993, for instance, seven out of eight winners were Russian. He also ensured the promotion of his favourite sport, mountain climbing.

In the mid-1930s, however, Nikolai found himself in disagreement with Andrey Vyshinsky over the power of the NKVD: Nikolai wanted to regularize his system of revolutionary justice, whereas Vyshinsky wanted the NKVD to be able to dispense arbitrary punishment in a less public manner. The end result was invariably the same, but Stalin would stand for no friction between his minions. Although Vyshinsky came over to Nikolai's view ten years later, it was too late for Nikolai: in the game of snakes and ladders he had been playing, he had landed on a snake. In the first session of the newly reorganized Supreme Soviet in January 1938, he was denounced by an up-and-coming Stalinist, Mir Jafar Baghirov, who cited Nikolai's mountain-climbing and chess-playing as evidence that he did not have a serious attitude towards directing the Commissariat of Justice. He was arrested at the end of January, and forced to sign a fantastic series of confessions. At his twenty-minute trial six months later, he just had time to withdraw his confessions before he was sentenced, taken out and shot. Thus he died in exactly the same manner as many – if not most – of the countless prisoners who had appeared before him over the preceding twenty years. There seems to be some justice in that.

As for his anti-Bolshevik sister Sophia, whom the GPU, the OGPU and then the NKVD had been watching since they seized that letter in 1922, it turns out that she had a son, André, born in Paris in March 1909 by another political activist, Max Mazower. Soon after the birth, Max Mazower decided to turn over a new leaf in England, whereas Sophia continued as a revolutionary agitator. Her son was about three-and-a-half when she had a daughter by another man, and at this point she sent André to be brought up by his father in England. (He later described himself as 'a piece of flotsam from the remote shipwreck of Imperial Russia.'[31])

How long she retained her job in Moscow I do not know; what is sure is that in 1935 she was sent to a broad-minded psychiatric hospital not far south of Moscow, where she was treated as an outpatient, allowed to live 'off campus'. Max Mazower's grandson, Mark, comments:

> The timing suggests that Nikolai had placed her there, sensing
> that his own position was in jeopardy, although whether he did so
> to protect her, as some in the family believed, or to protect himself,
> or both, we cannot know. Equally suggestive is the fact that she
> was released in the spring of 1938 once he was under arrest.[32]

Her freedom was short-lived: she was arrested by the NKVD two months later and sent for assessment at the Serbsky Institute, Russia's main clinic for forensic psychiatry, which later became notorious for diagnosing dissidents as being mentally ill. From there she was sent, along with her daughter and her sister Olga, to the NKVD's prison hospital for criminal patients at Kazan. She and Olga both died there during the war; her daughter was released many years later and allowed to return to Moscow.

Many are the witnesses who described Nikolai Krylenko working himself up into passions of anger against the prisoners who came before him, yelling at them, 'There is no law here but Soviet Law, and by that law you must die.'[33] Bruce Lockhart, who met Nikolai at the time when he was briefly in charge of the Red Army, described him as 'an epileptic degenerate ... and the most repulsive type I came across in all my connections with the Bolsheviks.'[34] When we recall that Max Eastman described Nikolai and Olga's mother as being completely 'absorbed in the one divine, all-encompassing, ultimate event – *the revolution*,' and that their father committed suicide, it is clear that they were obsessed by their ideals to a degree that might be classed as pathological today. Eliena escaped that, and thanks to Maxim Litvinov, Max Eastman and her dream of a life in America, she also escaped death in the great purges of the 1930s.

Sources

Brogan, Hugh. *The Life of Arthur Ransome.* Cape, 1984.

Bruce Lockhart, Robert. *Memoirs of a British Agent.* Putnam's Sons, 1933.

Carleton, Gregory. *Sexual Revolution in Bolshevik Russia.* U Pittsburg P, 2005.

Chamberlain, Lesley. *The Philosophy Steamer: Lenin and the Exile of the Intelligentsia.* Atlantic Books, 2007. Published in the USA by St Martin's Press as *Lenin's Private War: The Voyage of the Philosophy Steamer and the Exile of the Intelligentsia.*

Davies, Norman. *Europe: a history.* OUP, 1996.

Eastman, Max. *Love and Revolution. My Journey through an Epoch.* New York: Random House, 1964.

Gagarin, Princess Marie. *Reminiscences of Old Russia.* Privately printed, 1951.

Garnett, Richard. *Constance Garnett: a heroic life.* Sinclair-Stevenson, 1991.

Garstin, Denis. *Friendly Russia.* Fisher Unwin, 1915.

Harrison, Mark, and Andrei Markevich, 'Russia's Home Front, 1914–1922: The Economy.' https://warwick.ac.uk/fac/soc/economics/staff/mharrison/public/rgwr_postprint.pdf

Hill, George. *Go Spy the Land.* Cassell, 1932.

Irmscher, Christoph. *Max Eastman: A Life.* New Haven: Yale UP, 2017.

MacCullagh, Francis. *The Bolshevik Persecution of Christianity.* Dutton & Co, 1924. Sourced from Wikiquotes.

Mazower, Mark. *What You Did Not Tell. A Russian Past and the Journey Home* (2017). Penguin, 2018.

O'Neill, William L. *The Last Romantic: A Life of Max Eastman.* OUP, 1978.
Pipes, Richard. *The Russian Revolution.* New York: Knopf, 1990.
Solzhenitsyn, Aleksandr. *The Gulag Archipelago, 1918–1956: An Experiment in Literary Investigation.* New York: Harper & Row [1974–78].

Notes

[1]   Both quotations about the Krylenko parents are from Eastman, p.339. The italics are his.

[2]   Quoted by Brogan, p.171–2.

[3]   Hill, p.110.

[4]   Pipes, p.822.

[5]   Eastman, p.301.

[6]   Eastman, pp.303–4.

[7]   O'Neill, p.94.

[8]   O'Neil, p.100.

[9]   Eastman, pp.320 and 340.

[10]   Carleton, p.3.

[11]   Eastman, p.324.

[12]   Eastman, p.326.

[13]   Eastman, p.341 (his emphasis).

[14]   Eastman, p.340.

[15]   Eastman, p.391 (his emphasis).

[16]   Eastman, p.393.

[17]   Eastman, p.394.

[18]   Eastman, pp.362–3.

[19]   Eastman, p.364.

[20]   Eastman, p.367.

[21]   Eastman, p.422.

[22]   Eastman, p.421.

23 Eastman, p.409.

24 Eastman, p.431.

25 Eastman, p.431.

26 All these quotations from Eliena's memoir are taken from
    Eastman, p.433.

27 Eastman, p.434.

28 Eastman, p.407.

29 This document, dated 2 September 1956, is in the Lilly Library.

30 Irmscher, p.331.

31 Mazower, p.162.

32 Mazower, p.155.

33 New York *Herald* correspondent Francis MacCullagh, p.221.

34 Lockhart, Book IV: Chapter 5, p.257.

3 Natasha and Jack

AT THE BEGINNING of the twentieth century, almost no one in Britain could speak Russian, and very few knew anything of Russia and its culture. The Foreign Office could send diplomats who spoke no Russian to the British Embassy in St Petersburg, confident that they could depend on interpreters and the Russians' knowledge of the international diplomatic language, French. (This reflects a long-standing prejudice among the upper class in Britain that learning a foreign language – apart from public school Latin and Greek, of course – was beneath them.) As Bruce Lockhart put it with his tongue well into his cheek, when Moscow formally conferred on 'his Super-Excellency Sir George Buchanan, Ambassador Extra-ordinary and Plenipotentiary of His Britannic Majesty to the Emperor of all the Russias, the title of Honorary Hereditary Citizen of the City of Moscow', he knew not one word of Russian with which to express his gratitude, even though he had been in Russia for at least six years. So Benjie Bruce and Robert Bruce Lockhart (both of whom are properly introduced in later chapters) 'carefully rehearsed the Ambassador to say … *spasibo*, which is the shortest and most colloquial Russian term for "thank you."' The fateful moment came 'and in a firm but low voice Sir George was heard to say: *za pivo*, which, being interpreted, means "for beer!"'[1]

When Bruce Lockhart was posted to the Moscow Consulate in January 1912, he was determined to learn Russian as well as he could. His ambition was rewarded, as he put it in his *Memoirs*, by

an extraordinary stroke of luck. Every year half-a-dozen English officers came to Moscow to study Russian for their interpreter's examination. To meet their needs a certain number of Russian families specialized in teaching Russian. Most of them were squalid middle-class homes with nothing to recommend them in the way either of comfort or of intellectual uplift. By good fortune, the one family which had a vacancy at the time of my arrival was the Ertels, and to the Ertels by the grace of God I went.

Madame Ertel ... a plump and rather delicate little woman of about fifty, very intellectual, [was] a born teacher. She had a large flat with an excellent library on the Vozdvizhenka. The other inmates of my new home were her daughter [Elena], a dark-eyed temperamental young girl more like an Italian than a Russian ... and a wondrously old lady, who was known as *Babushka* [Grandma], who rarely spoke, and who appeared only at meal times.... Every day I had a lesson from Madame Ertel and her daughter, and under their skilful tuition I made rapid progress. They did their best, too, to make me one of the family, and, although I feel that at times I must have been a sore trial to them, we never exchanged an unpleasant word....

Lockhart observed that the Ertels were

typical representatives of the intelligentsia. When at ten o'clock every evening they assembled round the samovar, they would sometimes sit far into the night discussing how to make the world safe by revolution. But when the morning of action came they were fast asleep in their beds. It was very harmless, very hopeless, and very Russian....

Many writers came to the house: old friends of the late M. Ertel; young men with plays to read and novels to place; painters, musicians, actors and actresses; and, much impressed, I worshipped at the feet of all of them. It was at Madame Ertel's that I first met Olga Knipper, the widow of Chekhov and the leading Moscow tragedienne. It was Madame Ertel who first took me to see a Chekhov play performed by the Moscow Art Theatre players in that sober, solemn theatre where applause was forbidden and where a late arrival was shut out for the whole act.[2]

This was the society that the Bolsheviks completely wiped out.

Bruce Lockhart does not mention that Madame Ertel had an elder daughter, Nataliya, who had been in England for the past six years at the suggestion of Constance Garnett (1861–1946), the most prolific translator of Russian literature into English. Garnett started translating almost by chance. In the autumn of 1890, she met a Russian exile, Felix Volkhovsky, who had managed to escape from Siberia, make his way to London and join its Russian émigré community of political thinkers and writers. Working as an editor at an emigré publishing house, the Free Russian Press, he rapidly became a close friend of Constance and introduced her to other Russians, including the revolutionary known as Stepniak. (Much to his friends' distress, Stepniak died in a train accident just before Christmas 1895.) Constance was fascinated by their unfamiliar culture and its language. When she was expecting her first child and was obliged to take prolonged bed rest, Volkhovsky suggested that she should seize the opportunity to start learning Russian, and handed her a dictionary and a grammar. She took up the idea and began translating a novel as a practical way to learn the language. She obviously had a gift for it: by the end of the decade she had published ten volumes of Turgenev's stories. That was just the start: in a career spanning thirty-five years, she translated more than seventy volumes of Russian literature into English, much of which had been almost completely unknown outside Russia until then.

In 1904, when Constance had just finished translating *War and Peace*, she paid her second visit to Russia. On this occasion, she was given an introduction to Aleksandr Ertel (1855–1908), a largely self-educated Russian novelist and short-story writer. He is not well known today, but Leo Tolstoy declared, in his admiring preface to the commemorative edition of Ertel's best novel *The Gardenins, Their Retainers, Their Friends, and Their Enemies* (1908), that anyone who wished to know the language of the Russian people should study Ertel's prose.

Like most Russian writers of his time, Aleksandr Ertel was critical of the Tsar's refusal to entertain any further thoughts of social reform once he had emancipated the serfs in 1861 (partly inspired, it should be said, by Turgenev's descriptions of them). Since it was a crime to question the existing system, Ertel was arrested in 1884 for allowing revolutionaries to use his address. As he was just liberal-minded rather than an activist, though, he was sentenced only to four years at Tver, a mere 180 kilometres (110 miles) north-west of Moscow: that was rustication, as opposed to exile in Siberia, more than 4000 kilometres away. At the time of Constance's visit, he had given up writing and turned to estate management, which provided him with a regular income and a house for his family. This being Russia, the area under his management was 'as big as England, scattered in a number of estates.'[3]

Accompanied by her twelve-year-old son David (always known as Bunny), Constance went to stay with him and his family in the country at Khludovo (200 km – 130 miles – due north of Moscow, not all that far from Tver). She was immensely impressed by them, and particularly by the elder daughter, Nataliya, whom they called Natasha, or just Tata. Such was the precocious development of her intelligence that they had been treating her 'as though intellectually grown up since she was about ten years old.'[4] She had been edu-cated at Mariya Stoyunina's Academy in St Petersburg, which dis-pensed an education for girls that was second to none in Imperial Russia, and was preparing to start at the University of Moscow that autumn, when she turned eighteen. (I might note here that Madame Stoyunina's daughter Lyudmila married the philosopher Nikolai Lossky, who taught at the school. Consequently, he was one of Natasha's teachers. When Lenin expelled Lossky and his family on one of the Philosophers' Ships in 1922, Madame Stoyunina was exiled along with them.)

Natasha's sister Elena, who had her fifteenth birthday during Constance's visit, was already a good pianist and taking further music lessons. As the girls had had an English governess from their earliest years, English was their second language. They also had a

French one as well at some point. This was not exceptional; educated Russians were in the habit of using French and English in the home, so that their children grew up multi-lingual.

In addition to their daughters, the Ertels cared for two other children. The first was a boy whom they had discovered as a tiny baby, wrapped in a bundle of rags in the snow at the roadside. They had named him Kirik Levin, after the character in *Anna Karenina*, and placed him with a peasant woman in the village. As he proved to be intelligent, they fostered him and at the time of the Garnetts' visit he had already gone on to study at a university.

Then there was Elena Goncharova, always called Lenochka, whom they had brought up after the death of her mother when she was very small. (Her father committed suicide in 1906.) In his auto-biography, Bunny Garnett described her as

> the most conventionally beautiful of the three [girls], taller, with a willowy figure, and beautiful large grey eyes with dark eyebrows and lashes and dark hair. She was always using her big eyes and pouting lips to mock any male creature that was around and was not above flirting with a boy of twelve.[5]

She was about a year younger than Natasha, and Bunny met her again when he went to Russia for a visit in 1910, by which time she was an actress under the great actor, director and originator of method acting, Konstantin Stanislavski at the Moscow Art Theatre.

Lenochka probably gained her entrée through Aleksandr Ertel: he was particularly fond of the theatre, and even four years after his death in February 1908 his Moscow flat was still frequented by actors and actresses (as Bruce Lockhart discovered). He was a particular friend of Stanislavski's sister, Zinaida Sergeyevna Sokolova, and her husband Konstantin Sokolov. With his encouragement, the Sokolovs, who much wished to help the peasants, left their jobs in Moscow to set up Russia's first 'peasant theatre' in a village not far from where Ertel was managing an estate. Under their direction, everything in the theatre, including the acting, was done by the peasants themselves. It still exists.[6]

Seated, L to R: Ursula Cox, Lenochka Goncharova, Elena Ertel (aka Lola), a friend with her son, and Mariya Vasilyevna Ertel, photographed in 1909

Constance's visit lasted rather longer than planned: calling on another writer, she imprudently drank unboiled water, which resulted in a nasty bout of gastric enteritis. The Ertels looked after her very kindly; she got to know the family well and to like them very much. Through them, she learned about their culture and their ever-present moral code. In particular, Aleksandr Ertel had never married his common-law wife Mariya, by whom he had Natasha and Elena, because he had previously been married to a woman whom he had repudiated. For the Russian Orthodox church, a couple remained married until one of them died, even though they might have agreed to separate or divorce.

After she returned home, Constance remained in contact with Aleksandr Ertel, and when Natasha's studies were disrupted by the student strikes and demonstrations of the 1905 revolution, which led to the closure of colleges and universities in Russia, she encouraged Natasha to come and study in England. (This first revolution was harshly suppressed, which made reformers of every persuasion all the more determined that the next should succeed.) She came, having done one year at Moscow, won a scholarship to University College London, and obtained a first-class MA in Philosophy.

In the eyes of Bunny Garnett, Natasha was 'a spirited and intelligent young woman, of formidably strong character [and] very Russian.'[7] Ursula Cox, who was living with her mother in close proximity to the Ertels in Moscow and was much the same age as Natasha, told Constance, 'I have unbounded admiration for Tata, and when she speaks to me her magnetic personality mesmerizes me into doing anything that she tells me to, and, what's more, into feeling an intense desire to do it.'[8] Everyone agreed that Natasha had a strong – and very likeable – personality.

Soon after she arrived in England, Natasha met the Rev. John ('Jack') Nightingale Duddington through their common interest

An early picture of Jack
and (right) Natasha in 1910

in Theosophy. He was the newly appointed Rector of Ayot St Lawrence and living alone, except for his young daughter Iris, because his wife Elizabeth – always known as Lily – whom he had married in 1893, had refused to move with him from his previous parish. After Lily declared that she wanted to live with another woman, they agreed to divorce. On the face of it, this looked to be a simple matter, but it became a messy business.

In those days, there was no divorce by mutual consent; there had to be a guilty party. Lily volunteered to play this part, and her friend provided affidavits that Lily had committed adultery with 'a man unknown' on various dates and in various places. As it proved impossible to identify this man (since he did not exist), the case proceeded without a co-respondent. The court pronounced a decree nisi on 13 June 1911.

However, it would appear that Lily's father – who was a solicitor – did not like this in the least. He lodged an objection in which Lily withdrew her admission of infidelity, and Jack was accused of having committed adultery with Natasha at various seaside places between December 1907 and December 1908. The decree nisi was rescinded on 11 November 1911 and the costs (which were by now considerable) were awarded against Jack as the guilty party.[9]

This placed Jack in a difficult situation. Although he was not divorced, press reports of the court case had revealed his infidelity and he was obliged to resign his incumbency, so he had no income. He also had to leave the Rectory, so he had no home. He took lodgings in the little village of Ayot St Lawrence, leaving his furniture in the Rectory. As his successor found the Rectory too inconvenient for his purposes, it was leased to George Bernard Shaw, who eventually bought it freehold. Today it is known as Shaw's Corner. For several years, Shaw rented the furniture that Jack had left in the Rectory, thus providing him with a little money.

We do not know what Natasha thought of all this. Right from the start, her father had lovingly warned her of what she was undertaking, emotionally, financially and socially. But Natasha knew her own mind and went her own way. She signed her publications 'Natalie Duddington' and lived with Jack for more than forty years, finally marrying him only after Lily died in 1954. (Jack died only four years later.) While her parents' marital situation had been very similar, Natasha's mother never had the satisfaction of marrying Mr Ertel, for he predeceased her. Nor was this the only irregularity in their relationship: Mr Ertel had a mistress, Anna Vasilyevna Pogozheva. She was very clever and translated a number of books into Russian; she corresponded with Ertel on philosophical and political topics. Natasha liked her very much.

No one thought to record what Jack's daughter Iris thought when her father fell passionately in love with a Russian girl just eight years older than herself, and twenty-two years younger than her father. At any rate, she remained in contact with him and Natasha for the rest of her life. In the summer of 1912, she visited Russia with them both. About this time, she became an actress and studied dance with Isadora Duncan's brother, Raymond Duncan.[10] She married late in 1914 and had three children.

Jack and Natasha had two children together: Anna (1913–97) and Alexander, always known as Sasha (1921–98). They bore the name Duddington and grew up speaking English and Russian, like their mother. Anna became a librarian at the Courtauld Institute, and Sasha a doctor and much-respected Jungian analyst. They both married and had children in England.

Everyone seems to have been struck by the contrast between Natasha and Jack Duddington. For Richard Freeborn, Emeritus Professor of Russian Literature at the University of London, 'they were hardly ideally suited.' Was it a case of 'opposites attract'? Ursula Cox told Constance Garnett of an occasion when

> Tata was talking to me about philosophy and I was listening, and had forgotten everything in the world but what she was saying, and suddenly Jack [Duddington] came in and we seemed to drop down to earth with such a thump, and as I looked at the two I thought how incongruous they were.[11]

Whatever others may have thought, there is no doubt that Jack was devoted to Natasha, and Constance 'always spoke of Jack Duddington affectionately.'[12]

In 1914 Natasha went to Moscow with Jack and baby Anna to see her mother and her sister Elena (Mr Ertel having died in 1908). They must have returned for a third visit, for Natasha was photographed on the verandah of her family's house in the summer of 1916.[13] During one of these visits, Jack Duddington is said to have served as honorary Chaplain to the British Consulate in Moscow, thanks to the good offices of Natasha's mother. Having left the Church, it was hard for him to find a fresh niche in life. During First World War, he is believed to have volunteered to help the Red Cross in London and worked fifty-six hours a week as a stretcher bearer in the railway stations where the war wounded arrived from France. After the war, he became the Secretary – and later the Director – of the Whitechapel Art Gallery, where he remained until his retirement in 1947.

Right from the start, Natasha helped Constance Garnett with her translations. Eventually she became her principal assistant: as Constance had to spare her eyes as much as possible, Natasha would read her the Russian text, sentence by sentence, and write down the English translation to Constance's dictation. Thanks to her intelligence and the sensitivity to language she had inherited from her father, Natasha could give Constance a better sense of Russian style, elucidate difficult passages, and supply cultural information as only an educated Russian could; thus the final version was the result of close collaboration between the two of them, although this was rarely acknowledged. When their translation of *The Cherry Orchard* was questioned in 1911 because it diverged from earlier translations, Constance swore that, having compared their English version with the original, word for word, she and Natasha could vouch for it being faithful and correct. Their opinions on many things – religion and politics, to start with – were widely different, but when it came to Russian literature, they saw eye to eye. Natasha was one of very few people of whom Constance could say that their minds *met*; they became life-long friends. In 1922 Constance developed so strong a dislike for Vladimir Chertkov's *Last Days of Tolstoy*, which they had translated together, that she invited Natasha to publish it under her own name. When Constance was very old, Natasha would bring her each week a fresh home-baked loaf of Russian bread, yellow with the egg-yolks in the mix – a gift much appreciated during wartime rationing.[14]

Natasha greatly admired Dostoevsky's novels and successfully campaigned for them to be translated. As a result, Heinemann gave Constance Garnett a contract at the end of 1910, and by 1920 she and Natasha had completed all twelve volumes of his works, about two-and-a-half million words in all, a staggering achievement, particularly when Constance found Dostoevsky 'so obscure and so careless a writer.' In this way, Natasha was instrumental in bringing one of the monuments of world literature to the English-speaking public. Sometimes Natasha's place at Constance's side was taken by Sibyl Wilson; on these occasions Natasha was entrusted with revising and proofreading their work, which she could do at home while attending to her daughter. Constance and Sibyl would call on her whenever they hit a tricky passage.

Between them, Natasha and Constance made translations of the works of those great Russian writers – Chekhov, Turgenev, Tolstoy, Dostoevsky, as well as selected texts by Herzen, Goncharov (not the same family as Lenochka's) and Ostrovsky – that were to have such an impact on British readers and British writing in the twentieth century. Until now, Natasha's share in this has remained almost entirely unnoticed. She modestly refused to take any credit for 'Mrs Garnett's amazing understanding of the subtleties of the Russian language.'[15] She admitted only to helping with the grammatically complex sentences, yet it is perfectly clear that her contribution was crucial both to Constance's prodigious output and its fidelity to the Russian.

Constance and her husband, the writer, critic and literary editor

Edward Garnett, lived largely independent lives; he was seven years younger than her, and their partnership was intellectual rather than physical, although they had had a son together. In the house that Edward and Constance built for themselves, they lived separate lives and slept in separate bedrooms; he read manuscripts while she translated. He also had a flat in London where he stayed for a couple of nights each week while he reported to the publisher he worked for and collected fresh manuscripts to read. From the turn of the century onwards, he had a mistress, Nellie Heath. His wife encouraged this relationship, for 'Nellie represented no threat to those elements of her marriage that Constance really valued, added to which she was extremely fond of Nellie.'[16]

A recent biography of Edward Garnett has revealed that he and Natasha were lovers too. Although Natasha made no secret of her admiration for him, finding him 'exceptionally fascinating... kind' and 'generous', they were very discreet about their relationship. He did not date his letters to her, and someone – probably his son Bunny – destroyed her letters to him, so we have no firm dates, but their affair seems to have coincided, more or less, with the First World War. Constance never learned of it and, so far as I know, nor did Jack, but Nellie Heath did. More than twenty years after Edward's death, she recalled the moment when, towards the end of the war, she 'suddenly realized that his love was divided: the shock was terrible and the agony was often unbearable.' Helen Smith, Edward's biographer, adds that 'unanswered questions gnawed away in Nellie's mind for years.'[17] Natasha, on the other hand, took after her father and apparently had no qualms of conscience.

After the First World War, Constance's production slowed and Natasha had time to translate books of her own choice, principally works of philosophy but also other genres. In an independent career that lasted sixty years, she turned some three dozen works into English. She became quite as good a translator as Constance, who has been criticized for the nineteenth-century flavour of her prose. While Natasha's phrasing and fluency suggest that she learned a good deal from Constance, her idiom was more modern – and she was more sensitive to the style and nuances of the Russian texts. Professor Freeborn, who himself regularly translated Russian literature into English, wrote recently of her 1929 translation of *Oblomov*, for instance, that 'in its particular sensitivity to the subtlety of Goncharov's Russian, in its liveliness and its elegance, it has about it a freshness of manner that admirably matches the same enduring quality in the original.'[18]

After graduating, Natasha read widely, in both in English and Russian, and remained in contact with her London University professors, attending meetings and debates. In 1916, she became one of the first three women to be elected to the Executive Committee of the Aristotelian Society.[19] This in itself tells us that after just ten years in England and in her thirtieth year, she was accepted among the most brilliant minds of the day. In 1918, she read a paper to the Society on her favourite topic of philosophical debate, 'Our Knowledge of Other Minds.'[20] It was critically reviewed in an issue of *Mind,* to which she wrote a considered response: 'Do we know other minds mediately or im-mediately?'[21] Both pieces are remembered and cited to this day: in January 2017, Anil Gomes, a Fellow and Tutor in Philosophy at Trinity College, Oxford, opined that 'her two essays on our knowledge of others' minds are great fun, in both style and substance. They bear the imprint of the Oxford Realist conception of knowledge and give expression to one powerful source behind the claim that our knowledge of others' minds is perceptual.'[22]

Among her other publications, an article on 'The Religious Philosophy of Vladimir Solovyov' appeared in *The Hibbert Journal,* volume 5 for 1916–17, signed 'J. N. Duddington'. That this is actually Natasha's work is confirmed by a manuscript in the New Atlantis Foundation Dimitrije Mitrinović Archive at the University of Bradford: '"The Religious Philosophy of Vladimir Solovyov" by Mrs J. N. Duddington (Natasha A. Ertel).' This was not the first mis-attribution: when the Stage Society put on *The Bread of Others* by Turgenev in 1909, the programme announced that it was translated by 'J. Nightingale Duddington' – who at this point knew almost no Russian! (George Bernard Shaw and his wife were closely involved with the Stage Society, and it is possible that they facilitated the mounting of this play, a first in Natasha's career.) She was always modest about her work – and very discreet about her life. Even her grandchildren know few details of it.

Natasha's interest in Solovyov (1853–1900) – his name is also spelled *Soloviev* – is quite understandable when we remember that he is widely thought to have inspired the characters of Alyosha and Ivan Karamazov in Dostoevsky's *Brothers Karamazov* (1879–80). Moreover, his philosophical study on *The Meaning of Love* (1894) was written in reaction to Leo Tolstoy's *Kreutzer Sonata* (1889), so in him two of Natasha's fields of interest were united. I believe her first published book-length translation was Solovyov's *Justification of the Good: an essay on moral philosophy*, which appeared in 1918. She returned to his work thirty years later, bringing out *A Solovyov Anthology* in 1950.

Solovyov – and Natasha's article and her translations – are of particular relevance to this book, for he was a leading contributor to the development of the modern concept of human rights (as in the 1948 Universal Declaration of Human Rights). Solovyov was Russia's greatest religious philosopher; his thought belongs to the tradition of Russian neo-idealism, which 'combined Orthodox Christian personalism with a Kantian conception of human dignity to produce a theoretically sophisticated defence of human rights.'[23] Nikolai Berdyaev (1874–1948), another of the Russian philosophers expelled by Lenin, brought this way of thinking to the West, where it greatly influenced Jacques Maritain; the Universal Declaration has been called the embodiment of Maritain's thought.[24]

In 1919, Natasha translated Nikolai Lossky's *Intuitive Basis of Knowledge: an epistemological inquiry*, which was directly relevant to her interest in how we know other minds. In fact, as Lossky had been one of her schoolteachers, he himself may have awakened that interest. She must have been in correspondence with Lossky at this time, for during the famines of 1920 and 1921 he and his family owed their survival to the food parcels that Natasha sent them from England.[25] Her interest and sympathy for Lossky will have been heightened when she learned in 1922 that he had been expelled by Lenin. Six years later she translated his *World as an Organic Whole*. Not content with this, she wrote an article on 'The Philosophy of N. Lossky', which appeared in the *Dublin Review* in 1933 (vol. 192).

Lossky was not the only exiled philosopher whom Natasha translated. In 1946, she put *God with Us: Three Meditations* by Semyon Frank (1877–1950) into English, followed by his *Reality and Man* in 1965. Frank was a high-profile exile, having been appointed to the chair of philosophy at Moscow University in 1921, alongside the philosopher Nikolai Berdyaev, who was directing the Free Academy of Spiritual Culture at the time. After his expulsion, Frank settled in Germany, but when the Nazis began persecuting the Jews he and his family were obliged to move on. (Although Frank had converted to Orthodox Christianity many years before, he was born a Jew and bore a Jewish name, which condemned him in the Nazis' eyes.) Whereas his children managed to reach England by themselves in 1939, Frank and his wife spent the war in hiding near Grenoble, and only rejoined their children in England in 1946. Lossky's colleague, Berdyaev, was another philosopher whom Natasha translated: she brought out his *Destiny of Man* in 1937. These are not easy books; they were written by philosophers for philosophers. It took someone with Natasha's unique competence in philosophy, Russian, and English to translate them.

Yet another survivor of the Philosophers' Ships was Sergei Bulgakov (1871–1944), and Natasha contributed translations to *A Bulgakov Anthology* in 1976. She was no doubt moved by the expulsion of Lenin's 'undesirables', and may well have chosen to translate them partly because she was one of the few people in the English-speaking world who could appreciate their ideas and make their work better known.

From 1920 until the outbreak of the Second World War, Natasha translated a book a year. Notable among them is a collection of *Forty-Seven Love Poems* (1927) by Anna Andreyevna Gorenko (1889–1966), who wrote as 'Anna Akhmatova'. They belong to the first period of Akhmatova's writing, which ended with the Revolution of 1917. The Bolsheviks denounced her poetry for its introspective 'bourgeois aesthetic', reflecting only feminine pre-occupations. Yet even when all those close to her had managed to leave Russia, or were shot, Akhmatova chose to stay, although she had no hope of publishing her poems. For the rest of her life, under constant surveillance by Stalin's secret police, with her work officially banned, her first husband arrested and executed, their son Lev imprisoned on numerous occasions on spurious charges, she courageously stood firm. Even her common-law husband, Nikolai Punin, the art scholar, ultimately died in the gulag in 1953.

In the Second World War, she was evacuated from St Petersburg during the siege, almost died of typhus, and returned in 1945 to find the city a mere ghost of itself. Even then, the intimidation was unrelenting: in 1949 her son Lev was arrested yet again and sentenced to ten years in a Siberian prison camp; he was released in 1956 (along with a great many other gulag prisoners). Throughout this time, Akhmatova still managed to compose poetry. It was too risky to write in notebooks or anything like that; she kept her poems in her head until a trusted friend could visit; then she would hastily write them out; the friend memorized the lines, and they immediately burned the paper she had written on.

At the end of the 1950s, Akhmatova managed to re-compose these poems and get some published. Immediately recognized as the greatest Russian woman poet of the first half of the twentieth century and particularly the Silver Age, she was nominated for the Nobel Prize for Literature in both 1965 and the following year. She died in March 1966, shortly after being permitted to visit Oxford to receive the Taormina Prize and an honorary doctorate. On this occasion, Natasha was able to meet Akhmatova for the first time and hear from her own lips that she thoroughly approved of Natasha's translation.

In one of Natasha's articles on 'New Russian Philosophy,' which appeared in *The New Atlantis* for January 1934, she discussed works by several Russian thinkers. They included *Etika Preobrazhennogo Erosa* ('Ethics of the Transfigured Eros', 1931) by Boris Vysheslavtzev (1877–1954), another survivor of the Philosophers' Ships. Natasha used the Old Orthography, *'Preobrazhennogo'*, for the second word, rather than *'Preobrazhennavo'*. A poem by the Scottish poet Hugh MacDiarmid appeared in the same issue of *The New Atlantis*; he obviously read Natasha's article, for when he subsequently titled one of his poems (in *Stony Limits*) 'Etika Preobrazhennavo Erosa', he repeated this spelling. Vysheslavtzev's philosophy, or at any rate Natasha's account of it, 'is relevant primarily to the poem's references to spiritual aspiration and the sublimation of the self in a larger force.'[26]

Natasha's name also appears in the list of contributors to volume 4 of *The Encyclopedia and Dictionary of Education* (1922) by Professor Foster Watson. She clearly made a place for herself in philosophical thinking in Britain, and greatly contributed to our knowledge of Russian philosophy and literature. She died in May 1972, at the age of 85.

Until now, her life has remained unsung and almost entirely forgotten, yet she not only brought Russian literature and Russian philosophy to the West, she also helped raise our awareness of the persecution of Soviet citizens by their own rulers, and helped some of them survive famine. She was enabled to do this first by Constance Garnett, who encouraged her to come to England, and then by Jack Duddington, who loved and encouraged her from the moment they met.

On the other hand, her family in Moscow did not do so well. Her sister Elena married a D. F. Tupikov, about whom I know nothing, although it is noteworthy that, after the death of Konstantin Sokolov in 1919, the running of the country theatre that he and his wife had established was put in the hands of a local teacher, L. F. Tupikova. The coincidence of the same family name combined with the same initial of the patronymic suggest that Elena's husband was quite possibly this woman's brother.

Natasha's mother Mariya died in 1919, in one of the outbreaks of typhus that swept through Russia's cities soon after the Revolution. Elena, who was also a translator (from English into Russian) and her husband caught typhus too – they were probably all living together. Tupikov died, while Elena survived; she also survived the years of famine that followed the Revolution. Since Natasha sent food parcels to the Lossky family, there is every reason to think that she will have sent them to her sister as well. In 1927 Elena managed to escape from the Soviet Union and join Natasha in England. On this occasion, Constance Garnett was 'very active in getting her a residence permit,' even writing to the Home Secretary in support of her application, which was granted in 1930.[27] Like most refugees from the Bolsheviks, Elena did not speak of the nightmare she had left behind, but delighted Natasha's grandchildren with her piano-playing.

Of Natasha's adoptive siblings, Kirik Levin wrote a brief history of the Decembrist uprising of 1825; it appeared just a year before the 1905 revolution and was reprinted in volume 1 of *A History of Russia in the 19th Century* (1907). He went on to write a study of Alexander Herzen, *A. I. Herzen. Personality, Ideology*. It came out in 1922, the year Kirik died, aged only 46 (which suggests that he may have starved, or been executed).

As for Lenochka, she married an officer in the Imperial Army. After the Revolution, he joined Denikin's anti-Bolshevik army. When that was routed by the Red Army, he and Lenochka travelled hundreds of miles by horse and cart through Kazakhstan and succeeded in joining Admiral Kolchak's army just before it made 'the Great White March' along the route of the Trans-Siberian Railway in the direction of Vladivostok.[28] Lenochka survived and in later years lived in Prague with her second husband.[29]

Natasha in her sixties

It may well be that Elena's escape and the stories she had to tell decided Natasha to translate the harrowing accounts of the hardship and horror of living in Soviet Russia – and the difficulty of escaping from it – by Tatiana Tchernavin, *Escape from the Soviets* (1933)[30] and *We, Soviet Women* (1935).[31] Tatiana Tchernavin was an old school friend of Natasha's from Madame Stoyunina's academy.

Significantly, these translations are signed 'N. Alexander' – Aleksandrovna being Natasha's patronymic – which suggests that she chose to mask her identity in case Stalin's agents decided to punish either her (for revealing to the Anglo-Saxon world the reality of life in Soviet Russia) or her sister (for fleeing from that life).

Sources

Bruce Lockhart, Robert. *Memoirs of a British Agent.* Putnam's Sons, 1933.

Chamberlain, Lesley. *The Philosophy Steamer: Lenin and the Exile of the Intelligentsia.* Atlantic Books, 2007. Published in the USA as *Lenin's Private War: The Voyage of the Philosophy Steamer and the Exile of the Intelligentsia* by St Martin's Press.

Garnett, David. *The Golden Echo.* Volume 1. New York: Harcourt, Brace, 1954. Volume 2: *The Flowers of the Forest.* Chatto & Windus, 1955.

Garnett, Richard. *Constance Garnett: A Heroic Life.* Sinclair-Stevenson, 1991.

Goncharov, Ivan. *Oblomov.* Trans. Natalie Duddington. Intro. Richard Freeborn. New York: Everyman's Library, Knopf, 2014.

Krueger, Joel. 'Direct Social Perception.' In *Oxford Handbook of 4E Cognition,* eds. Newen, de Bruin, & Gallagher. OUP, 2017.

Graham, Stephen. *Part of the Wonderful Scene. An Autobiography.* Collins, 1964.

Poole, Randall A. 'Integral humanisms: Jacques Maritain, Vladimir Soloviev, and the history of human rights.' in Vestnik Sankt-Peterburgskogo Universiteta, Filosofiia i Konfliktologiia. 2019, 35, 92–106. 10.21638/spbu17.2019.108. Consulted August 2019.

Smith, Helen. *The Uncommon Reader. A Life of Edward Garnett.* Cape, 2017.

Tchernavin, Tatiana. *Escape from the Soviets.* Trans. N. Alexander. Hamish Hamilton, 1933.

—— *We, Soviet Women.* London; Hamish Hamilton, 1935.

Tchernavin, Vladimir. *I Speak for the Silent: Prisoners of the Soviets.* Trans. Nicholas M. Oushakoff. Boston & New York: Hale, Cushman & Flint, 1935.

Waithe, Ellen. *A History of Women Philosophers.* Vol. 4. Kluwer, 1994.

Whitworth, Michael. 'Forms of Culture in Hugh MacDiarmid's "Etika Preobrazhennavo Erosa".' *International Journal of Scottish Literature.* Issue 5, Autumn/Winter 2009, p.3.

Woodcock, Andrew. 'Jacques Maritain, Natural Law and the Universal Declaration of Human Rights' in *Journal of the History of International Law / Revue d'histoire du droit international.* 2006, vol.8, issue 2, pp.245–66. https://doi.org/10.1163/157180506779884455. Consulted August 2017.

Notes

1. Bruce Lockhart, Book iii, Ch.6, p.154.
2. Bruce Lockhart, Book ii, Ch.2, pp.65–6.
3. Richard Garnett, p.211.
4. Constance Garnett's words in a letter to her husband, dated 9 July 1904, quoted in Smith, p.149.
5. David Garnett, Vol. 1, p.78.
6. See https://thetheatretimes.com/big-theatrical-legacy-brought-life-tiny-russian-village/ (dated 23 September 2012).
7. David Garnett, Vol. 2, p.251.
8. Undated letter quoted by Richard Garnett, Vol. 2, p.251.
9. See *The Times* of 5 December 1911, p.3.
10. Information from Philippa Parker.
11. Introduction to the 2014 Everyman edition of *Oblomov.*
12. Richard Garnett, Vol. 2, p.251.
13. See Graham, facing p.33.

[14]   Richard Garnett, p.344.

[15]   Quoted by Richard Garnett, Vol. 2, p.304.

[16]   Smith, pp.99–100.

[17]   Smith, p.298.

[18]   From the Introduction to the 2014 Everyman edition of *Oblomov*.

[19]   Quoted by Richard Garnett, p.304.

[20]   *Mind*, 19: 147–178.

[21]   *Mind*, 30 (118): 195–197.

[22]   See Krueger on 'Direct Social Perception.'

[23]   Poole, p.92.

[24]   See Woodcock, passim.

[25]   See Chamberlain, p.22.

[26]   Whitworth, p.3.

[27]   Richard Garnett, p.339.

[28]   Information from David Garnett, Vol. 2, pp.182–3.

[29]   Personal communication from Sebastian Garrett.

[30]   The Tchernavins' son Andrei (1918–2007) was twelve when he escaped with his parents. He described their hazardous trek across the border into Finland in Angus MacQueen's documentary *Gulag* (2000), which was filmed on location in the Russian Arctic.

[31]   The American edition of 1936 has no comma in the title.

4 Lola, A.K., and D.

It was November 1916. Lola Kinel and her twin sister Rita were on a train to St Petersburg where their father was now working. They had barely seen him, or their big brother, for the past six years. Ever since their mother died, they had been on the move, staying with various members of their extensive family in Poland, Austria, Switzerland, and Germany. They had just spent a year with an uncle and aunt in America, adding yet another language to their collection. They were actually Polish, and they spoke Polish with their dear Granny (who would also be waiting for them in St Petersburg), but much of Poland was a province of Russia, so their passports were Russian. What is more, they were born in Russia itself, for their father worked as an Inspector for the government Monopoly on the sale of alcohol, principally vodka, and he moved around the country a good deal. So they received their first education in Russia. Then they went to various schools across Europe, including France.

Long journeys were nothing new to them. The worst had been when they were evacuated from their school in Germany at the outbreak of the Great War: three weeks crossing Sweden and Finland in cattle trucks, boats, and refugee trains. Only two years had passed since then, yet it seemed such a long time ago, so much had happened. And at eighteen Lola felt quite grown up compared with the child she had been then. Looking back, she realized that she had found their escape a thrilling, breath-taking adventure!

Life in St Petersburg would surely be exciting too, compared with New York and Los Angeles, where the people they had met were dull and disappointing, interested only in playing bridge and golf.

At least she had learned some practical things in America, like typing and stenography, and she hoped to use them in her first job.

The train crawled on through the endless Finnish landscape of trees and lakes. Walking up and down the corridor to stretch her legs, Lola noticed a man in the next compartment: a young *chinovnik*, a high-class St Petersburg office worker, dressed after the English fashion. He was teaching himself chess, solving problems from a manual while he balanced the travelling chessboard on his knee. Hearing Lola and Rita speak English together, he tried to chat them up. People of his class were always impressed by English; 'it was the language of the Russian aristocracy, whereas French was merely the language of the bourgeoisie.'[1] The twins didn't like him, but Lola could not resist offering to play him at chess. It was so long since she'd had a game.

As they played, she noticed another man casting curious glances through the open door of the compartment. He was tall, wearing a Russian military greatcoat and a fur cap, though without any insignia. He had long red moustaches that completely hid his mouth, and bright, smiling eyes. Eventually, he put his head in through the door and asked if he could watch the game. He spoke in Russian with an accent that Lola could not quite identify. After she had beaten the *chinovnik*, he asked if he too might play against her. This time, to her amazement, he spoke in English – not American, but a different kind that sounded much nicer to her ear. She had never heard Oxford English before, and she realized that it fitted the language of the books she liked to read far better than the American accent. They played, and she lost.

The next day, she played another game against the man with the walrus moustache; he was very pleasant. Aside from the accent, he might have been Russian, a really nice Russian. His eyes twinkled and he laughed readily; when she told him she was planning to get a secretarial job in St Petersburg, he smiled with his eyes and said nothing. After quite a battle, she lost to him again and vowed to look up all the openings when she got home.

The train pulled into the last stop before St Petersburg. Idly glancing through the window, Lola suddenly gave a loud shout, '*Tatusiu!*' and slapped the window with both hands. There was her father on the platform! All at once she was a little girl again and couldn't wait to be in his arms. He joined them in the compartment, the same old Daddy, genial and handsome, with his deep, hearty laugh. It was so like him to spring this surprise on his daughters.

Witnessing this joyful reunion, the English-speaking man tactfully got up to leave. Lola and Rita begged him to stay; they liked him and wanted him to meet their father. The two men exchanged visiting cards – huge cards they were in those days – and the girls peeped to see the name of their new friend. 'Artur Kirrilovich Ransom, correspondent *Daily News*' it said in Cyrillic.[2] (I suspect that Lola's memory was at fault here: this patronymic is usually spelled *Kirillovich*.) Below it, in small Latin type: 'Arthur Ransome'.

He had been in Russia for much of the past three years, fleeing an utterly impossible wife, learning Russian, and writing. He had finished a cultural guide to St Petersburg in little more than two months and then written *Old Peter's Russian Tales,* in which he found the narrative voice that we were not to hear again until *Swallows and Amazons* was published in 1930. The cultural guide was never published, rendered obsolete by all the changes brought about by the Revolution, but the *Tales* were published and have remained in print ever since. They brought in little money; he earned his keep by writing for the London *Daily News.*

What Ransome did not mention was that he was in direct contact with the British Secret Service (known at this point as MI1c). It all began in January 1916 when he approached the British Ambassador, Sir George Buchanan, with the idea of placing pro-Russian stories in British newspapers. Buchanan passed the idea on to London, where it was approved and a British-run propaganda organization, the International News Agency, was set up. At that point, of course, the aim was to strengthen the ties between Britain and Russia, who were allied in fighting the Germans.

As he had been introduced, Ransome was permitted to visit the family. Lola, who had a secret hope that one day she might become a writer, liked him more than Rita did. Having studied music at the Conservatory, Rita was more interested in renewing her contacts with the world of music in St Petersburg. One day Lola went to see Ransome in his huge room in an old boarding house. It was the first bachelor pad she had ever seen.

> It had a desk and typewriter in one corner; in another a bed, night table and dresser, all behind a screen; then a sort of social arrangement consisting of an old sofa, and a round table with some chairs. And *books*. They were everywhere, heaped in rows on the dresser, heaped on chairs, heaped on the sofa and even on the floor.

And everywhere there were old socks, holed and dirty. 'Doesn't anyone ever mend your socks for you?' she asked, gingerly holding one up between two gloved fingers. Apparently mending was not a service performed by Russian laundresses. So he just bought new ones.

> 'And look at your desk – all this dust! Doesn't the maid ever dust in here?'

> 'I would wring her neck if she did!' he snorted.[3]

Soon they were good friends, despite the disparity of age: Ransome turned thirty-three in January 1917, while she would not be nineteen until March. He called her 'Little Twin' – Lola being the smaller of the two – and she called him 'A.K.' after the initials of his Russian-style name on his card. He became quite fond of her, although irritated by her failure to appreciate the wonderful revolution that was taking place under her very nose. They were rather like an uncle and his favourite niece; think of Uncle Jim and Nancy Blackett in *Swallows and Amazons*. (At no point in her autobiography did Lola give any sign that she had read any of Arthur Ransome's children's books.)

Dazzled by the personalities propounding an ideal of social equality, of an end to the exploitation and oppression of the underprivileged, Ransome tended to overlook the means by which these ideals were to be achieved. Yet he had been warned. When he first arrived in Russia, he stayed with an Anglo-Russian family, Harold Williams and his wife Ariadna Tyrkova. She told him of how, when she met Lenin in Geneva in 1908, she had commented that she had no wish to live in a Russia ruled by illiterate factory workers. Lenin informed her that this was exactly why, when the revolution came, she would be one of the first to be hanged from a lamp post. She had never forgotten the smile on his face as he said this, and how he savoured the French word for lamp post, *lanterne,* that he used. It was a direct allusion to the method of eliminating the aristocracy adopted by the mob during the French Revolution.

Being more pragmatic, Lola preferred to bide her time, wanting to see how the Bolsheviks would behave before she took sides. She found Ransome 'clever, yet childish, very sincere and kind and romantic.' He was a true bohemian, with 'a thorough contempt for men who dressed well, or the least conventionally. He forgave women if they were pretty, but he preferred most Russian women, who did not pose and were simple, to English girls.'[4] Lola could not know how this reflected his disappointment at the character that his wife had revealed after he married her.

Another view of Ransome at this time is provided by George Hill, who first met him in Moscow early in 1918.

He had radical views which he never hesitated to express, and he was not exactly persona grata with British officials in Russia. This was partly due to a trick he had of entering into an argument and deliberately exciting the anger of his opponent – I suspect because he found that this was one of the easiest ways of getting at the truth, and Ransome was pre-eminently a journalist out for news. He was extremely well informed, intimate with the Bolsheviks and masterly in summing up a situation. He was a tall, lanky, bony individual with a shock of sandy hair, usually unkempt, and the eyes of a small inquisitive and rather mischievous boy. He really was a lovable personality when you came to know him.

He lived on the same corridor as I did, but had no bathroom

attached to his bedroom and so used to come in early every morning to use mine. Our profoundest discussions and most heated arguments took place when Ransome was sitting in the bath and I wandering up and down my room dressing. Sometimes, when I had the better of an argument and his feelings were more than usually outraged, he would jump out of the water and beat himself dry like an angry gorilla. After that he would not come for his bath for two or three days, then we would meet and grin at each other, I would ask after the pet snake which lived in a large cigar box in his room, and the following morning he would come in as usual and we would begin arguing again, the best of friends.[5]

During the winter of 1916/17, while Lola was looking for work, Ransome invited her to read the daily newspapers for him and cut out articles that would be of interest to readers in Britain. She enjoyed doing this, but soon found that with her indifference to politics and ignorance of England she could not guess what (in his opinion at any rate) would interest his readers. Luckily, she soon found work as a shorthand typist in a newly opened American bank; however, that did not last long because they wanted someone with more experience. Then she was with an English firm supplying steel cables, but the Revolution put paid to that business.

Everyone could feel revolution coming. Russia was like a pressure cooker without a safety valve: they could all hear it simmering, and no one knew how to stop it before the lid blew off. In the autumn of 1916, when he was in London, Ransome had predicted that there would be two revolutions, one in March and one in October (Old Style), coinciding with the seasonal food shortages, and indeed it all started on 8 March 1917 with a demonstration by women against the shortage of bread. They were joined by strikers from a munitions factory. Other people, of all classes, descended into the streets, some of them simply curious to see what was going on. At first, Cossacks stood by and did not intervene. Then, two days later, on Sunday the 10th, the army started shooting, and that turned the riot into a revolution.

It must have been on that day – for she was not at work and there were no trams running – that Lola walked all of the four miles to Ransome's flat. When she arrived, he was just going out to see what was happening, and she joined him. 'We went toward the river,' she writes,

> and soon noticed a large detachment of soldiers walking to one of the bridges. With a correspondent's nose for news, A.K. decided to follow them.... Just as we were approaching the bridge, right behind the soldiers, we saw a detachment on the other side of the river approaching the same bridge. A.K. was excited. The soldiers in front of us walked a little slower, in a more compact group; the others came straight on. When they were about two hundred feet away from us, they halted. Our soldiers halted too. The soldiers in the front ranks of the other detachment began to kneel down. Almost simultaneously they opened fire. The bullets began to whistle with the characteristic swishing sound, the crack of the report coming a bit later. A.K. and I watched intensely. It was like a show, only more vivid. The bullets came faster, one going right between our two heads. Holding my hand, A.K. watched with shining eyes.
>
> All of a sudden he shouted, 'Christ, Twin, I forgot you were here!' and, pulling me by the hand, he began to go back, still watching the fight.
>
> 'I don't want to go. I want to watch!' I said, stubbornly. But he pulled harder and began to run, dragging me along.
>
> 'Oh, A.K., I want to watch some more,' I begged, hanging back. Instead of arguing, he raised me in his arms and began to run. Only when we had left the bridge and turned the corner did he set me down.[6]

Lola kept her cool when under fire on another occasion. She was in her father's top-floor office when snipers on the roof above started shooting at the demonstrators in the street. Back came a hail of bullets, shattering the office windows. Mr Kinel made everyone lie down on the floor, where they remained for some three quarters of an hour. The snipers, the staunchest supporters of the old regime, were on suicide missions, for if they came down the rioters would tear them to pieces. So it was a matter of waiting until they had all been picked off. Finally, the shooting died down. Shaking off the broken glass, the office workers got up to find themselves surrounded by spent bullets that had failed to reach the roof. No one was hurt. At once, despite her father's protests, Lola decided to walk home, wanting to see what was going on in the streets. She was not particularly courageous, just curious, protected by her teenage belief in her invulnerability.

This belief was put to the test a few months later. By the summer of 1917, Lola was thin and weak from lack of food. The bread ration had been cut to a few grammes a day, and the bread itself got darker and darker; soon there was chaff and straw mixed in with the flour, and it became almost indigestible. Yet there was still food out in the countryside. Lola took a week's holiday at Gdov, beside Lake Peipus, which was well stocked with fish, and ate good meals in a local guest house. Each day she borrowed a rowing boat and went down the river to swim in the lake. Not having brought a bathing costume, she used her American union suit.

This raised questions. One day her landlady took her aside: 'The boys say that when you swim you wear some garment that covers you completely. Do you have unsightly moles or something?' So she abandoned the prudery she had learned in America and swam naked; the boys took no notice of her after that. They were used to nude girls in the water; it was the body suit that had intrigued them. (It was not for nothing that the American humorist and film-maker Will Rogers, who was a sharp observer of the world, called one of his travelogues, 'There is not a bathing suit in Russia.')

One warm evening she decided to take a midnight swim. Resting on a sandbank, she was surprised by the arrival of a group of soldiers, who had borrowed a rowing boat for an excursion on the lake. She remained motionless, hoping to pass unnoticed. They saw her – but decided she was a corpse and hastily rowed away, wanting nothing to do with it. Lola was greatly relieved, for in those lawless days, many women were raped, and not only by soldiers.

On this holiday, Lola stayed in a fisherman's cottage, but for her midday meal she went to a boarding house not far away, which led her to make a perceptive observation about the effect of Lenin's Order No 1. A famous cavalry division was quartered nearby,

> and about a dozen of the officers came to this table d'hote, where we met at two each day. They looked like the old-time officers ... but there was something about them, nevertheless, which had subtly changed. They seemed lost, these elegant young men, and their swagger was a little forced. Out on the street, when the soldiers met them they now often omitted to salute, and this made the officers feel funny, I think.[7]

One day, between the two revolutions, she dressed in her shabbiest clothes to go and hear Lenin speak, being curious to see the man that her father dismissed as a demagogue. For all her indifference to politics, Lola knew that 'demagoguery is part of every great revolutionary's equipment.' She had read Lenin's speeches in the newspapers, and learned how he proclaimed that

> all the power should go to the Soviets; that the soldiers should fraternize with the enemy and make their own peace and... that all banks and property should be nationalized and a workers' government take control.
>
> And the soldiers and workers and cooks and maids and small artisans and common tramps, and all the motley people of Russia who live much of the time on the street, listened to him spellbound, as he hammered these simple ideas into their heads.... And why the bourgeoisie, so terrified by it all six months later, did not pay any attention to him in those early days of April and May, will remain one of the mysteries of history....

They were hypnotized, like rabbits caught in the headlamps of a car rushing towards them.

> There was a good reason for this. As Lola herself points out,
> the people who had never had free speech and a free Press, who

had been dammed up for three hundred odd years, were suddenly allowed to speak. And as Russians are inveterate speakers anyway, the thing became an epidemic. But whereas they used to speak mostly in the privacy of their own homes (on politics, I mean) or at secret meetings or secret clubs, now they could speak anywhere. They spoke on the streets and in trains and in tramcars. People forgot their stops, because they were engrossed in discussions.[8]
The feeling of freedom was exhilarating. 'Russia would be a happy, free country. A democracy! Like other countries! Free!... *Svobodnaya Rossia!* (Free Russia!) How we revelled in this phrase!'[9]

Lola did not tell her family that she had been to hear Lenin. Nor did she tell Ransome, although she had become a regular visitor to his flat, borrowing books. One evening when she dropped round unannounced, he was playing chess with a young man. Chess was one of the many ways in which Ransome made friends with important people; he could glean all kinds of information from them when their minds were on the game. One of these friends was Captain Francis Cromie, whom Ransome saw as 'one of the very few [people] capable of inspiring trust on both sides of the ever-widening divide' between the British and the Bolsheviks.[10] We'll be hearing more of him later.

On this occasion, Lola did not know Ransome's chess partner. Embarrassed to have disturbed them, she quickly chose some fresh books and prepared to take her leave. The young man looked up.

'"Do you play chess too?" he asked.

'"I do. Not as well as Ransome though,"' and she looked at the man for the first time. 'He was handsome. Young and tall and slender and dark, with brown eyes that were both clever and shy. And with an imperious chin.

'"May I have a game with you sometime?" he asked.

'"Why, yes."

'"When shall we play? Tomorrow?" He spoke with a sort of desperate shyness.'[11]
'Tomorrow is fine,' she answered, and left.

So they played the following evening, and on many others after that. D – Lola never revealed his full name, and I have been unable to discover it – was twenty-four and worked in the British Embassy. He was well bred, had travelled a good deal, and read widely. His modesty was equalled only by his perfect manners. Lola soon fell for his typically English charm; he was so unlike the Russian boys she had met. They usually played two games; then D's landlady would bring in tea or cocoa for them. And they would talk. About books – Russian and English; about life; and about themselves. Outside, the great Revolution was taking place and they never mentioned it.

In September 1917, Ransome was in a poor state of health, suffering from ill-nourishment (to the point where he actually fainted in the street one day), so he made another trip to London and consequently missed the second Revolution too. By the time he came back, the joy of the first had been forgotten. Having tasted six months of freedom, the Russians bowed beneath a fresh yoke that grew heavier by the day. Thanks to his contacts in London, Ransome returned with an introduction to the new People's Commissar for Foreign Affairs, Leon Trotsky. He interviewed him at once and his article was published in Britain on 31 December. It made a great impression. He followed it up with two more interviews. He was so busy that Lola hardly saw him any more. She never guessed that he had fallen in love.

As it was, her free evenings were spent with D, and her days were devoted to the *Russian Daily News*. This was St Petersburg's only English-language newspaper, a shoestring operation. Having no reporters of its own, it depended largely on articles in the Russian press, hastily translated and printed a day later. Lola was its Girl Friday: secretary to the editors, translator, proof-reader, and general factotum. When the night editor expected news to come in by phone, he would call her to his side, and she would type to his dictation. He amazed her. While listening on the phone, he could turn what he heard into ready copy, in crisp newspaper style, neatly paragraphed. But what they printed was mostly rumours, rumours that comforted their readers. 'The Bolsheviks won't last more than a month or two. They know nothing about government, or administration.'

But the Bolsheviks knew how to stifle the press. One by one, the old newspapers were closed down. Sales of the *Russian Daily News* increased. And then someone had the idea of printing half of it in Russian. It became popular – until they were visited by half a dozen Kronstadt sailors. These were the men who made the official arrests for the Bolsheviks. Suddenly, the Editor could not be found. The night editor, a young American, came forward. Lola told the sailors who he was.

'"Tell him," said one of them, "that we have come to close your paper for counter-revolutionary propaganda, and for printing false news."'

Lola translated. The night editor bowed his head and signed a receipt. The sailors left.

Faithful to the long-standing practice of pre-revolutionary Russia, the name of the paper changed to the *Morning Star*, and it appeared as usual the following day. A couple of weeks later, the sailors came back; the editor was again not available; and the *Evening Post* began to appear. This little game was repeated several times until the sailors came back with sledgehammers and smashed the composing machines and the printing press. Lola was out of a job.

She lost her boyfriend at about the same time. All the diplomatic staff in St Petersburg – British, American, and French, alike, and D along with them – were evacuated at the end of February 1918. He promised to write to her – as a friend. Lola would happily have slept with him, but his code of honour came from a country where things were simply 'done' or 'not done', a notion incomprehensible to most Russians. Pre-marital sex was routine among young people in St Petersburg at the time. 'When the Bolsheviks issued their new decrees about marriage and divorce which so shocked the Western

World, they hardly invented anything new; they simply legalized what had been going on for almost ten years,' observed Lola.[12] She found the way the English clung to everything that represented *home* for them, from morals to tweeds and pipes, quite hilarious. She could hardly stop laughing for a whole week after she discovered that Ransome travelled with *a rubber bath.*

Two weeks later, Trotsky moved his office to Moscow and Ransome moved there too, so Lola saw him less than ever. It was a terrible time. She lived on indigestible black bread and, like everyone else, dressed in her shabbiest clothes; to look like a bourgeois was to invite a bullet in the back of the head.

On one of his flying visits, Ransome had hardly sipped his watery tea when he came out with,

'Twin, will you do some shopping for me? I have to catch the train back to Moscow tonight.'[13]

He had a long list of books that he needed – titles like *The Mexican Rebellion, Partisan War, Guerilla War Tactics,* and so on – and she obligingly spent the entire day going round the second-hand bookshops in St Petersburg for him. (St Petersburg bookshops had always been good, but now they were particularly well supplied, as the intelligentsia sold off their libraries prior to fleeing the country.) At the end of the afternoon, she had so many parcels, each neatly wrapped in paper and tied with string, that she took a *droshky* home. Ransome was surprised and delighted. 'Trotsky will be so pleased!' he exclaimed. Having relinquished Foreign Affairs, Trotsky was now creating the Red Army.

'What? *Trotsky?*' She could hardly believe it. 'You are a pig,' she stormed, 'asking me to help your silly Trotsky with his army. A.K., I will never forgive you this!'[14] Three months later, though, she had reason to forgive him.

He paid one of his unexpected visits, his eyes sparkling, and his voice more intense than usual. Anticipating the Bolsheviks' suppression of the bourgeoisie, he had come to save Lola and her sister.

'Listen,' he said, 'if you and your Babushka [Granny] can pretend

you are German, I think I could get you out of Russia and back to
Poland.'

'But how?'

'Mirbach, the German Ambassador in Moscow, is arranging
with the Bolsheviks for the return of all German war prisoners to
Germany. Some of them will go through St Petersburg. The only
trouble is passports; if we can get over that – and I think we can –
you could board the train here, and when you get to Poland, you
just get off. No one will stop you there.'[15]

He talked it over with her father and soon it was all arranged.
(Ransome must have used his contacts in the Commissariat of
Foreign Affairs to obtain the false passports and have their names
added to the list of persons to be repatriated.) Posing as Germans,
Lola, Rita and their Granny left St Petersburg in June on a train
composed of wagons marked '6 horses and 1 man.' Each contained
about fifty German prisoners of war. Some had come from as far
away as Siberia. They had one suitcase each, which served as their
seat.

When they reached the area occupied by the Germans, they were
all ordered out into a camp to be deloused and inoculated against
typhus. When this was explained to Babushka, she drew herself up
and asked to see the commanding officer. With quiet dignity she
explained to him that they had come from St Petersburg and not a
prisoner of war camp; neither she nor her granddaughters had ever
had lice, nor was there any typhus in St Petersburg. (This was perfectly true at the time, but there was a nasty outbreak almost
immediately after they left, swiftly followed by cholera.) They were
clean. 'If I have to stay in this camp,' she said calmly, 'I shall surely
become ill and may die. I am an old woman and I want to go home
and die in peace.'[16]

Such was the force of Babushka's character that within minutes,
their lovely fake passports had been stamped; in an hour they were
on a fast train, in a proper carriage with seats; and the next day they
were in Warsaw. Lola only realized how lucky they had been when,

in 1919 and 1920, other members of her family dragged themselves home, more dead than alive, having survived persecution and terror, disease and starvation. Among them was her father, whose flight had taken him down to the Black Sea and back to Poland through Bulgaria. Her big brother had been with the Imperial Army, in a port on the Caspian Sea, when the Revolution broke out and they never heard from him again. She and Rita owed their salvation to Arthur Ransome.

After that, she lost contact with him, so he never learned of her further adventures. In Warsaw she worked as the secretary to the local director of the American-Jewish Relief Mission (AJRM), organizing the distribution of food to starving peasants. During this time, she received a postcard from D, forwarded from St Petersburg. Eventually, he was posted to Danzig (Gdańsk today), and it was to Danzig, when the Bolsheviks unexpectedly stormed Warsaw in July 1920, that Lola made another dramatic escape, this time by car with the American Vice-Consul and other diplomats. So after two years of separation, she and D met up again. She found a job as an administrator in a refugee camp, with its daily litany of heart-breaking personal tragedies, and saw D quite often. With his help, she managed to get two little boys, who had nothing and no family, just the address of an uncle in London, the British visas that had previously been denied them.

But her relationship with D did not work out. 'If I could have foreseen the misery that fate had in store for us I should never have replied to that card.... D was still chock-full of principles and, what was worse, conventions' that kept her at arm's length.[17] (I suspect that he was homosexual, to which he not possibly admit at that time, any more than she could recognize it.) Lola continues, 'Perhaps I loved him even more for that, just as I loved his strong jutting chin, his fine eyes, and his whole beautiful, chiselled face.'[18] In the end, though, she sorrowfully went her separate way.

When they arrived in Poland, her sister Rita found a job as a pianist, accompanying silent films from 5 p.m. to midnight in a third-rate cinema. Having a rare talent for improvisation, she could make up an accompaniment as she watched a film from the piano placed behind the screen. It was exhausting work, playing for seven hours at a stretch. On Sundays, the films started at two in the afternoon, so Lola would take over from her for a while, but three hours was usually the most she could manage. And she needed a score.

One day Rita came home in great excitement. She had met and fallen in love with an eighteen-year-old violinist called Vic. He had been born in America, but when he and his sister were very young they had been sent to live with their maternal grandparents in Warsaw: their father was a singer with a touring opera company and after the death of their mother, he thought her Polish parents were better placed to bring them up. Realizing Vic's musical talent, his grandfather gave him a violin at the age of nine, and then enabled him to study at the Warsaw Conservatory. After graduating, unemployed and penniless like everyone else, he played all the time: in concerts, with the famous Warsaw Philharmonic, in a quartet, a quintet, and in between he gave lessons. Rita smuggled food from the table at home to help feed him. When Vic decided to return to America, Rita followed him and they married in April 1922.

Before Rita left, Lola was moved to Vienna by the AJRM; after three days, they sent her on to Berlin, which was full of Russian emigrés. Rather than be moved on yet again, to Paris, she parted company with the Mission and found employment as the secretary of a Berlin music magazine. As she was expected to attend concerts in the evening and write them up, in addition to her day job, she ended up working fifteen- and sixteen-hour days. That was too much. Wanting to make greater use of her language skills, she placed a small ad in Berlin's English-language newspaper and found herself engaged as private secretary to Isadora Duncan during her brief marriage to the Russian poet Sergei Yesenin. He spoke only Russian; Isadora had picked up 'a sort of Russian, a quaint language of her own, twisted, naive, and broken, but very charming, which quite sufficed for everyday use with Yesenin,[19] but when it came to lovers' quarrels, arguments about God, or the way people slept together in different countries, Lola had to interpret for them. She also had to explain to Yesenin the impossibility of providing him with faithful translations of his poetry into English. As the marriage broke down, Lola was caught in the crossfire. It was almost inevitable that she should be dismissed for not obeying an order from Yesenin, one day when he was more drunk than usual. (It was shortly after Isadora and Yesenin separated that Max Eastman met Isadora in Kislovodsk.)

Brief though her time was with this famous couple, Lola had the unforgettable experiences of seeing Isadora dance and hearing Yesenin recite his poetry. Everyone who attempted to describe Isadora's dancing was invariably lost for words; 'it was a thing beyond explanations, beyond analysis, above words.'[20] Lola tells us that her dances 'were full of profound meaning. They seemed to reveal all the different emotions through which a human being, or humanity itself, passes in a lifetime.'[21] On one occasion, Yesenin recited

> extracts from his dramatic poem, *Pougachyov*, the story of the great Cossack rebel who rose against Catherine the Great, led the peasants against her soldiers, and was Russia's first great revolutionary.
>
> I was instantly spellbound; Yesenin's voice of the Southern Russian peasant, soft and slightly drawling, ran an amazing gamut of expressions, from the very gentlest crooning, which was like a caress, to some utterly wild, hoarse shrieks. He *was* Pougachyov, the tortured peasant... at first long-suffering, patient, bewildered, and then wild, cunning, wrathful, terrible in his anger and desire for freedom and revenge... and then, at the end, when he was betrayed, humble and forlorn.[22]

After leaving Isadora Duncan and Yesenin, Lola could not find work in postwar Germany, so she returned to Poland, where a letter from Rita, writing from America, encouraged her to join her. So she emigrated in 1923 and spent the rest of her life in the US.

By the time Lola joined Rita and her husband, Vic Young, he had found that he could make more money working as a concert master in a movie theatre than as a violinist. The better cinemas had their own orchestras to accompany films, which now came with their own scores, and even an overture to play while the audience were taking their seats. Occasionally, Vic would compose an overture of his own, and from this he moved into writing music for radio plays and then films, for which he proved to have a particular talent. In the mid-1930s, he was 'discovered' by Hollywood and composed the scores for more than three hundred films, ending with *Around the World in Eighty Days* (1956), for which he received a posthumous Oscar, having been nominated no less than twenty-two times before without winning the award. One wonders what part Rita played in all this, she who could improvise film music on the piano for hours at a time.

Lola was less successful; she married in the mid-1920s, had a daughter, and divorced after her husband fell in love with his secretary. Thereafter she was a single parent, dependent on alimony and presents from her sister, for she was unable to find work – this was the start of the Great Depression, and she had no qualifications, no recommendations, and no experience that Americans recognized. She tried writing, and realized that although she was fluent in Russian, Polish, German, and English – and she was good at French too – her written English was not idiomatic. So she set about reading all the good books in English that she could lay her hands on, at the same time as observing their style and technique. She wanted to write fiction, but found that she could not predict how readers would react to what she wrote: she had not yet absorbed enough of American culture. When she began to write, in the early 1930s, it was to tell her life story, in very readable English. Published in America in 1937 as *This is My Affair,* it sold well enough. Published in England as *Under Five Eagles: My Life in Russia, Poland, Austria,*

Germany and America 1916–1936, it quickly sold out and was reprinted the same year. But it was her only book, and she wrote no novels.

Over the years that remained to her – she was aged 90 when she died – Lola did some translating and published a few articles. There's one article that shows her to be an early ecologist: noting that the flowers in her garden were overrun by aphids, she ordered a dollar's worth of ladybirds from a breeder and watched, with great satisfaction, as they feasted on her aphids. She recommends this natural solution to pest control, rather than insecticides, which kill the insect-eating birds. Almost all of her other articles warn of the danger of Soviet Communism, a not altogether different topic. She translated the memoir of a Polish woman who was deported from Poland by the Russians in 1940, along with tens of thousands of other Poles (Jews and Roman Catholics alike), to a slave labour camp in Siberia. Her story came out in 1951, one of the earliest first-hand accounts of life in a gulag to be published in the West. In 'How Karl Marx Won the Civil War', Lola reported on the mendacious representation of the history of America in Soviet schoolbooks. Both articles appeared in *Commentary* magazine, which was a major voicepiece of the American Jewish community, and resolutely anti-Communist and anti-McCarthyite.

She also wrote a memorable letter. As a member of the West Hollywood Democratic Club, Lola attended a meeting in May 1946 at which James Roosevelt was due to speak. He was prevented from doing so at the last minute, and Ronald Reagan was called upon to speak impromptu in his place. A few days later, Lola wrote a letter of appreciation to Reagan, adding, 'I noticed, however, that when you spoke for liberalism and said something to the effect that "we liberals can take care of the Communists ourselves and weed them out and need no help from the reactionaries" – there was a dead silence. I wanted to applaud,' she added, 'then stopped because of this funny reaction.' It had confirmed her feeling that the Democratic Party was being contaminated by Communism.

Lola, soon after she arrived in America:
'Look at her hair!' cried Rita. 'She *must* have it bobbed.'

Lola's letter has historic significance, for it provides evidence of the tipping point in Ronald Reagan's political career, when his opposition to Communism caused him to change from Democratic liberal to Republican conservative – with profound consequences for America and indeed the whole world. And she encouraged him, writing

I find that sticking for all the things which real liberalism means: freedom of the press, of speech, of religion, freedom from fear (and that is important. No one in Soviet Russia is free of fear) seems to put one right into the lap of the reactionaries. Kind of crazy, isn't it? ... What I wanted to say is that if you agree with me that it is important to keep American liberalism true to its real tenets of freedoms, please do speak up for it again whenever you might be called upon to speak. Please make this clear and firm; you have a wonderful talent, you can rouse people and you know how to present ideas forcefully and logically.

On 12 August 1946, Reagan wrote a personal answer to Lola, confirming his change in orientation.

This is a very belated answer to your letter of May 19. I appreciated your writing to me very much & I assure you I was very conscious of the silence that greeted my 'anti-communist' utterance in the address at 'Fairfax Hi'. Yes the entire 'liberal' movement has been invaded by the 'outright communist' element but there is cause for hope. Organized labour has started to rid itself of this 'red' influence – especially here in Southern Calif. And our own Democratic party is in the hands of a man who is well aware of the menace (Jimmy Roosevelt). No matter what he says publicly, I can assure you he resigned from the Hollywood Independent Citizens Committee [HICCASP] because the 'fellow travellers' are in complete control there. Speaking of that organization, some of us have been staging a fight to bring this issue to a head. We presented a resolution for adoption by the executive council which re-affirmed our desire for friendly relations with Russia but repudiated Communism as a form of government desirable for this

country. It only took an hour's discussion to reveal every communist on the council, so many of us who have been active on the
liberal front are resigning & leaving HICCASP to the 'Reds'.[23]

Lola Kinel witnessed the Russian Revolution, but she never found a
man with whom she could share her life. For whatever reason, she
gave her love to men who, like D, were unable to reciprocate,
or who, like her husband, lacked what it takes to make a lasting
commitment. She observed the infiltration of Hollywood by
Communist sympathizers – but never managed to do the writing
she had aspired to. Instead, she left a valuable record of her early
life and experiences, for which we are the richer.

Sources

Chambers, Roland. *The Last Englishman. The Double Life of Arthur
Ransome.* Faber, 2009.

Hill, George A. *Go Spy the Land.* Cassell, 1932.

Kinel, Lola. *Under Five Eagles. My Life in Russia, Poland, Austria,
Germany, and America, 1916–1936.* Putnam, 1937.

The RAAB Collection, https://www.raabcollection.com/presidential-
autographs/reagan-1946. Consulted 8 August 2019.

Notes

[1] Kinel, p.4

[2] Kinel, p.6.

[3] Kinel, p.14.

[4] Kinel, p.15.

[5] Hill, pp.192–3.

[6] Kinel, pp.22–23.

[7] Kinel, p.35.

[8] Kinel, p.29.

[9] Kinel, p.21.

[10] Chambers, p.239.

[11] Kinel, p.41.

[12] Kinel, p.61.

[13] Kinel, p.70.

[14] Kinel, p.71.

[15] Kinel, p.81.

[16] Kinel, p.84.

[17] Kinel, pp.115 and 125.

[18] Kinel, p.62.

[19] Kinel, p.232.

[20] Sheldon Cheney, in the Introduction to *The Art of the Dance* (1928) by Isadora Duncan, quoted in Kinel, p.213.

[21] Kinel, p.215.

[22] Kinel, p.217.

[23] These letters are quoted from the RAAB Collection website, which is where they were first published. I have made some insignificant changes, adopting British rather than American spelling.

Evgenia Shelepina
about the time she started working as a secretary

5 Evgenia and Arthur

WHEN THE FEBRUARY REVOLUTION broke out in 1917, Evgenia Shelepina, aged not quite twenty-three, was working in the typing pool at the Ministry of Trade and Industry in St Petersburg. Her family had been serfs until the Emancipation Reform of 1861, and she had the eminently pragmatic nature of a country girl, along with the physique of a farm labourer: big-boned, standing one metre ninety in her socks. On the other hand, she was quite well educated for a girl in those days – not the kind of education that young women from the aristocracy received in the vast Smolny Institute, but a good country education at the grammar school in Gatchina, about an hour's train ride south of St Petersburg. She was the eldest of the six children, three girls and three boys, of Peter Shelepin; he had risen through the ranks of clerkship to become the curator of the Tsar's Imperial Hospital and Charity Institute.

After her father died in 1912, leaving her mother a modest pension, Evgenia took herself off to study at the Stenography College, which was the only place in St Petersburg to provide the training for government secretaries. On graduation, she immediately found work in the Transport Office of the Ministry of Trade and Industry. In 1917, its windows provided her with a grandstand view of the demonstrations in the streets below; she secretly hoped that the people would win. Her father had supported the 1905 revolution and she shared his desire for greater civil rights.

Throughout that tumultuous time, she herself was never under fire in the streets, which made her quite jealous of her next youngest sister, Eroida, who also worked as a secretary in St Petersburg. To avoid the shooting, Eroida spent the first night of the February revolution at a friend's house. The following day, when things seemed quieter, she and another girl from Gatchina prepared to go home together. 'Almost as soon as they were in the street they had to lie flat on the ground because someone with a machine gun was firing at anything that moved. They had to lie down six times before they got to the station,' Evgenia recalled. 'It was just like Eroida to have all the experience when I really wanted to have it.'[1]

It is natural for young men and women to desire new experiences, but being under machine-gun fire is one that not many of us would 'really want to have'. Evgenia must have been like the teenage Lola Kinel, who so believed in her invulnerability that she did not flinch from gunfire. There may have been an another reason for Evgenia's feelings: At some point during the First World War, she had been engaged to a young man serving in the Imperial Army, and he had been killed. She must surely have wondered what it was like to find oneself under fire.

After the October Revolution, Evgenia's colleagues went on strike – to no effect, however: the Bolsheviks closed all the Tsarist Ministries and created new ones with Bolshevik staff. The only way to get a job in their administration was to join what was now called the Communist Party. (In this manner, the Bolsheviks created an electorate that was grateful for the advantages that accrued from membership, and that could be relied upon to vote for them in the *soviets*.) Luckily for the Shelepina sisters, they had a friend called Mara whose father was secretary of the Gatchina branch of the Party. Through her, all three of them got membership cards and found work with the new regime. (Two of their brothers did the same; only the eldest, Viktor, did not; having joined the Imperial Army in 1914, he fought for the Whites in the civil war.) So when Evgenia applied for secretarial work, and was asked what party she belonged to, she produced her trump card, and was taken on as a typist in the Ministry of Labour.

What she really wanted was to get back her old job in the

Ministry of Trade and Industry, and help run it as before. She made no secret of this when she talked with the head of the Committee of Mobilisation (which found staff for the various ministries). He and she were on good terms and he would laugh at her for being so

Trotsky at the time
Evgenia started working for him

anxious to return to her old post. Having an excellent sense of humour, Evgenia could see the funny side of it too. One day, he told her that he was looking for people for the Commissariat of Foreign Affairs. Did she know any foreign languages? She said she could tell one from another, but not speak any. 'That is unfortunate,' he replied. 'Trotsky wants a practical, sensible secretary, and you would be just right for the job. We can trust you, and you belong to the Party.' She reminded him of her wish to get her old place back, and he promised that this one with Trotsky would be only temporary, adding that he thought she should do it. So she accepted.

When the Bolsheviks took power in November 1917, they appropriated the Smolny Institute and made it their headquarters. (The building is so large that some employees used to ride bicycles down its endless corridors.) Evgenia found the new People's Commissar for Foreign Affairs in room 67, at the end of a corridor on the third floor.

There was just one table in the corner by the two windows. In a little room partitioned off was some dreadful furniture, particularly a green divan with a terrible pillow on it. You could see it had been the room of the resident mistress on that floor when it was still an institute for girls. Trotsky sat on one side of the table and

> I sat on the other. I did not hide from him that I was quite unfit for
> the work, but that I wanted to do anything I could.
>
> It was settled that I should begin at once. The first work I did
> was to make that dreadful room into a place fit to work in. Trotsky
> gave me a chit to take to the Ministry of Foreign Affairs to get a
> good typewriter, instead of the broken one that was in the room
> for show, and telephoned for his motorcar to take me there and
> bring me back with the machine and some furniture.[2]

At the Foreign Ministry, Evgenia found a good typewriter, plus a
table and some chairs, in a room that she soon appropriated for
herself; a smartly dressed sailor helped her carry them back to the
Smolny. She arranged everything so that by the next day she felt it
was possible to work there. She reserved the back of the room,
behind the partition, as Trotsky's private area.

One day, she found a girl aged about sixteen, with short hair like
a boy's, sitting in this private corner. She turned out to be one of
Trotsky's two daughters by his first marriage. Evgenia was taken
aback.

> I thought of Trotsky as of someone so great, and so high, all of
> whose time was given to work. It was almost a shock to me to find
> that he had a daughter. I did not think of him as having any
> human relations at all. I did not know how to address him. Once
> only I called him Comrade Trotsky. It came out very funnily, and
> he immediately called me Comrade Shelepina, and we both
> laughed. After that I always called him Lev Davidovitch, and he
> called me Evgenia Petrovna.[3]

So in Trotsky's office the traditional way of addressing someone –
their first name followed by the patronymic – prevailed over the
new Bolshevik style.

From then on, Evgenia typed most of Trotsky's correspondence,
official and private, including internal memos and notes to diplomats. At first, she was unaware of the historic importance of the
documents she was handling. 'For example, I tore up and threw
away all the replies of the Foreign Embassies to Trotsky's note invit-

ing them to join in discussions of general peace.'[4] Crucially, she controlled access to Trotsky. She soon became proficient in assessing visitors and rapidly deciding who to admit and who to exclude. The British secret agent George Hill left this eloquent picture of her:

> At first glance, one was apt to dismiss her as a very fine-looking specimen of Russian peasant womanhood, but closer acquaintance revealed in her depths of unguessed qualities.... She was methodical and intellectual, a hard worker with an enormous sense of humour. She saw things quickly and could analyse political situations with the speed and precision with which an experienced bridge player analyses a hand of cards.... I do not believe she ever turned away from Trotsky anyone who was of the slightest consequence, and yet it was no easy matter to get past that maiden unless one had that something. She was a glutton for work; morning after morning she would be at the office for nine o'clock and not leave it until well past midnight.[5]

Another glimpse is provided by Bruce Lockhart, who was sent to Russia early in 1918, tasked with trying to prevent the Bolsheviks from making peace with the Central Powers (Germany, Austria-Hungary, the Ottoman Empire, Bulgaria). He arrived too late, but he provides us with a telling description of Trotsky's office and the Smolny, shortly before the Bolsheviks moved the capital from St Petersburg to Moscow:

> I was piloted upstairs through a maze of corridors and classrooms to Trotsky's sanctum on the second floor. I made a mental note of the various notices still posted on the walls: Vth Class Dormitory, Linen Room, Drawing Class. Formerly these corridors had resounded to the gentle tramp of girls' slippers. Everything, one could be sure, had been immaculate; the only unseemliness a foolish giggle. Now all was dirt and confusion. Sailors, Red guards, students and working-men lounged against the walls. None of them looked as if he had washed for a fortnight. Cigarette ends and crumpled news-sheets strewed the floors.

Trotsky's own room was an exception. Lofty and well-lit, it con-
tained a red carpet. There was a fine birch-wood writing desk.
There was even a waste-paper basket. The habitual neatness of its
occupant was everywhere manifest.[6]
He was not yet aware that this neatness was actually the work of
Trotsky's secretary.

A few weeks later, the Bolsheviks requisitioned forty rooms in
Lockhart's hotel – most of them on the same floor as his – for the
new German Ambassador, Mirbach, and his staff. Furious at this
close proximity to representatives of the country that Britain had
been fighting since 1914, Lockhart went to Georgy Chicherin (who
by then had taken over from Trotsky as People's Commissar for
Foreign Affairs), and protested vigorously – to no avail. Chicherin
was apologetic, but threw up his hands, claiming he could do
nothing for him: accommodation was in such short supply.

In despair I went to Trotsky, who, at any rate, could be relied upon
to give a decision. He was not to be found. He had, however, an
extremely able and tactful secretary, Evgenia Petrovna Shelepina.
I told her that I must speak to Trotsky immediately and that the
matter was one of the utmost urgency. Within five minutes I was
speaking to him on the telephone.

Although he was in the middle of a Commissars' meeting at the
Kremlin, Trotsky agreed that the situation was intolerable and
promised to take immediate action.

He was as good as his word. Half-an-hour later he telephoned to
me to say that the matter had been settled. He had given categori-
cal orders that other quarters – he did not know where – were to
be found for the Germans. For several days they were lodged
uncomfortably in a second-rate hotel. Then they moved to a
magnificent private house in the Denejni Pereulok. This minor
triumph I owed entirely to Shelepina.[7]
None of this went to her head, although she was impressed when
guards leapt to attention as she passed. Evgenia was simply doing
her job.

In the last week of December 1917, an English journalist, who had just arrived from London, presented an introduction from Maxim Litvinov and requested permission to interview Trotsky. Only a few weeks earlier, Trotsky had appointed Litvinov as the Bolsheviks' official representative in London, so Evgenia had no hesitation about arranging a meeting for this 'Artur Kirillovich Ransom.'

Ransome and Trotsky had never previously met in person, although Ransome had of course heard Trotsky address political meetings. Trotsky may well have heard of Ransome; his positive attitude towards the Bolsheviks in his newspaper articles would have been noticed. In any case, Litvinov's recommendation spoke in his favour, as did Ransome's command of Russian. Trotsky received him warmly. Evgenia sat in on the interview, discreetly taking notes.

That evening, after working late, she was drinking tea with a few colleagues and her sister Eroida, who worked in the same building, when Ransome looked in through the door. He had already typed up his article and had come for the stamp of approval that the telegraph office required before it could be sent off. With Ransome in tow, Evgenia tracked down the censor; he had dozed off in his chair, leaving a pan of potatoes on a Primus stove. It had boiled dry and the potatoes were sending up black smoke. She seized the pan and tipped the contents out onto a sheet of Foreign Office stationery. 'Thank goodness!' she exclaimed. 'They've only just begun to brown.' Shaking the old man awake, she scolded him. 'You mustn't let the pot boil dry like that, or you'll have a hole in the bottom of it!'[8]

While they waited for the censor to find his wits and the rubber stamp, Evgenia took Ransome back with her to join Eroida round the samovar. Finding him good company, she invited him to join her and Eroida in celebrating Christmas ten days later. That proved to be an enjoyable occasion, for all three of them.

On the strength of this, they invited him to see in the Russian New Year with them, along with Trotsky's children (a ten-year-old son as well as two teenage daughters), plus Karl Radek and his wife

Rosa. Evgenia had got to know Rosa only a short while before, through her friend Mara. It turned out that Ransome had just met Karl Radek through a curious circumstance.

On his way back from London a fortnight before, Ransome had decided to lighten his load by leaving a suitcase in Sweden, to be forwarded to him care of the Press Bureau in the Smolny. Radek, a long-term friend and supporter of Lenin – it was he who had arranged with the Germans for the 'sealed train' to bring Lenin back to Russia in 1917 – had just been appointed Vice-Commissar for Foreign Affairs, second to Trotsky and in charge of Western Propaganda. Bruce Lockhart described him as 'a Puck full of malice

Karl Radek

and with a delicious sense of humour … an amusing and entertaining comedian and, kept in proper check, the most dangerous propagandist that the Bolshevik movement has so far produced.'[9] Intrigued by the weight of this suitcase from the West, Radek had opened it. Inside was 'a Shakespeare, a folding chessboard and chessmen, and a mixed collection of books on elementary navigation, fishing, chess, and folklore.'[10] This motley collection made him really curious, and he asked to meet the owner. He and Ransome got on at once. 'They were like a pair of brothers, both writers, both voracious readers, both self-proclaimed bohemians with a mortal scorn for flat-footed bureaucracy,' writes Chambers in his biography of Ransome. So that made for another pleasant evening.

Thus Evgenia and Ransome got to know each other, meeting almost daily in the Smolny, where Ransome interviewed Trotsky three times in the space of two weeks, or in the Foreign Affairs building, where she had the room that she had appropriated. Soon they were in love, but Evgenia had little free time to enjoy the romance, for major political events were taking place.

The Imperial Army had suffered badly on the Eastern Front; after the February revolution in 1917 and more particularly Order No 1 a few weeks later, all discipline evaporated; conscripts began to lay down their rifles – some shot their officers first – and return home; Russia's defence collapsed. In December, faithful to Lenin's slogan of 'peace, land, and bread,' the Bolsheviks demanded a ceasefire, adding that the belligerents should fraternize. The Central Powers seized the opportunity to peacefully overrun the Russian defences. At once, a conference was called at Brest-Litovsk (on the Bug River which now marks the border between Poland and Belarus).

The first round of negotiations, held between 22 and 28 December 1917, was something of a farce. Trotsky sent his trusted friend Adolf Joffe, accompanied by Lev Kamenev, an old Bolshevik confidant of Lenin's, to represent the new Soviet Russia. But along with them, in support of their claim to represent the proletariat, went a motley crew of bohemians and ex-convicts, plus Roman Stashkov, whom they picked up along the way as 'a representative of the peasantry.' When they arrived at Brest-Litovsk, their German hosts had prepared a good meal for them. Stashkov was seen stuffing food into his mouth with both hands; when asked which wine he preferred with his meal, red or white, he asked, 'Which is the stronger?' The world of diplomacy had never seen anything like this before.

The various delegations had vastly different aims. Count Ottokar Czernin, representing Austria-Hungary, was in haste to conclude an agreement, having been warned that the Dual Monarchy would fall if the negotiations lasted too long. He announced that, if the Allies would join the conference, the Central Powers would give up all claim to territories conquered during the war. This infuriated the Germans, incensed the Bulgarians, and alienated the Turks. The Bolsheviks, on the other hand, were playing for time. Lenin and Trotsky firmly believed that copycat revolutions would shortly break out among the workers of western Europe. It was with this in mind that Trotsky had released the terms of the secret Sykes-Picot Agreement (discovered when the St Petersburg Foreign Office was ransacked by the Bolsheviks) to the *Manchester Guardian* in November 1917. This revealed that Britain and France, with the assent of Russia and Italy, had secretly agreed, once the war was over, to share out the Ottoman Empire into 'spheres of influence' between themselves. Trotsky expected right-thinking citizens to be revolted by such blatant imperialism and to follow Bolshevik slogans such as, 'German comrades, throw off your Kaiser, just as your Russian comrades have thrown off their Tsar.'[11]

Rather unwillingly, for he felt like a fish out of water in the company of diplomats, Trotsky decided that his presence was required at Brest-Litovsk for the second round. The Russian delegation looked very different after he arrived: very smartly dressed, he gave something of a virtuoso performance, picking holes in the draft documents prepared by the Germans, and speaking to them in his fluent German whenever he wanted to get a point across quickly. His straight-talking brought about an adjournment of the conference on 28 December for the participants to think things over.

During the night that followed, two Austro-German delegations, in all fully sixty people, arrived in St Petersburg, the first hoping to discuss ways of stopping the naval war, and the second to arrange an exchange of prisoners. Evgenia was run off her feet. She had been following negotiations at the Brest-Litovsk conference through the telegrams that arrived for and then from Trotsky, and the answers that she typed for him, but she hardly expected to find them continuing in her office. The German Ambassador Wilhelm von Mirbach, dressed in full formal attire, had presented himself at the People's Commissariat for Foreign Affairs, looking down his nose at the Soviet staff in their shabby everyday clothes.

Ten days later, negotiations were resumed at Brest-Litovsk, but soon after the arrival of Trotsky's delegation, the telegraph line went dead. At the People's Commissariat in St Petersburg, they had no idea of what of was happening. In a document she dictated to Ransome a few weeks later, Evgenia recalled,

Stalin (Lenin's right hand man) came into the room where I was and said, 'We must send some trusty person to bring back a report of how things really are.'

I said, 'Send me,' never thinking for a moment that they would. Stalin replied,

'Seriously, would you go?'

I said, 'Of course I would go if I were sent.'

He said, 'All right, the train goes at eight-thirty tonight.'[12]
It was a memorable journey.

Not only was it Evgenia's first experience of anywhere more than fifty kilometres from St Petersburg, but it involved crossing the no man's land between the Russian and German lines in mid-winter, on foot. Once her little party left the train, it was two kilometres before the first German officer appeared; it was four more before they found 'simple low sledges like the peasants use' waiting for them. 'We came at last to a low building of white logs.' Inside, the walls were decorated with typical soldiers' graffiti – 'primitive wit', as Evgenia put it. There they were given supper. As there was no train before the next morning,

> the officer asked me if I minded sleeping in a barrack. Of course it was all the same to me where I slept. We went out from the casino, and round several smaller buildings adjoining it, which I think must have been kitchens, and came behind it to the place he called the barrack. It was incredibly clean. The beds in it were made up with clean wood shavings.
>
> He took me to a room opening out of the main barrack, and said that it was his own room and that I could sleep there. He apologized for it, but I was really astonished at it. There was everything anybody could want. A washing stand so arranged that you could pour clean water on yourself from a jug and let the dirty water run away. I wondered how long they had been in this place. It seemed to me that they had fixed themselves up as if they meant to stay there for ever. I am sure no Russian officers take the trouble to arrange for washing so pleasantly. [She rather admired Ransome's rubber bath.] Then there were pictures on the walls,

photographs, comfortable chairs, everything as solid and nice as it could be. He said that he would have to lock the door from out-side, which he did, but I was too sleepy to have any particular feel-ing of imprisonment....

We reached Brest at 11 at night, and went at once to barrack No.7 in the fortress, where the Russian delegation was housed. Trotsky laughed when he saw me. 'When they said that a lady had come, I was sure it must be you, but I do not understand in the least why you have come.' I said I had come because I found it dull without him. Then, of course, I told him how it really was that I had come.[13]

This tells us more about Evgenia's character than any other docu-ment does, in particular her pragmatic self-confidence and the sense of humour that went along with it.

The battle-scarred town of Brest-Litovsk made a deep impression on her. 'Nothing had been done to mend the houses, but the streets had been tidied up, so that there was an impressive orderliness even in the disorder of the broken town,' she observed. While she supported change in the name of social justice, she disliked change in the material world around her, and would have preferred to see the town restored to its pre-war state. So the destruction wrought by the Bolshevik revolution offended her. Unfortunately for her, 'the credo of the Russian communist' (as Princess Marie Gagarin put it rather bitterly) is, '"We need no reforms. Our mission is to destroy utterly. Only out of ruins can a better state of things arise."'[14]

Evgenia continued: 'There were only two or three little shops open, selling necessary things, tobacco and thread and such things, and then there was a bookstore, over which, of course, Radek spent more time than over all the rest.' He was a pipe-smoker and had brought a plentiful supply of his usual plug, yet he also bought some cigarettes. When Evgenia asked him to buy some for her, he refused, saying that 'the Commandant did not allow him to buy any more.' Thus she learned that 'Radek had to get permission from the Commandant for every purchase he wished to make. This had the most terrible effect upon me. I felt I was going to choke.' It was even worse when they saw a party of Russian prisoners of war. They were dressed in rags, surrounded by an armed guard of German soldiers. 'It was a terrible sight. For the first time in my life, I really wanted to kill people,' she confessed.[15]

As before, Trotsky dominated the conference – and his delegation, insisting that they be well dressed and sleep and eat separately from the representatives of the Central Powers, abstaining from the free wine and champagne. Faced with choosing between accepting the current battlefront as the new border of Russia, or letting the Germans invade, he simply declared the state of war between the Central Powers and Russia was 'terminated'! The traditional diplomats on the other side of the table were apoplectic. This was unheard of. Then Trotsky delivered his punchline: it was 'neither war nor peace'. Picking up their papers, he and his delegation left the room and returned to St Petersburg.

What a story Evgenia had for Ransome on her return! His newspaper readers were agog with all the inside news that he was sending them. He and Evgenia probably had little time together, though, for the People's Commissariat for Foreign Affairs, and Evgenia with it, was unimaginably busy. Trotsky's gamble had not paid off. German forces were advancing unopposed through the Baltic states. After ten days of intense debate among the Commissars, Trotsky and Lenin drafted a telegram to Berlin announcing their acceptance of the proposed peace treaty. The agreement that Russia signed on 30 March may have brought the fighting between Russia and Germany to an end, but it amputated Russia of most of the Ukraine and all the Baltic countries. Ever since, Russian leaders, from Stalin to Putin, have been keen to recover these areas, as witnessed most recently by Russia's appropriation of the Crimean peninsula and occupation by proxy of eastern parts of the Ukraine.

March 1918 was a month of changes. Fearing invasion by the German forces in neighbouring Estonia, Lenin decided to move Soviet Russia's seat of government from St Petersburg to Moscow, appropriating the Kremlin to replace the Smolny. (Ransome spent some twenty hours helping Evgenia, Rosa Radek, and a Bolshevik historian named Pokrovsky to place the Imperial archives in packing cases for shipment to Moscow.) Simultaneously there was a ministerial shuffle, occasioned by the arrival of Georgy Chicherin.

An aristocrat by birth and a career diplomat in Imperial Russia, Chicherin had resigned his post in 1904, renounced his inherited estates, and become a Menshevik, devoting his fortune to the French Socialists and the British labour movement. Living in London during the First World War, he was arrested soon after the Revolution for speaking out against the war. Since he was being held in Brixton Prison without charge, the Council of People's Commissars (Sovnarkom) in St Petersburg retaliated by declaring the British ambassador in Russia, Sir George Buchanan, *persona non grata*. Along with other British nationals who had been trapped in Russia by the Revolution, he was exchanged for Chicherin. On his arrival in Russia, Chicherin was at once appointed Commissar for Foreign Affairs (with Litvinov as his deputy), replacing Trotsky, who became Commissar for War in place of Nikolai Krylenko, who went to the Commissariat for Justice. (This is the moment when Trotsky created the new Red Army – and 'made a very good job of it'[16] thanks in part to the books bought for him by Lola Kinel.) Chicherin's first duty was to sign the Brest-Litovsk peace agreement on behalf of Soviet Russia. In this move to Moscow and a new portfolio, Trotsky took Evgenia with him, and Ransome followed.

The threat of invasion by the Germans caused the Allied diplomatic missions to evacuate their staff from St Petersburg. On 28 February, the Americans headed east, to Vologda, 480 km away (300 miles). (Ironically, the Tsars used to send convicted revolutionaries there, where they could – supposedly – do less harm.) The British and the French opted to go north and in three days they were in Helsinki. Hardly had the Americans left than Chicherin sent Karl Radek after them, with Ransome as his interpreter, to try to persuade them to return. Radek made an unfortunate impression by addressing them with a large pistol hanging from his belt – his customary attire, but not what diplomats were accustomed to. They felt threatened. As Bruce Lockhart put it, Radek 'looked like a cross between a professor and a bandit.'[17] The Americans refused to budge, fearing that they might be taken hostage.

Radek always wore a pistol: the Bolsheviks remained in power by force, and they were well aware that someone might respond in kind. So they all had a weapon for self-defence, although they did not carry it all the time, and had no training in its use. (When attempts were made on Lenin's life, in January and August 1918, he either had no pistol or no time to pull it out.) Even Evgenia had a pistol, something she was quite unaccustomed to. One day, while fiddling with it in her office, she sent a bullet into the wall. There was already a bullet hole in one of the windowpanes. Trotsky soon put her at her ease, confessing that he too had accidentally let off his pistol one day, and his son had nearly frightened his chauffeur to death by doing the same in his car.

When Ransome was at Vologda with Karl Radek, the poor quality of communications with Brest-Litovsk caused Lenin to believe that the peace negotiations had broken down and that invasion must be imminent. In haste he sent a message to Vologda, asking the Americans to help defend Russia. It was Evgenia who transmitted Lenin's message, and she added to it a personal PS for Ransome. Assuming that he would react to the news by moving out of Russia, she wished him a safe journey and sent her love, revealing how close they had come to each other in the space of two months. Within hours, he was on his way back to her. Shortly after, though, Lockhart asked Ransome to return to Vologda, to seek accommodation into which the British diplomatic staff could move if they decided to return from Finland. But he could find nothing suitable.

That spring, food was desperately short in Russia's cities. Lola Kinel described the Bolshevik solution in a few blunt words:

A detachment of Latvians under a revolutionary officer went into the villages and requisitioned food for starving St Petersburg. When the peasants hid it, or refused to deliver the required quota, they were lined up in a row and every tenth one of them was shot. It was a very efficient method: the villages handed over their quotas obediently.[18]

In Moscow, Evgenia's sister Eroida accompanied 300 Baltic sailors on such an expedition, returning with – according to Ransome – over a million poods (16,300 metric tons) of corn. (The Bolsheviks generally employed soldiers from the Baltic states, especially Latvians, for these expeditions because they could not trust Russian soldiers to fire on their own peasants.)

For a few days, Ransome lived in a requisitioned flat in Moscow with Evgenia and Eroida (who had been promoted secretary to the head of the Eastern Department of the Commissariat of Foreign Affairs), and the Radeks. (Karl Radek was the Deputy Commissar of Foreign Affairs and the Head of the Press Bureau.) The Cheka must have considered this a major security risk and indeed we know from Ransome's telegrams to London that Evgenia was passing on to him detailed information on the intentions of the Bolshevik leadership and its attitude towards Britain in particular. Brogan was surely right when he speculated that Evgenia would have been 'required to report on her lover to the authorities [i.e. the Cheka], an unpleasant and alarming task, even though he was so reliable from the Bolshevik point of view.'[19] Any hint that Ransome may have dropped to her that he was working for the British Secret Service would have put her in an untenable position: withholding information from the Cheka was tantamount to committing suicide.

Little wonder then that, as Chambers puts it, 'their love affair proceeded like a jagged cardiograph through stormy scenes and ecstatic reconciliations. Evgenia could at times be sweet tempered; at others fiercely moody, given to "barometric" swings.'[20] She must have been fiercely debating within herself: could she really be unfaithful to her job, her family, her country? To throw in her lot with Ransome would mean abandoning everything she knew and loved. Even to leave Russia with him was incredibly risky. Before permission to travel was granted, she would have to provide the Cheka with the names and addresses of every member of her family in Russia. And it was clearly spelled out to everyone who went abroad that if they voiced any criticism of Soviet Russia and the conditions of life there, their relatives would be arrested. Leaving clandestinely was therefore out of the question.

Neither she nor Ransome left any record of the next few weeks, although we know that it was at this time that Ransome went to rescue Lola Kinel, along with Rita and their Granny, by enabling them to escape to Poland. We also know that by 19 June love had prevailed: Evgenia had agreed to leave Russia with him.

Ransome turned to Bruce Lockhart, who asked the Foreign Office for permission to put Evgenia on Ransome's passport – for services rendered to the Allied cause – as though she were his wife, although everyone, Evgenia included, was perfectly aware that he was already married. In London, the Foreign Secretary himself, Arthur Balfour, gave the OK, aware of the value of the information that Ransome and Evgenia would bring out of Russia. In the event, she never needed to make use of this special dispensation.

Accompanying Radek to Vologda for the third time, Ransome took the opportunity to ask the British chargé d'affaires for an introduction to the British Ambassador in Stockholm, making it clear that on arrival in Sweden he would inform the British of all he had learned from his Russian contacts. Meanwhile, Evgenia managed to persuade Trotsky to let her go and work for the Soviet delegation in Stockholm. How she managed this, and Trotsky's thoughts on her relationship with Ransome, we shall never know, but his consent suggests how much he liked and trusted the two of them.

It took time to finalize all their arrangements, which were complicated by the murder of the Tsar and all his family at

Ekaterinburg on 16 July, closely followed by the precipitate departure of all the Embassies at Vologda for Archangel – they had been advised of the Allied plans to land troops there, and decided to make a quick exit from Russia lest they be taken hostage. As it was, travel to Sweden was severely restricted by civil war in Finland.

Finally they were off: Evgenia left for Berlin at the end of July, travelling as the secretary of Vatslav Vorovsky, who was returning to his post representing Soviet Russia in Stockholm. Ransome went by train and boat, using his British passport to leave Russia and entering Sweden on 4 August as a Bolshevik courier, carrying a Soviet diplomatic bag. The 'bag' – actually his suitcase – contained three million roubles in cash to fund Communist propaganda in Stockholm. (This sounds an enormous sum, and it is, but the rouble had already lost more than ten percent of its pre-war value.) Evgenia joined him in Stockholm on 28 August.

It was perfect timing. The Allied expeditionary force had landed on 3 August. As anticipated, the Bolsheviks responded by declaring that no Allied citizen would be allowed to leave Russia; they closed the British and French missions and took hostage more than four hundred foreign nationals. Evgenia and Ransome had managed to leave just before this came into effect. They settled down to enjoy each other's company in peace and quiet – for the first time – in a little cottage at the mouth of the harbour.

The peace was only relative. Ransome had arranged, presumably with Karl Radek, for 'all Russian Government publications, newspapers, both official and other,' to be sent him twice a week.[21] And the news they brought was dramatic. On 30 August, the head of the St Petersburg Cheka was assassinated; in Moscow on the same day, Fanny Kaplan attempted to kill Lenin. (It is speculated that the stress of this attack, and the bullet that lodged under his right collarbone – which was never removed because Lenin refused to go to hospital for the operation – may well have contributed to the strokes that killed him.) As Fanny refused to implicate anyone else, the Cheka shot her on 3 September. This was in accordance with a decision taken the day before by the All-Russian Central Executive Committee authorizing the Cheka to punish counter-revolutionaries without recourse to courts or tribunals. In addition, they were authorized to run their own prisons and open their own concentration camps. It was the birth of the gulag. The Cheka made full use of its new rights: in September alone, they shot 2,600 people in Moscow; in St Petersburg, they shot 512 in one day, and in the Kronstadt fortress they dispatched a further 500 in a single night. (These are official figures released at the time. Historians multiply them *ad libitum*.) It was the start of the Red Terror.

The bad news continued: on 31 August, the day after the attempt on Lenin's life, Ransome's friend and fellow chess-player Francis Cromie was killed by the Cheka while defending the British Embassy. Then came the shattering news that Bruce Lockhart had been arrested, released and then re-arrested two days later, accused of fomenting a plot to overthrow the Soviet government.

Lockhart was just an envoy, but he had been granted diplomatic immunity. The accusation of plotting against the Soviet state was therefore most serious. Before he was arrested, Britain should normally have been presented with the evidence and asked to waive his immunity; the Bolsheviks had jumped the gun. Immediately after the Revolution, Maxim Litvinov had been named the Bolsheviks' ambassador in London; recognized as such, he enjoyed full diplomatic immunity. In a tit-for-tat reaction to Lockhart's arrest, Whitehall had Maxim Litvinov arrested and imprisoned, without charge. (By coincidence, it was to protect a Russian ambassador that Britain first guaranteed diplomatic immunity to a foreigner, in 1709.) Official hostage-taking like this had not been seen among civilized countries for centuries. As it was, Radek wrote to reassure Ransome that Lockhart would not be shot; he was to be exchanged for Litvinov.

Ransome must have realized how extraordinarily lucky he and Evgenia were to have left Russia when they did. As a friend and close associate of Bruce Lockhart, he would surely have been taken in for questioning too. Which would have brought his relationship with Evgenia into question. It did not bear thinking about. Up to this point, Ransome had been a supporter of the Bolsheviks. He knew how much the Russian people had aspired to a change of regime, to free speech and basic civil rights. This had been one of the things that had struck him most when he first arrived in the country. Having got to know and like some of the protagonists of the Revolution, he believed in their good intentions. The rise of the Cheka – with the Bolsheviks' blessing – and the launch of the Red Terror in September unsealed his eyes. But it took time and more evidence for the full implications of it to sink in.

Ransome was a journalist and lived by writing articles about Russia. It was part of his cover as an agent for MI6 that he should write uncritically of the Bolsheviks; in that way they were pleased with his work and were happy to speak to him, knowing that their words would be reported accurately in the British press. To do this, he had to go back to Moscow. But in London there were those who had no idea of the purpose his articles actually served, and they talked of having him arrested and tried for treason. So while he congratulated Bruce Lockhart on his escape, as he passed through Sweden, Ransome also needed to ask for him to put in a good word for him. Once back in London, Lockhart vouched for Ransome's integrity and pointed out that, since he himself had been expelled, Ransome was the now only person who could talk with both the Bolsheviks and officials in London. This resulted in the *Daily News* renewing Ransome's contract. It was not just his cover: he needed a salary to live on, and a visa to enter Russia.

We have no idea what Evgenia thought of all this, nor for that matter do we know just how much Ransome had confided in her by now. In Sweden she will have discovered, for the first time, what life was like outside Soviet Russia and what the outside world thought of the Bolsheviks. She was probably glad that Ransome had not whisked her off to England, where she would no doubt have had to face a great deal of antipathy, not just as a Bolshevik but also as

Ransome's Red mistress. The cottage by the sea must have felt a safe haven. Meanwhile she was employed at the Soviet Legation in Stockholm, which also provided Ransome with a desk and a type-writer.

Exchanged for Lockhart, Litvinov arrived in St Petersburg on the first anniversary of the November Revolution, and was promptly entrusted with a peace mission in Stockholm. In exchange for an immediate cessation of hostilities, he offered Britain, France, Italy, Japan, and the United States the return of Allied prisoners, the repayment of Russia's war debts, and the opening of trade. But the Allies turned a deaf ear: they were preparing the Paris Peace Conference (from which Soviet Russia was excluded). Ransome took this opportunity to interview Litvinov while he was in Stockholm, finding in him another congenial chess player. Faithful to his brief, he reported Litvinov's words without censorship or criticism, which gave his handlers in MI6 exactly what they wanted to learn, but antagonized all those who were not in the know, which included MI5 and the Foreign Office.

MI6 wanted to get Ransome back into Russia, for it was now harder than ever to get good intelligence out of the country. They arranged for Sweden to expel the Soviet legation, and Evgenia along with them. As they were preparing to go back to Russia, Ransome was informed that the Bolsheviks did not want him. It seemed that he and Evgenia were doomed to be separated. Early in 1919, however, MI6 resolved the problem for them by arranging for Lockhart to give a public lecture in which he complained that Ransome could not be trusted as a reporter on Russia when he had not set foot in the country for the past six months. This reached the ears of the Bolsheviks who invited him back again: they wanted their mouthpiece. He and Evgenia were together – but back in the lion's den.

There is no doubt that the Soviets needed Ransome to bring their point of view to the rest of the world. They could not even make their voice heard at the Paris Peace Conference. The war had ended, yet there were Allied – mainly British – troops on Russian soil in the north-west and also in the farthest east, where they were supporting Kolchak's White Army. Ransome did his best for both the Bolsheviks and London with a book titled *Six Weeks in Russia*, which served its purpose very well. 'No one could read that book,' observed Ransome in his *Autobiography*, 'without feeling that the Russian war could not be justified, if only because the people in the book, from Lenin downwards, were quite obviously human beings and not the fantastic bogies that the Interventionists pretended.'[22] He was treading cautiously. Yet the Bolsheviks treated him well, putting him up in a hotel reserved for Soviet officials and delegates. Evgenia was given a job in the Commissariat for Education.

Thanks to Litvinov, who proved 'a firm ally' to Ransome,[23] he received a letter signed by Lenin commanding all commissariats to assist him 'in every possible way.'[24] Lenin himself granted no less than three interviews. After one of them, Ransome noted,

> more than ever, today, Lenin struck me as a happy man. Walking home from the Kremlin, I tried to think of any other man of his calibre who had had a similar, joyous, happy temperament. I could think of none. Napoleon, Caesar, did not make a deeper mark on the history of the world than this man is making: none records their cheerfulness. This little, bald, wrinkled man who tilts his chair this way and that, laughing over one thing and another.[25]

Lenin had good reason to be delighted at this point. Two Americans, William Bullitt and Lincoln Steffens, had been sent over from the Paris Peace Conference to sound out Moscow on the possibility of an armistice, the re-establishment of economic relations, and the withdrawal of Allied troops. Their first port of call was St Petersburg, where Litvinov received them and sent them on to Moscow to meet Lenin and Chicherin, with an introduction to Ransome as their intermediary and guide. In the space of a week, they obtained an agreement and Bullitt 'compiled an extensive report on conditions there. While acknowledging the economic hardships facing the Russian people, Bullitt asserted that the violent phase of the Bolshevik Revolution had ended and that the Bolsheviks enjoyed popular support.'[26] Since Chambers tells us that 'over the next three days, Bullitt and Steffens enjoyed the very best that the Bolsheviks had to offer – champagne, caviar, a night at the opera with seats in the Tsar's royal box,[27] – it is hard to see how Bullitt could have compiled his 'extensive report' without a great deal of help from Ransome.

In the event, the American mission came to nothing. The Report on it in the Archives of the Department of State concludes:

Although Lloyd George privately assured Bullitt that he was sympathetic to the Bolsheviks' offer, he repudiated it once news of Bullitt's mission had been leaked to the British press. Clemenceau had opposed any overtures to Lenin from the start. [President] Wilson was in poor health and was focused on achieving a breakthrough in negotiations with the French concerning the peace treaty with Germany.... Finally, news from Russia indicated that anti-Bolshevik forces would soon capture Moscow, thus obviating the need to negotiate with Lenin. Consequently, the April 10th deadline for the Allies to respond to Lenin's offer passed without any word from the Allied side, and Bullitt angrily resigned from the U.S. delegation on May 17. The failure of the Allies to agree to the proposal secured by the Bullitt mission delayed official U.S. recognition of Soviet Russia for many years.[28]

It had not been for lack of effort on the part of Ransome and the Bolsheviks.

During Ransome's six-week stay, he was the only non-communist to attend the founding meeting of the Third International; he declined an invitation to accompany Trotsky on an armoured train heading north towards the Allied expeditionary force. He preferred to remain in Moscow and meet Dzerzhinsky, with whom he visited British prisoners of war in the Butyrka prison, and Yakov Peters, with whom he discussed the Lockhart case – of which more in the next chapter – in Peters' own office in the Lubianka. He had already met Peters a year before and, like Lockhart, found him a polite and agreeable man, who spoke quite good English. (Richard Deacon reports that 'those who knew him testified to many small kindnesses which he performed when off duty'.[29]) During their meeting, Ransome noted that there was a copy of *Mr Britling Sees It Through* by H. G. Wells on Peters' desk; he did not know that Peters had loaned this very book to Lockhart to help pass the time during the five days he spent in the Lubianka. (Peters was probably not aware that Gorky much admired this novel and had had it translated into Russian by Mikhail Lykiardopoulos, who was a good friend of both Bruce Lockhart and Arthur Ransome. It proved immensely popular in Russia.)

As Ransome prepared to leave with hundreds of pages of notes in preparation for his book, Lenin gave him a message for the Estonian ambassador in Finland: if Estonia would agree to a cease-fire, Russia was prepared to honour its independence. For Ransome, it had been a fruitful visit – but Evgenia refused to leave with him. Neither she nor he has left us any explanation for this refusal; I suspect that the Cheka will have had a hand in it. So Ransome was obliged to leave without her, not knowing when or how they would meet up again. With a heavy heart, he set out for London, passing on the message for Estonia as he went.

On arrival, he was arrested by Scotland Yard and brought before the Assistant Commissioner, Sir Basil Thomson, who had just been made Director of Intelligence at the Home Office. Sir Basil, 'extremely grim', looked hard at Ransome as he sat 'in that famous chair' where so many criminals had sat. After a moment's silence, Sir Basil said,

'Now, I want to know just what your politics are.'

'Fishing', I replied.

He stared. 'Just what do you mean by that?'

I told him the exact truth, that in England I had never had any political view whatever, that in Russia I believed that this very fact had let me get a clearer view of the revolution than I could otherwise have got, that I now had one clear opinion, which was that Intervention was a disastrous mistake, and that I hoped it would come to an end and so release me to turn to my ordinary interests.

We talked for some time, in a manner more and more friendly. I told him just why I thought that, win or lose, the effect of Intervention must be bad for our future relations with Russia under any government whatsoever.[30]

After that, he had Sir Basil's trust – but not everyone in Whitehall or the Intelligence services followed suit. Worse, the *Daily News* reviewed its politics and the editor who had been taking Ransome's articles moved to the *Daily Chronicle*, leaving him with no newspaper prepared to get a Russian visa for him.

In mid-April, the White Army under Admiral Kolchak, having 30,000 Allied troops guarding his supply line along the trans-Siberian railway, began pushing westwards. Simultaneously, General Denikin's army, using British spotter planes, began advancing northwards. If the Red Army failed to contain them, Moscow could fall to the counter-revolutionary forces, who spared no one with a Party membership card. It was becoming urgent to extract Evgenia.

Thanks to Sir Basil Thomson, Ransome managed to obtain permission for her to come to England, accompanying a Red Cross representative through Finland. Sending her precise instructions, he begged her not to 'act the fool' and to escape while she could.[31] She remained where she was. Publication in June of *Six Weeks in Russia* brought an unexpected invitation for Ransome to work for the *Manchester Guardian;* on top of a good salary, the editor proposed to get him a visa for Russia and to pay his costs. It took weeks to set it up and it was October 1919 before he was back in Stockholm. From there he went on to Estonia, where the government was most grateful for the peace proposal that Ransome had brought from Lenin in the spring and was anxious to send their response by the same means. Only this time, the message was so secret that it had to be delivered by word of mouth. Ransome was happy to oblige and, safely crossing the battlefront between Estonia and Russia, arrived in Moscow, where he delivered his message to Litvinov and was reunited with Evgenia, on 22 October.

They left only six days later, with no problem: it would be easy to assume that it was thanks to all Ransome's friendly contacts, from Lenin downwards, that the Bolsheviks raised no objections to Evgenia's departure with him. It is quite possible that Ransome thought so too – until they arrived in Estonia, where Evgenia had an appointment with Soviet agents, and handed over to them the thirty-five diamonds and three strings of pearls (valued at 1,039,000 roubles) that, unknown to Ransome, she had smuggled out. To obtain much-needed foreign currency, Soviet Russia carried on a discreet export trade in confiscated goods, through a Department of External Trade that was masterminded by the Cheka. Women were targeted as 'mules' for this purpose because they could carry – even wear – jewellery without awakening suspicion. Learning what Evgenia had done put Ransome in a state of nervous collapse. She, on the other hand, having kept her cool, nursed him back to health. It was the last service she rendered to her home country, for as soon as he had recovered, he typed up and had her sign the following affidavit, in both Russian and English:

> Dear Arthur, I hereby promise you on my word of honour that I will undertake no political commissions in England from the Bolsheviks or any other political party, and further that I will engage in no conspiratorial work whatsoever without expressly informing you that I consider this promise no longer binding.[32]

It was a remarkable marriage vow. I believe that it showed Evgenia how deeply he cared for her and his determination that she should not endanger them again. The mention of 'conspiratorial work' refers to the risk that the Cheka might pressure her to work for them once they reached England.

On all its fronts, the Red Army was throwing back the counter-revolutionaries, benefitting from the extra troops withdrawn from the Estonian front. As a result of the messages that Ransome had carried, a peace treaty had been signed between Russia and Estonia, where Ransome's help was duly recorded. It was, he noted ruefully, 'the only time that anybody has ever said "Thank you" for any of my amateur meddling in public affairs.'[33] Things were less peaceful on the home front as far as Ransome's wife, Ivy, was concerned. Although he had not lived with her for almost ten years, she haggled with him over the terms and conditions of their divorce, retaining his prized collection of books, most of them signed by their authors. Until agreement was reached, he and Evgenia had to 'live in sin' and remain outside England. They settled down in Estonia, close to the capital, Tallinn. And they were very happy together. Evgenia caught Ransome's passion for sailing and joined him on many sea trips; she also set about learning English properly and, according to Chambers, after four years 'she could write like a native.'[34]

During those four years, Ransome made several more visits to Moscow. One of them resulted in another book, *The Crisis in Russia* (1921), and a long report for the Foreign Office. Another in May 1923 resulted in what must be accounted Ransome's greatest – and least publicized – intervention in Soviet-British relations, on the occasion of the so-called 'Curzon ultimatum': the British Foreign Minister, Lord Curzon, charged the head of the Mission in Moscow, R.M. Hodgson, to hand over a document without comment and without discussing it in any way with the Russians. It demanded that the Russians cease forthwith and for ever from fomenting revolution against British interests in India, and that they should fully and unconditionally agree to this within ten days; failure to comply could lead only to a break in diplomatic relations, and possibly war. After lengthy discussions with Chicherin and Litvinov, and equally long discussions with Hodgson, Ransome arranged for Hodgson and Litvinov to meet 'by chance' in the grounds of a country house outside Moscow. While the two men talked, Ransome walked up to the big house where he was immedi-ately challenged to a game of chess by Nikolai Krylenko, who happened to be staying there. The diplomatic encounter ended in almost as friendly a manner as the chess game: the Bolsheviks agreed 'not to spread discontent or to foment rebellion in any part of the British Empire.'[35]

It is striking that although Ransome was frequently in Moscow during the twenty months or so of Max Eastman's stay there, and saw Litvinov on every visit, he and Max do not seem to have met. Nor does Ransome ever mention meeting Litvinov's secretary, Eliena Krylenko. Yet it chanced that, after his divorce finally came through, Ransome married Evgenia on 8 May 1924, less than a month before Max married Eliena. While Max and Eliena left for England within minutes of their marriage, Ransome and Evgenia took their time. Equipped with a brand new British passport, Evgenia even paid a visit to her sisters in Moscow; she was not to see them again for fifty years. Although Evgenia was the eldest, they looked far older than her by then, having lived much harder lives – but they had survived, thanks to those Party membership cards. It was November when Ransome and Evgenia arrived in England and settled in the Lake District.

Journalism occupied him for the next five years, and it was only after the grandchildren of his friend and mentor, W. G. Collingwood – Taqui, Susan, Mavis (known to her family as Titty), Roger and Brigit – inspired him to write *Swallows and Amazons*, that he became a full-time writer. Evgenia encouraged him, although she had no hesitation about expressing her opinion of his books. In fact, her denunciation of *The Picts and the Martyrs* as recycling, 'pale imitations of something that happened many times before,'[36] may well have contributed to ending the series.

Much of the charm of those books lies in their evocation of a quiet and safe pre-Revolutionary and pre-First-World-War child-hood. They implicitly celebrate the values of honesty, integrity, and consideration for others that are close to the heart of British culture. The one book in which Ransome's ethos is made clear – but never spelled out – is *Missee Lee*, in which the crews of *Swallow* and

Amazon fall into the hands of a charming Chinese pirate, Missee Lee. She can serve them a 'Camblidge bleakfast' (with *Oxford* marmalade though, *if* you please) at one moment and calmly talk of cutting off heads ('chop, chop') the next. It was the nearest Ransome ever came in his stories to evoking the ambivalence of his experience of the Bolsheviks.

Although 'no political party in Russia interested' him at all,[37] he had embraced the February revolution, and defended it passionately. The uprising delighted him as a sudden, inexorable blow for democracy, throwing off the yoke of the Tsar. What more could an ex-Bohemian wish for? And how could a son of the Victorians fail to be impressed by the will, determination and ruthless moral conviction with which the Bolsheviks seized power in November 1917, saving the first revolution from the impotent vacillations of Kerensky's provisional government? That he took so long to realize what the Bolsheviks were actually doing is indicative of his romantic belief in their good intentions; they were after all people whom he had met and liked. And I'm sure that Evgenia, who had shared his hopes for Russia and liked Trotsky, will have also shared his disillusionment.

Sources

Adelman, Jonathan R. 'Soviet Secret Police'. In Adelman, Jonathan R. (ed.), *Terror and Communist Politics: The Role of the Secret Police in Communist States*. Boulder: Westview Press, 1984.

Archives of the Department of State, 'The Bullitt Mission to Soviet Russia, 1919'. https://2001-2009.state.gov/r/pa/ho/time/wwi/99847.htm, consulted August 2019.

Brogan, Hugh. *The Life of Arthur Ransome*. London, Cape, 1984.

Bruce Lockhart, Robert. *Memoirs of a British Agent.* Putnam's Sons, 1933.

Chambers, Roland. *The Last Englishman. The Double Life of Arthur Ransome.* Faber, 2009. [I am aware that the *New York Times* considered that this book 'relies too much on uncertain argument and indifferent scholarship'.]

Deacon, Richard. *A History of the Russian Secret Service.* (1972) Revised and updated edition. Grafton, 1987.

Gagarin, Princess Marie. *Reminiscences of Old Russia.* Privately printed, 1951.

Hart-Davis, Rupert (ed.). *The Autobiography of Arthur Ransome.* Cape, 1976.

Hill, George. *Go Spy Out the Land.* 1933. http://www.gwpda.org/memoir/Hill/Hill_1.pdfHill,

Kinel, Lola. *Under Five Eagles. My Life in Russia, Poland, Austria, Germany, and America, 1916–1936.* Putnam, 1937.

Milton, Giles. *Russian Roulette.* Sceptre, 2013.

Shelepina, Evgenia. 'Evgenia Shelepina and the October Revolution.' Like 'The Journey to Brest' (below) this is one of two documents hosted on the Russian Arthur Ransome website. The site explains: 'Either just before the move to Moscow or just after,

Evgenia set down in various notes her experiences and feelings about the early days of the Revolution and her subsequent employment as Trotsky's secretary.' These notes, dated 'Moscow 18 March', appear to have been typed by Ransome to Evgenia's dictation. Identified as 'Shelepina on the Revolution' in the Notes below. https://arthur-ransome.ucoz.ru/index/0-8

Shelepina, Evgenia. 'Journey to Brest.' A memoir composed soon after her trip to Brest-Litovsk. Not paginated. https://arthur-ran-some.ucoz.ru/ index/evgenia_shelepina_journey_to_brest/0-12.

Notes

1   Shelepina on the Revolution
2   Shelepina on the Revolution
3   Shelepina on the Revolution
4   Shelepina on the Revolution
5   Hill, p.191.
6   Bruce Lockhart, Book iv, Ch.6.
7   Bruce Lockhart, Book iv, Ch. 6.
8   Chambers, p.181. The words are Ransome's but Chambers does not identify the source.
9   Bruce Lockhart, Book iv, Ch. 6.
10 Chambers, p.184.
11 This much-quoted slogan was carried as a banner by Bolshevized German prisoners of war in the first May Day parade, 1918.
12 Shelepina, 'Journey to Brest'
13 Shelepina, 'Journey to Brest'
14 Gagarin, p.28.
15 Shelepina, 'Journey to Brest'
16 Deacon, p.160.
17 Bruce Lockhart, Book iv, Ch.6.
18 Kinel, p.67.

[19] Brogan, p.191.

[20] Chambers, p.221.

[21] Chambers, p.235.

[22] *Autobiography*, p.269.

[23] *Autobiography*, p.264.

[24] Chambers, p.264.

[25] Chambers, p.269.

[26] Archive of the US Department of State.

[27] Chambers, p.271.

[28] Archive of the US Department of State.

[29] Deacon, p.168.

[30] *Autobiography*, p.279.

[31] Chamberlain, p281.

[32] Chambers, p.293.

[33] Chambers, p.292.

[34] Chambers, p.325.

[35] Quoted from Milton, p.335.

[36] Quoted by Brogan, p.387.

[37] *Autobiography*, p.217.

6 Moura and Her Many Lovers

This chapter comes with a health and safety warning.

THERE ARE TWO RECENT BIOGRAPHIES of Moura, Baroness Maria Ignatievna Zakrevskaya Benckendorff Budberg (1893–1974). The first, written in Russian by Nina Berberova and translated into English in 2005, is titled simply *Moura*. The cover (and only the cover) adds a subtitle: *The Dangerous Life of the Baroness Budberg.*

The second, *A Very Dangerous Woman* by Deborah McDonald and Jeremy Dronfield, appeared in 2015. It too has a subtitle: *The Lives, Loves, and Lies of Russia's Most Seductive Spy.*

Moura's daughter, Tania Alexander, has left us an account of her childhood in which she confirms her mother's duplicity and dishonesty, but tells us nothing of her spying.

As we know from the James Bond films, sex and spying make exciting bedmates – in fiction. In real life, they may go together, but are never revealed in such lascivious detail, for they are conducted – for the most part, at any rate – in secrecy. There are few secrets as to Moura's lovers; she chose them from among the most famous names of the first half of the twentieth century. As for her spying, on the other hand, hard evidence is thin on the ground; she was suspected by Russia, Germany, Italy, France and Britain; their agents amassed voluminous case files, but none ever came up with sufficient evidence to prosecute her. Perhaps it was not in their interest to do so; no one knew who she was actually working for.

So I must add my own warning: I do not claim to know the truth. I write only to the best of my knowledge and belief.

☭

Human beings tend to fear what they do not understand, and the authors of these books did not understand Moura; hence the suggestion that she was dangerous. I am not sure that I have understood her any better than they have, but I can at least offer an explanation for her behaviour. Although Nina Berberova lived with Moura for three years in the entourage of Maxim Gorky (1868–1936) and met her on numerous other occasions over a long period, she confessed to being at a loss when, aged eighty, she finally tried to pin Moura down in a book. Rather significantly, though, she reveals that Gorky's nickname for Moura was 'Iron Woman'. For Berberova, this was an allusion to the Man in the Iron Mask, whose face no one ever saw. They could see he was *there* – but no one knew *who* was there, behind the mask. This is a typical response to a person like Moura, who suffered, I believe, from the Narcissistic Personality Disorder.

We all know the myth of Narcissus who fell in love with his own image and we are most of us aware (more or less consciously) that a degree of self-love is essential to our psychological health. It keeps our self-esteem intact, protecting us from damage inflicted by others. Moreover, without sufficient narcissism, there is a risk of self-hatred and even self-mutilation. But few people are aware of the extreme form that, since the 1980 edition of the *Diagnostic and Statistical Manual of Mental Disorders*, has been called the Narcissistic Personality Disorder (NPD). Unlike Narcissus, persons suffering from NPD do not have a beautiful self whose reflection they can fall in love with, but a false self, constructed from the admiration and flattery (termed Narcissistic Supply – the capital letters denoting technical terms relating to Narcissism) that they elicit from others.

Their strategy can be reduced to: 'Tell me how wonderful I am!' leading to 'I am wonderful, since everybody tells me so.' Consequently, Narcissists are forever in search of fresh sources of praise and adulation to maintain this self-delusion. They develop an uncanny skill at assessing other people, and of saying the very words that will prompt others to give them the love and attention they crave. Berberova writes of Moura's 'profound ability to understand her interlocutor after hearing only half a word,' and 'the fact that everyone who spoke to her or even just sat next to her was somehow convinced that he or she alone was more important to Moura in that moment than anyone else in the world.'[1] Moura's daughter Tania writes in the same vein: her mother could make someone 'feel that they were the most important person to her, that they alone mattered.'[2]

Narcissists are very clever; they calculate every move they make, every word they say, for the positive return it will bring them. Tania says that Moura's letters to Gorky 'were carefully thought out and designed to give the image she wanted to present of herself, often distorting the truth.'[3] Narcissists feel no disinterested love; they profess love – most convincingly, as they are consummate actors – only in order to be loved back. They perceive other people as useful only to the extent of their ability to provide Narcissistic Supply. So Narcissists are serial seducers.

They always aim high: believing that they themselves are 'special' and unique, they invariably seek the company of people of high social status. The greater the degree of social recognition achieved by their victims, the greater the gratification in being loved by them. Narcissists particularly favour writers and editors, because they are read and admired by many people. Moura's first high-profile lover was Robert Bruce Lockhart (1887–1970), who wrote of their 1918 affair in his *Memoirs of a British Agent* (1932); it was a bestseller, and filmed two years later as *British Agent,* with Leslie Howard as Lockhart and Kay Francis as Moura. That was a Narcissist's dream come true.

It is extremely difficult to imagine a person without a personality, and this makes Narcissists hard for us to recognize. They move and behave much like anyone else, but there is always something enigmatic about them – and we know the seductive power of *that* – for they have no durable self; there is no *person* behind the mask. As they create a new self with every social situation, the idea of being *true to oneself* is unimaginable for them. (A sufferer once asked me, in all seriousness, 'What do people mean by *sincerity*?') So they have no integrity, no honesty, no conscience – and therefore no morals. Having nothing to keep them in check, Narcissists are inherently dishonest and masters of duplicity. (In the 1930s, Moura used her daughter 'as an accomplice or an alibi, [or] forced [her] into telling lies for her.'[4]) Narcissists say whatever suits them best in the moment. This requires constant vigilance on their part, not to be caught in self-contradictions. (And when they are caught out, they typically say, 'Oh, I miscalculated there,' and dismiss the subject. Apologies are unknown to them.) Consequently, they develop almost perfect recall of everything they have ever said, to whom they said it, when, and where. It is extremely disturbing, to say the least of it, to meet one of these people and realize that, for all their undoubted ability (and the many skills they claim to have) *there is no one* (in the everyday sense) *inside that body of theirs.*

Tania Alexander concludes that

> those who would understand Moura are confronted and challenged with a paradoxical character full of deep divisions; with a story where rival versions conflict and the truth is elusive. Those who knew Moura testify at once to her courage, her charm, and her self-confidence: even her sharpest detractors do not deny her good humour, her warmth and her affection. And yet at the same time they also acknowledge the lack of scruple, the disregard for truth, the insatiable need of admiration and attention. She was somebody supremely attuned to the power of the impression she left: she behaved always according to the image she wanted people to have of her.[5]

This is one of the best lay descriptions we have of someone suffering from NPD.

It is not known exactly how or when a person becomes a Narcissist, for they rarely consult and prove almost impossible to treat. (They deny that they have a problem.) It must begin very early. In the case of Moura, she was her mother's darling, beautiful and talented, and her father 'spoiled her unashamedly'.[6] When she was very young, he would set her on a table and have her sing or recite for guests. Soon she was hooked on applause and admiration. Once on the treadmill of Narcissism, she worked hard – not always honestly of course – to win fresh supplies of admiration. She learned to charm – and seduce – everyone she set her sights on.

Moura's father, Ignaty Zakrevsky (1839–1905), was an important lawyer in the service of the Tsar, with a large estate in the Ukraine. He married Maria Nikolaïevna Boreisha (1858–1919), and they had four children: a son in 1881, and twin girls, Alexandra and Anna – always known as Alla and Assia – in 1884. Another daughter, named Maria after her mother but always called by her pet name Moura, was born in 1893. Shortly before she arrived, Mr Zakrevsky took in a young Irishwoman, Margaret Wilson, as a nanny who would speak English with his children. She remained with the family for the rest of her life, never properly learning Russian and thus ensuring that two generations of Zakrevsky children, who all called her Micky, spoke English fluently. Moura developed a mother–daughter bond with her. Moura's first language was English, and she spoke Russian with a slight English accent. This bond was reinforced when Moura's father died of a heart attack in 1905, leaving his family in much diminished circumstances, for he had left a significant proportion of his fortune to the Freemasons.

Between the ages of twelve and seventeen, Moura lived a frustratingly solitary life on the family estate, not going away to school as her sisters had done. They went on to marry well, Assia to Nikolai Ionoff, a diplomat, in 1907 or 08 and, at about the same time, Alla to another diplomat, Arthur Engelhardt, who came from a family of diplomats. Very soon after, Alla had a daughter, Kira – or so some believe; the alternative story is that sixteen-year-old Moura seduced her new brother-in-law and the child was hers. Whoever the mother really was, Kira spent all her life with the Zakrevsky family, and then Moura's family, instead of Alla's, and

Moura as a young woman

was looked after by Micky. She went to England in the 1930s, married well, and became the grandmother of the English politician and former deputy Prime Minister, Nick Clegg.

When Moura turned eighteen, Assia, whose husband had been posted to the Russian Embassy in Berlin, invited her to join them there. This was just the opportunity that Moura had been waiting for, and she plunged into the glittering social life of Berlin. Soon she was engaged to an aristocratic diplomat, Djon Alexandrovich von Benckendorff, and married him in 1911. (The name Benckendorff has an ominous ring for historians of social oppression in Russia. Following the Decembrist coup of 1825, Tsar Nicholas I established a special corps of the Gendarmerie, the Third Section, under Count Konstantin Benckendorff, charged with preventing any further uprisings. The Count laid the foundations of the total police state, with its system of espionage and counter-espionage.) When not in Berlin, where Djon worked at the Russian Embassy alongside Assia's husband, Moura shared her time between Djon's apartment in St Petersburg and his estate in Estonia. When she became pregnant, she summoned Micky from the Zakrevsky estate, and Kira came with her. Moura had two children by Djon – Pavel in 1913 and Tania in 1915 – and Micky brought them up, with Kira as their big sister. Mothering is of no interest to a Narcissist; babies can neither admire nor flatter, so Moura was rarely at home with them. Tania recalls meeting her mother 'for the first time' when she was five years old: 'there was a great deal of embarrassment on both sides which prevented any closeness between us.'[7]

There is a tale that Moura and her husband paid an extended visit to London in 1911, during which Moura met two of her future lovers, Robert Bruce Lockhart and H. G. Wells (1866–1946). This was surely one of her fantasies (or lies, if you prefer), just like the degree from Cambridge that she claimed to hold, and the sixty volumes of Russian literature she was reputed to have translated. The grain of truth behind these myths may be the winter course that she once followed at Newnham College to improve her English –

though I have yet to find independent evidence that even this actually took place. Grossly exaggerating their achievements and talents and presenting them convincingly is the hallmark of a Narcissist.

On the outbreak of the First World War, Djon joined the Imperial Army and became a staff officer on the north-west front. Moura remained in St Petersburg, where the high life of the upper class continued – muted but uninterrupted – until the revolution of February 1917. As the world she had thrived on collapsed around her, Moura organized one last summer party on Djon's estate, Yendel, in Estonia. Among those present were Ambassador Buchanan's daughter Meriel; Edward Cunard (a secretary in the Embassy); Captain Francis Cromie, who was in charge of the British submarine fleet in the Baltic Sea – he was gunned down a year later while defending the St Petersburg Embassy against a Cheka raid; and Captain Denis Garstin, who was attached to the Embassy as member of the Anglo-Russian Commission. After the British landed troops at Archangel on 2 August 1918, he managed to reach them, but he was killed by a Red sniper on 15 August.

Nineteen seventeen was a year for rumour quite as much as revolution in Russia. It was widely believed, even at high levels in Whitehall, that Lenin and Trotsky were German agents, sent to bring about the collapse of Russia. Twenty years later, Moura told H. G. Wells that she had been spying on the Germans for the Russians; caught, she was turned and obliged to spy on the Russians on behalf of the Germans – but her daughter Tania dismissed this as pure myth-making on the part of her mother. Yet there are stories of indiscretions by Imperial Army officers, at parties hosted by an otherwise unidentified Madame B— in St Petersburg, somehow reaching the ears of German intelligence. Moura also let people believe that she became the mistress of Alexander Kerensky (1881–1970),* who led the short-lived

---

* In *A Very Dangerous Woman*, McDonald and Dronfield take this story for true coin.

Provisional Government between the two revolutions. What is independently attested is that, following the October Revolution, when food became desperately short in Petrograd, she found work as a translator in the British Embassy. There, on the last day of January 1918, she threw a party for Captain Cromie's birthday, at which she met Robert Bruce Lockhart.

It is tempting to portray Lockhart as a classic, flag-waving ex-public-schoolboy, for he was an enthusiastic Scotsman who loved sports. When he learned, as a small boy, that he had a second brother, he immediately exclaimed that that would be perfect for cricket, 'one to bat, one to bowl, and one to keep wicket.'[8] Arthur Ransome described him as 'a cheerful young man with a taste for gypsies, wine and dancing.'[9] He brought this enthusiasm to all the other areas of his life. Sent out to Malaya as a young man to manage a rubber plantation, he managed to fall head-over-heels in love with a local princess, who was already married – but divorcing her husband and due to remarry shortly after. He declared his love, and in the interval between her marriages, she lived with him. This idyll was brought to an abrupt end by malaria and he was shipped back to civilization, more dead than alive, to recover his health and his heart.

Joining the Foreign Office, Lockhart was appointed Vice-Consul at Moscow in 1912. On arrival, he was mistaken for his younger brother John, who had an enviable reputation as a sportsman at Cambridge. On the strength of this, Lockhart was invited by the English manager of a textile-factory football team to play for them; his team won the 1912 Moscow league championship. He also won the heart of Jean Haslewood, whom he married in 1913, but she soon returned to England, disheartened by the early death of their child and her husband's philandering. Much later, they had a son, who survived to write a popular biography of his father's friend and fellow agent, Sidney Reilly, titled *Ace of Spies* (1967).

Without a spouse in Moscow to keep him in check, Lockhart had a number of affairs, the last of which was rather too public; in

September 1917, the Ambassador regretfully asked him to take 'sick leave' in England. Hardly was he home when the Revolution took place. On 15 December, Trotsky informed the Allies that he was seeking to end the war by making peace with the Central Powers. This was not at all what Britain wanted; peace on the eastern front would enable the Germans to divert more troops to the western one, which Britain and her Allies were barely managing to hold. Whitehall suddenly realized that Lockhart was just the man they needed in St Petersburg to establish unofficial relations with the Bolsheviks and prevent them, or at least discourage them, from making peace.

In an unbelievably off-hand fashion, Lockhart's important mission

> was arranged over the table at a Lyons tea shop in the Strand. The two contracting parties were represented by [Maxim] Litvinov and [Theodore] Rothstein on the Russian side and [Rex] Leeper and myself [i.e. Bruce Lockhart] on the English side.* There was to be no recognition – at any rate for the present. Unofficially, both Litvinov and I were to have certain diplomatic privileges, including the use of ciphers and the right to a diplomatic courier.... On the rough linen of a standard Lyons' table, Litvinov wrote out my letter of recommendation to Trotsky.[10]

He arrived back in what was now called the Russian Soviet Republic at the end of January, too late to confer with Trotsky before he left for the Brest-Litovsk conference, but just in time for Moura's party. She pounced, and he was soon head-over-heels in love with her. It was a spontaneous honeytrap.

It seems that it was soon after this that Moura began working for the Cheka. As the wife of a diplomat who had worked in Berlin, and then with her history of translating at the British Embassy in St Petersburg, she would in any case have been 'a person of interest' to them. On the other hand, she belonged to the class that the

---

* These men are fully identified in Chapter 8.

Bolsheviks were trying to eradicate; the very fact that she was neither arrested nor deported suggests that she was useful to them. Lockhart should have been more suspicious of her, for she told him quite openly that she cultivated the acquaintance of Francis Cromie because he might be charmed into revealing secrets that she could use. (Although Cromie was fascinated by Moura – and who wasn't? – he was well protected, having both a wife in England and a beautiful young mistress in St Petersburg, Sonia Gagarin, the daughter of Princess Marie Gagarin, whose autobiography has been one of my source books.) How much Lockhart confided in Moura we shall never know, but as she was living in his flat, she was in a good position to read any documents that he may have left around, and to overhear conversations between him and his colleague Hicks and their visitors. Moreover, Lockhart always kept the code book which he used when communicating with Whitehall locked in a drawer in his flat; she could easily have gained access to it and copied it. It was summer when Lockhart was warned by the Swedish mission that the Bolsheviks had had his codes for two months. A rational man would have suspected Moura; being completely besotted with her, Lockhart was beyond reason by then.

I must open a parenthesis here to tell you about Captain William Hicks, or 'Hickie' as everyone called him, for he too fell in love with a Russian girl, Liuba Malinina, in 1918. She was the niece of Mikhail Chelnokov, the Mayor of Moscow and Lockhart's 'best friend in Russia'.[11] According to Moura's daughter Tania, Liuba had 'a tiny face and large blue eyes,' along with 'endless energy.'[12] I would have written a chapter about them were it not for the dearth of information. In July 1916, Hickie had been seconded from the Liverpool Regiment as a temporary captain to liaise with the authorities in St Petersburg on the poison gases that were used by all the belligerents in the First World War. Lockhart had got to know him there, and chose to take him with him on this mission, for Hickie was

> a man of great personal charm; he was popular with Russians and understood their mentality. He was, too, a good linguist with a first-

class knowledge of German and a working acquaintance with Russian. His views on the situation were in tune with my own. I never regretted my decision. He was a most loyal colleague and devoted friend.[13]

In mid-March 1918, however, Hickie was delegated to represent Britain, alongside an American, in an investigation into the rumour (which they quickly disproved) that the Russians had turned large numbers of their prisoners of war and were preparing to use – or even already using – them as fighting forces on their own side. So the trusted colleague who shared Lockhart's flat was not there for six weeks to keep an eye on things for him.

The arrival of Bruce Lockhart in Moscow with an introduction to Trotsky was a red flag – excuse the metaphor – to the Bolsheviks. Britain's attitude towards them was confused and variable, which made them suspicious of any apparent good intentions. As it was, Lockhart's own attitude towards them evolved rapidly, for he soon realized that, following the collapse of the Imperial Army, it would take the Bolsheviks years to build up an effective Red Army. And then he witnessed the brutality with which the Bolsheviks suppressed everyone who did not support them. So he started to hope that a way might be found to overthrow them. Meanwhile, because German forces seemed likely to reach St Petersburg before the Brest-Litovsk agreement could be signed, the British Embassy was closed in March 1918 and its staff withdrawn to Murmansk, leaving Lockhart without anyone in authority over him. Having been given *carte blanche* by Whitehall, he became a loose cannon.

While Moura was getting the love and admiration that she needed from Lockhart, she slipped away to the Ukraine for a brief visit. By signing the Brest-Litovsk treaty, Trotsky had signed away the Ukraine and the Baltic states to the Germans. At the end of April, they dissolved the Central Council of the Ukrainian People's Republic and installed an anti-socialist government, called the Hetmanate, in its place. The Bolsheviks took exception to this, so the Cheka sent Moura to her homeland to spy for them. She met some of the leaders of the Hetmanate (who had been friends and colleagues of her father's), and they soon signed a peace treaty with the Bolsheviks, although Moura's role in this – if any – is quite unknown. As it was, the Hetmanate collapsed in December 1918, and the Ukrainian People's Republic was re-instated in the form of a Directorate.

It must have been during this trip to Kiev that Moura realized that she was pregnant. As she and Lockhart each had a legitimate spouse, they hatched a plan: she would return to her husband's estate in Estonia, and sleep with Djon. That would give a nominal legitimacy to their child. But Estonia was now occupied by the Germans; although there was no fighting on the border, it was by no means open to all comers. Moura was away ten days, and always told fantastical accounts of her journey. Did she actually make it? At any rate, there was no further talk of legitimizing her pregnancy; instead she named the foetus 'Peter'.

By now, it was August 1918. When the Allies landed at Archangel with a mere fifteen hundred French and British troops, the Bolsheviks were in two minds; some wanted to have all French and British nationals in Russia rounded up and expelled; others, led by Karl Radek (of all people) wanted them publicly shot. In this uncertain situation, two Latvian soldiers approached Cromie with a plan. Cromie sent them on to Lockhart, who arranged a meeting with the French and US consuls. The plan, as it evolved, was to mount an armed attack by discontented Latvian soldiers on the All-Russian Congress of Soviets that was due to be held on 28 August. Unfortunately, the French brought to the meeting a journalist who was a double agent, and he warned the Cheka. The Congress was cancelled and everyone involved in the plot was arrested.

There is another version of this story, according to which the Latvian soldiers were actually Cheka agents. There are also two versions as to what was going to happen after the Latvian soldiers attacked the Congress: the British line was that Lenin, Trotsky, and other leaders were to be taken prisoner. One schoolboyish idea was to remove their trousers and have them marched through the streets with their shirt-tails flying: defeat through ridicule. The Bolsheviks' version was far less facetious: according to *Pravda*, their leaders were to be shot and 'the intention of the Allies, as soon as they had established their dictatorship in Moscow, was to declare war on Germany and force Russia to fight again.'[14] I don't think anyone had actually imagined that; it was just Bolshevik paranoia.

Although Lockhart had not attended the meeting with the French and US consuls, he was arrested by the Cheka, along with Moura and Hickie, but he was released after twenty-four hours. Moura was not. Realizing this when he got back to his flat, Lockhart returned to the Lubianka to demand news of her, and was immediately re-arrested, for in the meantime Fanny Kaplan had shot and wounded Lenin. As this occurred straight after the plan to attack the Congress had been thwarted, the Bolsheviks jumped to the conclusion that British agents must have been guiding Fanny Kaplan's hand too, and arrested everyone they could think of.

While the other Britons were taken to the Peter and Paul fortress, where they were crammed into small cells, Lockhart was held in the Lubianka (where he was confronted with Fanny Kaplan, just hours before she was shot, to see if they recognized each other.) Moura was rapidly released and after five days Lockhart, considered to be an important political prisoner, was transferred to the Kremlin. He was most fortunate in being lodged in a clean and comfortable apartment that in former times had been reserved for one of the Ladies-in-Waiting. The sole disadvantage was that its two windows opened onto a corridor, so that there was no fresh air.

Another prisoner that Lockhart encountered in the corridors of the Kremlin was Maria Spiridonova, the leader of the Left SRs who had advocated assassinating the German ambassador. They greeted each other, but otherwise exchanged no words. The Communists persecuted her for the rest of her life, which she spent largely in internal exile, until she was finally executed in 1941.

Lockhart's principal interrogator was Yakov Peters. 'As between

Yakov Peters

prisoner and gaoler, our relations were pleasant,' he reports, and Peters told him about his years of exile in London, during which he had participated in various robberies aimed at raising funds for the Party. He had actually been one of the gang of thieves (referred to as anarchists in the British press at the time) who had tried to break into the back of a jeweller's shop in Houndsditch, in December 1910. Caught in the act, two of them holed up in a house in Sidney Street, and opened fire on the police, triggering the notorious 'Siege of Sidney Street' which ended with the deaths of three policemen, one fireman, and both the anarchists. When the police came for Peters, he made no attempt to resist arrest. In May 1911, he and three other Latvian members of the gang were tried in the Old Bailey. Although Peters had been seen dragging away one of the injured thieves, he was acquitted on both the charges of conspiring to commit a burglary and of murder, for lack of evidence on both counts. His positive experience of British justice undoubtedly rendered Peters more considerate towards Lockhart, especially when his own experience as a prisoner in Tsarist Russia had been quite otherwise: he showed Lockhart his fingernails as proof of the torture he had been subjected to as a prisoner in Riga.

Moura was allowed to bring clothes, books, tobacco, and such luxuries as coffee and ham to Lockhart; the food was particularly welcome, as the diet in both the Lubianka and the Kremlin consisted of tea, thin soup, and potatoes. Lockhart adds, 'Peters apologised for it, stating that it was the same as that supplied to himself and his assistants. From what I had observed during my stay in the Cheka headquarters, his statement was true.'[15] Food was indeed in short supply. As far back as April, Cromie had warned London that any British officials being sent out to Russia should bring six months' supply of food with them. So it is amazing that Moura's gifts were not seized by Lockhart's jailors for their own consumption.

As it is, many people have speculated why Moura should have had such an easy time of it, for she was released after spending less than a week in the women's wing of the Butyrka prison. The Russian girlfriends of British nationals who were arrested at this time were thoroughly grilled by the Cheka, and records have survived of what they said, but there are no records relating to Moura. The Cheka surely knew all about her already and probably decided that she would be more useful to them if she was released. Some people claim that she offered sexual favours to Peters. One thing is certain: at some point during the month that Lockhart was in prison, she had a miscarriage and lost 'little Peter'.

September was a most anxious month for Lockhart. For several weeks he expected to be executed at any moment – the newspapers that his jailors brought him reported the resolutions of Bolshevik groups demanding the death sentence for him – and in the early days of the month, there was a high probability that he would indeed be shot. But the Bolsheviks feared the political repercussions, and so they agreed to exchange Lockhart for Maxim Litvinov and a couple of other lesser figures. At the end of the month, he was released on house arrest, with two days to pack his bags and prepare to leave. He was allowed visitors, one of whom was Liuba Malinina, who came to ask if he could obtain one hour of freedom for Hickie so that they could marry before he was expelled alongside Lockhart. He promised to do what he could.

When the Bolsheviks began mass arrests of Allied nationals, including diplomatic representatives, half-a-dozen officials, including Hickie, had taken refuge in the American Consulate General. Rendered cautious by the consequences of their raid on the British Embassy in which Cromie was killed, the Cheka resolved rather to starve them out, and cut off both the electricity and the water supply. What they did not know was that Allen Wardwell, the head of the American Red Cross Mission in Moscow, who was charged with ensuring that relief supplies from America were safely delivered from Murmansk to St Petersburg and Moscow, had placed a stock of food in the cellar of the Consulate. Even better, there was one tap from which water continued to flow; far from starving or dying of thirst, the beleaguered Allies were living rather well. To improve the jape, whenever there was any rain, they hurried out with bowls, and even a bath, to collect water. This completely fooled the Cheka (for once).

On the evening of Liuba's request, Yakov Peters came round to Lockhart's flat to wish him goodbye. By now, Lockhart knew just how to handle Peters, who had asked him to take a letter and a photograph of himself to his English wife in London.* So Lockhart

> put the question to him in the half-joking, half-sentimental way which I knew would appeal to him. He was amused. 'No one but a mad Englishman,' he said, 'would make a request of this nature at a time like this. Nothing is impossible to such a race. I'll have to see what I can do.' He did, and 'Hickie' and Liuba were duly married the next day.[16]

They spent their honeymoon on the journey to Britain, along with the other Allies who had been expelled at the same time: more than ten days on the train, and sixteen days on the ship to Aberdeen. It must have been galling for Lockhart and Moura to see Hickie and Liuba safely united when they were parting, with only a promise from Lockhart that he would tell Moura as soon as he could when she should join him in Stockholm.

---

* Not long after, Yakov Peters' wife and their daughter Maisie (born in 1914) joined him in Russia. After that, Maisie was never allowed to leave; she died in the USSR in 1971. In 1937, Peters was arrested, along with Karl Radek and a large number of other Old Bolsheviks, accused of plotting with Trotsky to overthrow the Soviet government and restore capitalism. They were all found guilty and were either executed or died in labour camps. Peters was shot on 25 April, 1938.

Moura came to the station to see him off – accepting the separation with dignity – and left accompanied by Allen Wardwell, who had carried the letters that she and Lockhart exchanged while he was in the Kremlin. Wardwell was no doubt the source of the food she took to Lockhart. He was a good person to know: his father had been the Treasurer of Standard Oil, and he was a partner in the firm of Davis, Polk and Wardwell, the legal agents of Morgan and Rockefeller's interests. (His fellow partner Davis ran for President in 1924.) Tania Alexander tells us that 'this kindness forged a link between our two families that has lasted even to the present day; in 1940, he sponsored Kira and her two children to come to America to escape the war.'[17]

After a long wait at the border for news that Litvinov had safely reached Bergen, Lockhart was allowed to continue his journey to London (where he faithfully delivered the letter to Mrs Peters). He spent the following months patching up his marriage and his life; he never managed to meet Moura in Stockholm and wrote rarely – and cautiously – to her. Nor, of course, did he ever return to Russia. Along with twenty or so Russians, most of whom had worked for the Americans or the British in Moscow, he was tried *in absentia* by the Bolsheviks, in a case presented by procurator Nikolai Krylenko before the Supreme Revolutionary Tribunal. The trial concluded on 3 December 1918 with two defendants sentenced to be shot and various others sentenced to terms of imprisonment or forced labour for up to five years. Lockhart was sentenced to death, to be applied if ever he set foot in Soviet Russia again.

Hickie died of consumption (as tuberculosis was called in those days) in Berlin in the spring of 1930, leaving Liuba almost nothing. She moved to London, where she kept a small dress shop, on the lookout for another husband. She was successful: on 3 April 1935, she married Sir Lionel Fletcher,[18] who was well off, kind and undemanding. In 1946 they emigrated to Tanzania where they lived until his death.

Returning now to Moura at the end of 1918, she spent the following months writing loving and increasingly despairing letters to Lockhart. She was living with her mother in St Petersburg, in the flat that her mother owned. (How this was managed, we shall never know: private property had been abolished, and Madame Zakrevskaya belonged to the upper class that the Bolsheviks pretty well exterminated.) At the end of 1918, Moura was informed that her husband's safe deposit box at the bank was to be officially broken open and its contents confiscated. (The Bolsheviks had been doing this systematically ever since the Revolution.) Moura insisted on being present and worked her customary magic to keep the contents for herself, commenting to Lockhart that the 'boys' at the bank were 'perfect infants in arms as far as any training of the mind goes.'[19] But her magic could not conjure up food for her meals or wood for her fire. As it was impossible for Djon to send her any money from Estonia, she was obliged to sell her jewellery and her best clothes – starting with her Court ball gown.[20] But that was a limited expedient: she had to find work.

At this point she became involved in a short-lived and therefore little known project, which introduced her to her next lover, Maxim Gorky. When the Bolsheviks seized power in 1917, they instituted a Commissariat for Enlightenment (Narkompros: Soviet Organization for Education and the Arts), charged with the promotion of art and culture as well as the censorship of literature through the control of all publishing in Soviet Russia. It also aimed to create an image of Russia as a progressive state concerned to educate its citizens by providing them with the best of world literature in Russian translation; to this end, a World Literature Publishing House was established within the State Publishing House. This was something that Gorky, by far the best-known writer to support Communism, had been dreaming of for more than fifteen years. So when his *Novaya Zhizn* (*New Life*), the chief mouthpiece of the Mensheviks, was finally shut down in July 1918, long after all the bourgeois newspapers had gone, his appointment to direct the World Literature project was more than just a sop.[21]

He embraced the project with enthusiasm, and charged Korney Chukovsky with selecting European works for translation.

Korney Chukovsky (1882–1969) was an Anglophile writer and poet, who had already gained a reputation that lasts to this day as an idiosyncratic and much-loved poet and story-teller for children – the nearest thing to a Russian Dr Seuss, with a bit of Edward Lear thrown in. He became the chief editor and translator of English and American literature in this World Literature project. Moura knew him for his having been the official interpreter at the Embassy in St Petersburg. At Christmas 1918, she told Lockhart that Chukovsky had called on her, offering translation work. According to Arkady Vaksberg, it was the other way round: she appealed to Chukovsky for help. I have found no evidence that she did any translating for him, but he certainly did give Moura some kind of office work and – more importantly – a food ration card.

Nineteen nineteen was a pivotal year in her life: her mother died in the spring, either from illness or else as a result of a medical procedure intended to relieve that illness. Her husband Djon also died, in suspicious circumstances. Moura had assured Lockhart that she would get divorced; after their long separation, it was simply a matter of obtaining his signature. But it was as difficult as ever to reach Djon. He was still living on the family estate, Yendel, in Estonia, in an area where a civil war was raging. The family house had been plundered and as a precautionary measure he had moved his children, along with Micky and Kira, to the dower house, an inconspicuous pavilion, Kallijärv, at the remote end of the lake on the estate. Nevertheless, in April, Moura set out with her divorce papers, fully intending to have him sign them. She entered Finland; from Helsingfors it was only a short sea crossing to Estonia. Shortly before making the crossing, she wrote of her plan in a letter to Lockhart, but it breaks off with the words 'I hope to get—'. The following page is missing. The day after, Djon was shot dead on the path between Kallijärv and the family house. He was found by his children and their nanny, who had set out to look for him when he did not return for lunch. There were no witnesses, and no formal investigation into this murder. Moura returned to St Petersburg, without anyone having seen her at Yendel, or anywhere in Estonia – so far as went recorded. It may have been a coincidence – but it was terribly convenient for Moura. Ten days later, she wrote to Lockhart that she had been informed of her husband's death. She was free (and reverted to her maiden name, Maria Zakrevskaya). Lockhart did not respond.

That summer, Moura was arrested by the Cheka, for no known reason. At that time, quite as much as any other in Soviet Russia – or Imperial Russia too, for that matter – you could be arrested by the secret police simply because you were in the wrong place at the wrong time. Solzhenitsyn tells the story of a woman whose neighbour was arrested, leaving a small child in her flat. She went to the Cheka to ask what she should do about her neighbour's abandoned child. 'Sit there,' she was told, 'and we'll deal with you in a few minutes.' Of course, they forgot about her, and when the lorry came round to take the day's haul of prisoners to the gulag, she was taken along with them, despite her protests. As she had not been sentenced, there was no official record as to how long she was to be detained; so she was kept indefinitely. In Moura's case, Chukovsky complained to Gorky, and he had her released, taking her into his little community in a twelve-room flat on the Kronversky Prospekt in St Petersburg. Soon he had made her his personal secretary-translator, and mistress.

Like all the men whom Moura decided to seduce, Gorky was hopelessly lost from the word go. When she arrived, he was proud to receive her and acted like a peacock displaying its feathers. 'Even though she magically attracted men, Moura was different because of her rationalism, perhaps even calculation and reserve, which is often called coldness, although she was never at a loss for warm – even hot – words, both spoken and written,' recalled Chukovsky.[22] Of the Russian writers who remained in the country after the Revolution, Gorky was the most tempting target for a Narcissist, being both famous and popular. By 1920, he had written more than twenty works of fiction and essays, plus over a dozen plays.

Gorky's real name was Alexei Maximovich Peshkov; quite early in life he had adopted the pseudonym (meaning 'bitter') by which he was always known. He and Lenin had been friends since 1902, and shared similar political views, but after the Revolution they diverged increasingly, until Gorky felt that the Bolsheviks had betrayed the ideals that he and Lenin had shared. Once he called them 'real barbarians, just like those that ravaged Rome.'[23] Lenin returned the compliment; he now despised Gorky: 'You allow yourself to be surrounded by the worst elements of the bourgeois intelligentsia and fall for their whimpering.'[24] Gorky did indeed make good use of his privileged position to protect and preserve his friends in literature and the arts from the hardships that prevailed in post-Revolutionary Russia. In particular, he demanded extra ration coupons for his collaborators on the World Literature project. When writers like Yevgeny Zamyatin, author of *We*, were arrested, Gorky at once intervened through Grigory Zinoviev, the chairman of the St Petersburg *soviet*, and many of them were eventually released. The list of those who claimed that he saved their lives, if only by helping them to leave Russia, is very long.

Gorky married his first wife, Ekaterina Pavlovna, in the summer of 1896, and had two children with her. But the death of their daughter from meningitis estranged them; at the same time, Gorky met an actress, whose stage name was Maria Fyodorovna Andreyeva. She became his second wife in 1903. When Moura joined the community in his large flat – actually two adjoining flats which they had made into one by knocking a hole in the dividing wall – both his estranged wives were regular visitors, despite having busy lives of their own. Ekaterina Pavlovna had done great work for orphaned children during the First World War, starting out by heading a commission that organized volunteers to search for minors separated from their parents by the battle front. Thereafter she worked in Russia for the International Red Cross, and continued to do so after the Revolution, visiting prisons. The Cheka did not like this and in 1919 harassed her by accusing her of being a member of the Left SRs – but she was never arrested and the case was dismissed in 1922. Undeterred, she set up an organization called the Pompolit to help the Red Cross search for Polish captives in Russian prisons and camps; it was banned by the NKVD in 1938.

Meanwhile, Maria Andreyeva had been actively promoting classical theatre to the masses even before the war. Only after the October Revolution did these endeavours bear fruit, when she was instrumental in the establishment of the Bolshoi Drama Theatre, which opened in 1919. Between 1918 and 1921, she was Commissar of Theatres and Public Shows in St Petersburg. In January that year, Anatoly Lunacharsky, the head of the art section of Narkompros in St Petersburg, nominated her as his deputy. The St Petersburg Soviet refused to confirm this nomination, but Lenin intervened in her favour and the appointment went ahead. From 1922 she represented the film industry in the Commissariat of External Trade, and from 1931 to 1948, she directed the House of Scientists in Moscow.

Gorky had had other, short-term mistresses, but only Moura could flatter herself that she was his 'third wife'. She was quickly accepted in his little commune, presiding over the soup bowl at meal times and nicknamed 'Titke' (Auntie). That did not prevent her from slipping into H. G. Wells' bed when he visited Gorky.

Right from the launch of the World Literature Publishing House, Wells had been in Gorky's mind as the one Englishman whose approval of the project he sought. They had first met in 1906, and he much admired Wells' novels. On 9 January 1919, he told Lenin:

Soon we will finish printing the catalogue of books proposed for publication.... I think it would be good to translate these lists into all the European languages and to send them to Germany, England, France, the Scandinavian countries, and so forth, in order that the proletariat of the West, and all people such as Anatole France, H. G. Wells ... can see for themselves that the

Russian proletariat is not simply barbarous, and that we understand internationalism much more broadly than they, cultured
people, do. In the most dire conditions possible, we could manage
something that they should have thought of long ago.[25]

An invitation was duly issued, and Wells came in the autumn of
1920. He was a tempting target for Moura: he was internationally
known for his fiction, as well as his progressive social views. She
served as the interpreter during his meetings with Gorky, just as
she had done when Bertrand Russell had visited only a few weeks
previously. Russell later confessed that this young woman had been
so fascinating that he found it hard to concentrate on the conversation. Wells was even more powerfully captivated, despite his long
experience of young women falling in love with him: 'no other
woman has ever had that much effectiveness for me.'[26] It was the
beginning of a relationship that lasted until the end of his life.

Moura also served as Wells' guide to St Petersburg. On one occasion, when Gorky came with them, they visited the abandoned
British Embassy – the site of so many memories for Moura – and
marvelled at

> room after room piled high with beautiful lumber … big rooms
> crammed with statuary; never had [Wells] seen so many white
> marble Venuses and sylphs together … stacks of pictures of every
> sort, passages choked with inlaid cabinets piled up to the ceiling;
> a room full of cases of old lace; piles of magnificent furniture.[27]

Had they recognized them, they might have spotted some of the
ballerina Tamara Karsavina's prized possessions. Little did they
know that Gorky's private museum in his flat was supplied from
sources such as this. Nor – for that matter – were they aware as yet
that Maria Andreyeva was deeply involved in the export of abandoned and confiscated goods like these in exchange for foreign
currency through the Department of External Trade.

Before he left, Wells promised Moura that he would make a
detour through Estonia on his way home, to check on the well-
being of her children. Faithful to his promise, he reported to her, in

A telling group portrait of Wells, Gorky, and Moura in 1920,
photographed by M. S. Nappelbaum

a carefully worded letter, that Tania and Pavel were safe and well. On learning this, Moura decided to go and see them, choosing a time when Gorky was paying a visit to Moscow. It was February 1920, when the Gulf of Finland was frozen over. Having no passport or travel papers, she opted to walk across the ice to the coast of Finland, a matter of 15 km as the seagull flies (about 9 miles) at the narrowest point, and more like 21 km (13 miles) if one uses the islands, including Kronstadt, as steppingstones. (It was across this same stretch of ice that the Bolsheviks launched their attack on the Kronstadt sailors, just a year later.) Somewhere along the way, Moura was picked up by the Cheka and taken to their prison in St Petersburg. Informed of this, Gorky wrote directly to Zinoviev, demanding her release. The Cheka refused, even though Gorky was an old and valued friend of Dzerzhinsky. Then Maria Andreyeva stepped in with an extraordinary letter to the head of the Chekists in St Petersburg:

> I respectfully ask you and the Commission of the Cheka to release
> into my custody Maria Ignatievna Benckendorff, who attempted
> to cross the border somewhere outside St Petersburg. It is known
> to me that she was going to see her children, aged six and seven,
> living under the care of an uncle and in very bad conditions in
> Estonia. I will bet my life that, having given me her word, she will
> not attempt to repeat this dangerous undertaking, even for her
> children, therefore in the worst case scenario I give you my word
> to shoot me: knowing this and seeing my signature here, she will
> not lift a finger without your knowledge. She is a mother and a
> very good person.[28]

Moura had worked her magic once again.

A year later, Gorky started planning to leave Russia, aware that another winter in the spartan conditions of the Kronversky flat would be fatal to him, for he had only one functioning lung, the consequence of a teenage attempt at suicide. He encouraged Moura to go and stay with her children, and helped her obtain the requisite papers – or rather Maria Andreyeva did, since she was in better favour with the local Cheka. She may also have been pleased at this opportunity to separate Moura from Gorky. It is possible that the Cheka was happy to see her go as well, for they were convinced that she was a British spy. Early in her stay with Gorky, they had raided the flat. They barely glanced into the other rooms and concentrated on Moura's, spending two hours examining absolutely everything. Of course, they found nothing.

Thus she was enabled to travel by train to Estonia, leaving a note for Gorky telling him, 'You are my joy, my big true Joy.'[29] This journey proved to be a turning point in Moura's life: she never lived in Russia again, paying only brief visits in Gorky's final years, after he returned. It also marked a change in her relationship with Lockhart, for on the day before she left she heard that he had had a son; 'little Peter' had been successfully replaced. However, she soon had another problem to take her mind off Lockhart: the moment she stepped off the train in Reval – now renamed Tallinn, for Estonia had become independent of Russia, and the old Estonian place names had been revived – she was arrested for working with the Cheka. Her Benckendorff in-laws had petitioned that she be declared unworthy of looking after her children and expelled from the country. She took a lawyer and fought as only Moura knew how, winning a three-month residence permit. She hastened to rejoin Kira, Tania, Pavel, and of course Micky, who was far more pleased to see her than any of the children were. For Tania, Moura 'only became a real person to me when she turned up in Kallijärv' in May that year.[30] She had not seen her mother since 1917.

The next three months were a busy time. She spent much of the working week in Tallinn, returning to Kallijärv at the weekend. Only many years later did she admit that she had been working for a Dutchman of the Urvater family who dealt in gold and diamonds. Her source of supply was surely Maria Andreyeva. (The British and American governments were not happy with this illicit trade; at this point MI5 opened the first of its many files on Moura.) She also had to find a way to extend her residence in Estonia. Her lawyer proposed a solution: Baron Nikolai Budberg, a local Estonian just a little younger than Moura, was looking for a spouse who would pay off his debts: after inheriting his title very young, he had squandered his fortune.

They soon reached agreement: thanks to funds from Maria Andreyeva, Nikolai's debts were paid, and the happy couple married in November. Moura gained an Estonian passport and – which pleased her even more – the title of Baroness; she used it for the rest of her life. They did not live together for long, though: within a few months, Nikolai decided (with Moura's help) to emigrate to Rio de Janeiro. Five years later, the marriage was dissolved; neither party appeared at the hearing in Berlin.

This enabled Moura to effect a return to Gorky with no strings attached except for her waning attachment to Lockhart. In 1923, when she was visiting Hickie and Liuba in Vienna, she learned that Lockhart was in Prague, working for a bank, having abandoned his career in the Foreign Office. She spoke to him on the telephone, and Lockhart came over to Vienna for the weekend. But the spell was broken; Lockhart had become an anonymous bank employee whom Moura would have considered beneath her notice were it not for their shared past. 'It would be a mistake,' she told him, to renew their relationship. 'Don't let us spoil something – perhaps, the one thing in both our lives – that has been perfect.'[31] Lockhart could only nod in assent. But they kept in contact with each other.

Just so long as Gorky lived outside Russia, she remained at his side much of the time, acting as his literary agent in the West and, in later years, translating some of his works into English. When not with him, she was generally in Berlin, where she was involved in administering the foreign rights to his work, and in publishing. During these visits to Berlin she gathered information on now-exiled former members of the Hetmanate government, who included her brother-in-law, Assia's new husband Prince Basil Kotchoubey. (Her first husband had died of tuberculosis in 1917.) This activity ended in 1929, when the exiles discovered that Moura had spied on them in 1918.

In the mid-1920s, Gorky moved to a villa in Sorrento, with a splendid view across the Bay of Naples to Vesuvius. On more than one occasion, Moura brought her children for a summer holiday there, and Gorky impressed Tania as a friendly old man. However, Moura realized that Italian agents were spying on them – unlike Gorky, she spoke Italian fluently. Engineering a meeting with Mussolini, she complained to him of this surveillance, since Gorky was a perfectly legal resident in Italy. Mussolini laughed her off: 'It's not Gorky we are watching; it's you!' Apparently a Russian émigré had denounced her.

Only when Stalin induced Gorky to return to Russia in 1929 (by withholding his Russian royalties and offering a luxurious lifestyle) did Moura cease to live with him, and she continued to act as his agent in the West until 1939, three years after his death. Such was Stalin's determination to keep Gorky in a golden cage in Russia that, in his last years, Moura would occasionally be ordered over from England for a visit. She must have been the only ordinary citizen in the free world who could visit Russia at the drop of a hat; no visa required. A car from the Russian Embassy in London would pick her up at her door and she would be flown to Moscow and back with never a stamp in her passport! It is now widely believed[32] that she was working for the NKVD at this point, reporting directly to its director Genrikh Yagoda, who regularly visited Gorky. She is said to have met Stalin three times and brought him an accordion as a present. According to C. P. Snow, she was 'the only woman Stalin would speak of with respect.'[33] Perhaps she was not such an ordinary citizen after all.

These visits to Gorky very nearly broke Moura's relationship with H. G. Wells, for he was unaware that she was Gorky's mistress. She had written to Wells frequently in the 1920s, flirtatiously keeping the old flame gently flickering. After she finally managed to get to London in 1929, she rekindled it to the point where Wells started asking her to marry him. She always refused, for now she valued her independence and the freedom to visit Gorky when necessary. In 1934, Wells invited himself to Russia in the vain hope (in both senses of *vain*) that he could effect a rapprochement between Stalin and President Roosevelt. Moura had steadfastly refused to accompany him, assuring him that she was unlikely to be allowed into the country and, once in, she would probably not be allowed out. Worse, she might even be shot. During his visit, Wells took the opportunity to go and see Gorky, and casually mentioned his plan to make a break in his journey home by visiting Baroness Budberg in Estonia. 'Oh,' said the translator, 'she was here only last week.' And Gorky added that he had seen Moura three times in the past year. Wells was almost apoplectic, and immediately wrote a codicil to his will, cutting her out of it entirely. He did stop over in Estonia, though, intending to make a clean break with her – and by the time he left Moura had managed to heal the breach sufficiently for their relationship to continue, stormily at times but nevertheless

unbroken, until he died in 1946. As Anthony West, Wells' illegitimate son by Rebecca West, put it, Wells 'could not reason himself
out of his intoxication' with Moura: he forgave her sufficiently to
leave her several legacies. She was beside him in his last hours, just
as she had been with Gorky, and would be with Bruce Lockhart too.

After Wells' death, Bertrand Russell, whose sense of humour
never deserted him and who had never forgotten meeting Moura
back in 1920, quipped, 'She's welcome to a place in my bed.'[34] She
did not take him up on that. But she did have other lovers, including Count Constantine Benckendorff (a distant cousin of her first
husband, Djon). That affair lasted from 1929 or '30 until shortly
before Wells died, and he never knew about it, although Moura
once had effrontery to get herself and Wells invited to a weekend
with the Count and his wife.

Her post-war lover was the Hungarian-born film producer,
director, screenwriter, and ultimately movie mogul, Sir Alexander
Korda (1893–1956), for whom she worked in the filmscript department. At the same time, Moura developed the lifestyle that was to
make her famous throughout the 1950s and 60s. Already well
known for her drinks parties (and she could drink practically anyone under the table), she turned her flat into a salon, a hub of the
postwar social world in London. Everyone who was anyone in the
arts came, and politicians too. Moura knew them all, and was
prized for the introductions she could offer people. No wonder the
spies Burgess and Mclean were regulars in the year or so before
they defected.

Moura's reputation for being a spy never left her; British Intelligence spent a fortune tapping her telephone, opening her mail, and
watching the coming and going at her flat. Around 1950, the spook
whose job it was to watch her was 'Klop' Ustinov (the father of
actor and film director Peter Ustinov). His nickname, which means
bedbug in Russian, had been coined by his wife who recognized
that he was expert at learning secrets from women by sleeping with
them. The amusing thing here is that one of H. G. Wells' mistresses

cruelly nicknamed Moura 'Bedbug' (from her married name Budberg, but also because of the ease with which she slipped from bed to bed). So here we have one bedbug watching another.

Nicknames aside, Klop decided that it might be more advantageous to make Moura work for MI6; so he tackled her and she promised to pass on any tidbits that came her way. One of the first things she revealed was that Anthony Blunt – one of the Cambridge Five along with Burgess and Mclean – was spying for Soviet Russia. This was more than ten years before he was arrested and twenty-eight years before he was publicly exposed. At the time when Moura denounced him, Blunt was a highly respected figure: he had worked for MI5 during the war; he had been appointed Surveyor of the King's Pictures in 1945, and become both Professor of the History of Art at the University of London and the director of the Courtauld Institute of Art. MI6 cautiously marked Moura's accusation, 'take no action'. Should we conclude that it takes a spy to spot a spy?

In 1974, she decided to retire to Italy, close to the farm where her son Pavel (now Paul) was living. She went out there by car with a trailer full of private papers, some of which the intelligence services of both Britain and Russia (to mention only two countries) would have dearly loved to get their hands on. The story goes that the trailer caught fire during the journey, and Moura did nothing to extinguish the flames. She died a few months later, and her secrets died with her.

Moura's love affair with Sir Robert Hamilton Bruce Lockhart, KCMG, was certainly the most famous romance of the Revolution, thanks to his *Memoirs of a British Agent* and the film adaptation soon afterwards. She carefully vetted the manuscript before it was published and they colluded in omitting almost as much as they revealed. So we shall never know just how deeply involved he (and probably she) was in what the Bolsheviks called 'the Lockhart Plot', or the full extent of her collaboration with the Cheka. This secrecy makes it stand out among Moura's many love affairs.

Sources

Alexander, Tania. *A Little of All These. An Estonian Childhood.* Jonathan Cape, 1987.

American Psychiatric Association (ed.). *Diagnostic and Statistical Manual of Mental Disorders.* Fourth Edition, Text Revised (DSM-IV). Washington, D.C.: American Psychiatric Association, 2000.

Berberova, Nina. *Moura.* Trans. Marian Schwartz and Richard D. Sylvester. New York: NY Review Books, 1988.

Chamberlain, Lesley. *The Philosophy Steamer: Lenin and the Exile of the Intelligentsia.* Atlantic Books, 2007. Published in the USA as *Lenin's Private War: The Voyage of the Philosophy Steamer and the Exile of the Intelligentsia* by St Martin's Press.

Day, Peter. *The Bedbug. Klop Ustinov: Britain's Most Ingenious Spy.* 2nd ed. Backbite, 2015.

Gagarin, Princess Marie. *Reminiscences of Old Russia.* Privately printed, 1951.

Garstin, Denis. *Friendly Russia.* Fisher Unwin, 1915.

Hart-Davis, Rupert (ed.). *The Autobiography of Arthur Ransome.* Cape, 1976.

Khotimsky, Maria. 'World Literature, Soviet Style: a Forgotten Episode in the History of the Idea.' *Ab Imperio,* 2013, no.3, pp.119–54.

Lockhart, Robert Bruce. *Memoirs of a British Agent.* Putnam, 1932.

——— *Retreat from Glory.* Putnam, 1932.

McDonald, Deborah, and Jeremy Dronfield. *A Very Dangerous Woman: The Lives, Loves, and Lies of Russia's Most Seductive Spy.* London and New York: Oneworld paperback edition, 2016.

Smith, Michael. *Six: the Real James Bonds, 1909–1939.* Biteback, 2010.

Vaksberg, Arkady. *The Murder of Maxim Gorky: A Secret Execution.* Trans. Todd Bludeau. New York: Enigma Books, 2007.

Notes

1   Berberova, p.165.
2   Alexander, p.59.
3   Alexander, p.76.
4   Alexander, p.150.
5   Alexander, p.148.
6   Alexander p.27.
7   Alexander, p.67.
8   Lockhart, *Memoirs,* part i, ch. 1, p.4.
9   Ransome, p.231.
10 Lockhart, *Memoirs,* part iv, ch, 1, p.203.
11 Lockhart, *Memoirs,* part iii, ch.2, p.114.
12 Alexander, p.126.
13 Lockhart, *Memoirs,* part iv, ch. 1, p.205.
14 Smith, p.232.
15 Lockhart, *Memoirs,* p.330.
16 Lockhart, *Memoirs,* p.345.
17 Alexander, p.47.
18 From a professional wedding photograph of the couple available from TopFoto.co.uk through https://www.europeana.eu/portal/en/collections/photography.
19 Letter to Lockhart, 24 Jan. 1919, quoted by McDonald and Dronfield, pp.172–3.
20 Alexander, p.53.
21 Berberova, pp.93 and 95; Kinel, pp.75–76.
22 Vaksberg, p.98.
23 Quoted by McDonald and Bronfield, p.189.
24 Vaksberg, p.93.
25 E. A. Bialik et al. (Eds.). *V. I. Lenin i A. M. Gor'kii.* Perepiska. Vospominaniya. Dokumenty. 3rd edition, Moscow, 1969. p.138, quoted by Khotimsky. (Lightly edited.)

26   *H. G. Wells in Love* (p.164), quoted by McDonald and Bronfield, p.199.
27 *Russia in the Shadows* by H. G. Wells (pp.51–2), quoted by

7 Tamara and Benjie

DURING THE FIVE YEARS that preceded the First World War, Sergei Diaghilev's Ballets Russes revolutionized the performing arts in Western Europe and far beyond. Its avant-garde choreographers, composers, artists, and dancers collectively introduced almost everything that we now call Modern. Breaking with convention in music and costume design, rhythm and movement, it was hailed with delirious excitement (bordering on hysteria) by the young and open-minded, and reviled as primitive and obscene by the staid and conservative. The break between Nijinsky, the principal male dancer, and Diaghilev in 1913, closely followed by the war, put a halt to these innovations.

Of Diaghilev's three ballerinas, Anna Pavlova, Tamara Karsavina, and Lydia Lopukhova (whose name has been Anglicized as Lopokova), who shared in this explosion of originality, Tamara was the one who created most of the lead roles. She starred in Fokine's *Les Sylphides* (the first version of 1908), *Cléopâtre* (1909), *Carnaval* (1910), *Firebird* (1910), *Le Spectre de la Rose* (1911), *Narcisse* (1911), *Petrouchka* (1911), *Le Dieu bleu* (1912), *Thamar* (1912), *Daphnis et Chloe* (1912), Nijinsky's *Jeux* (1913),

Tamara in *Le Coq d'or*

Papillons (1914), and *Le Coq d'or* (1914). Inexcusably, Tamara is barely remembered in Britain today, yet she was also one of the founders of modern British ballet, which would never have happened had she not fallen in love, quite unexpectedly, with an Englishman.

With hindsight, it might be said that Tamara, who was born on 10 March 1885, was destined for greatness as a ballet dancer. Her father, Platon Karsavin, had been First Soloist with the Imperial Ballet in St Petersburg, but, due to some irreverent off-stage miming, he had fallen into disgrace, with the result that his family always lived from hand to mouth. Withdrawn from the stage, he taught at the Theatre School in St Petersburg for a few years. His wife Anna was educated in the Smolny Institute for upper-class girls that the Bolsheviks took over as their headquarters after the Revolution.

Their two children reflected this dual heritage, combining their father's artistic skill with their mother's intelligence. Their son Lev, who was two years older than Tamara, excelled as a student of history. On graduation, he carried out research in Italy and France and published his findings on medieval monastic life in 1911. He became a professor of cultural and medieval studies – and was one of the philosophers that Lenin exiled in 1922.

Even when Lev and Tamara were very young, their maternal grandmother used to tell them of the infidelities of her long-dead husband and how 'he often confessed his peccadilloes and said, "Mary, my angel, you will understand and forgive me."'[1] Both Lev and Tamara became unfaithful spouses, as we shall see.

In her autobiography, Tamara added an anecdote about herself which reveals how intelligent she was, and also has its own significance here. When Lev was seven years old, and Tamara therefore only five, their mother taught him to read.

There was no fixed time for these lessons. Mother came into the nursery whenever she had time to spare, bringing her work with her. I was allowed to play quietly by, or to look at a picture-book.

But I had an ambition to learn; and, partly from listening to the
lessons, partly by asking what this or that letter was, I soon picked
up a lot. I was not fully aware then that I could read: nor was anybody else.
Soon there came a day when Tamara was looking at some pictures
in the newspaper, and read out a caption.

Mother was surprised, but thought I must have learnt it by heart.
She bade me read out a few sentences, which I did with a slight
hesitation. Then she called to my father: 'Listen, Platon, Tata has
learnt to read all by herself.' To me she said: 'But newspapers are
not reading for children.' I pleaded with her to let me read a serial.
'And what is this serial?' she asked. The answer must have
sounded very odd, especially as I still lisped. 'The Victim of
Passion: A criminal novel.' Mother was startled, but Father
laughed to tears, and said: 'Let her read "The Victim of Passion".
It won't do her any harm.'[2]

Tamara was a 'happily married woman' when she fell in love with
her Englishman. A victim of passion? She never saw it that way.

It was by no means evident to everyone that Tamara was to be
a ballet dancer. Her father was against the idea, at any rate. Anna
privately thought otherwise, noticing how, as a very small child,
her daughter loved dressing up and looking at herself in the
mirror. This was not nascent narcissism. A great ballet dancer
needs many things; high among them is perfect awareness of how
her least movement appears to her audience. Anna arranged for
Tamara to be coached and it was soon discovered that she had a
natural ability for ballet dancing. Her father was informed; he
bowed to the inevitable and shared in training her, disciplining her
strictly. Given the family's straitened circumstances, there was a
practical consideration in this: even if Tamara never made it
beyond the corps de ballet, she would earn more than in any other
respectable profession. Although it was quite accepted that dancers
in the Imperial Ballet were often kept by their aristocratic lovers,
ballet remained a respectable career. The much-admired Mathilda

Kschessinska, a ballerina a generation older than Tamara, included the future Tsar and two Grand Dukes among her conquests.

Tamara passed the entry exam to the Imperial Theatre School in 1894, when she was nine and a half. Competition for places was fierce. Of the thousands of applicants, about a hundred boys and two hundred girls were selected for audition, preference being given to those who already had some connection with the performing arts; the annual intake was a dozen girls and six boys. The following years were a hard grind. In addition to the usual school subjects, there was all the physical training, the hours and hours of practice at the barre. Not a moment of the day was unregimented; in fact all the pupils were lined up and counted five times a day. All this left little time for Tamara to indulge her sense of fun or play pranks. Determined not to disappoint her parents or her mentors, she disciplined herself to the point where some fellow students called her 'a self-torturing fakir'. Among her teachers at the Theatre School was her godfather Paul Gerdt. He developed her natural ability, inherited from her father, to leap high in the air: her elevation became exceptional. His speciality was grace, though, especially expressive bearing and use of the arms. For a ballet dancer, every part of the body, from the toes to the eyelashes, has its role to play. This requires a high degree of self-awareness, so that when performing, the dancer is conscious of what she is doing with every muscle, every tendon, every sinew of her body. And this Tamara achieved to an exceptional degree. She also had superb acting skills: like her father, she was a born mimic, and eloquent miming enriched her dancing. The English dance critic, Cyril W. Beaumont, exclaimed, 'She remains the only dancer I have ever seen who was a born comedienne.'[3] For Edward Stark, she had an 'exclusive gift for turning the dance she performed into poetry.'[4] Lastly, she was one of the most intelligent ballerinas of her time, open to new ideas. Exceptionally (but not surprisingly), she was allowed to graduate six months ahead of the rest of her class, in the spring of 1902, just as she turned seventeen.

Mathilda Kschessinska described Tamara at this point as 'a beautiful girl, gifted, simple, and full of infinite kindness,' ill-adapted to the petty jealousies, rivalries and scheming of the world of professional dance. Her career was launched within a year of graduation, when she was given the lead role in a one-act ballet, *The Awakening of Flora.* It was a triumph, but Tamara was over-critical of herself and her confidence ebbed away. 'At the end, applause roared, and bouquets filled the stage,' she recalled. But 'it didn't cheer me up; I had sentenced myself as a failure.'[5] Shortly afterwards, she was diagnosed and treated for acute malaria. Thanks to a Chancery loan, she rested and took the waters at Roncegno, in the north of Italy, with her mother – and bounced back to health remarkably quickly (suggesting that it was not in fact malaria that she was suffering from, but possibly some nervous condition brought on by stress). Taking advantage of the proximity of Milan, she followed classes with Signora Beretta of the Scala, with whom Pavlova had studied not long before. Being out of train-ing after her rest, she fainted during her first lesson at the barre. As it was, the Italian approach was more vigorous than the Russian: it enhanced her endurance and expanded her breathing. It also boosted her confidence, and she returned to St Petersburg with higher jumps, stronger pointes and much improved precision. She now felt 'ready to justify the expectation of all those who had pinned their faith on me.'[6] And she did too. Already the darling of the popular audiences, she began to win the esteem and admiration of other dancers. Ever modest, she merely observed in her autobi-ography, 'My fellow artists, through thick and thin, had a generous belief in me.'[7] Full belief in herself was slower to come.

In her late teens, Tamara went out with a young instructor at the School called Michel Fokine; they fell in love and he begged her to marry him. But Tamara's mother, thinking perhaps of how her hus-band had brought the family so low, refused to let her throw herself away on a dancer. To replace Fokine, Anna Karsavina found a civil servant for her, Vasili Mukhin, and Tamara obeyed her mother, marrying him in 1907. Vasili was devoted to her and she became quite fond of him. But it was no love match.

Once spurned, Fokine would not talk to Tamara offstage, and married another dancer who looked (it must be said) rather like her. He was not just a dancer. He had revolutionary ideas for choreographing ballets, inspired in part by Isadora Duncan, who demonstrated her unique and intuitive style in St Petersburg at Christmas 1904. (It was on a further visit to Russia, seventeen years later, that she met and married Sergei Yesenin.) Duncan also made a lasting impression on Tamara: 'I remember that the first time I saw her dance, I fell completely under her sway. It never occurred to me that there was the slightest hostility between her art and ours.' Later, Tamara came to 'feel many discrepancies between her ideals and her actual performances.' Yet however much she may have disagreed with Duncan's theories, she continued to recognize that 'those wonderful steps of hers with [their] simplicity and detachment could only come through the intuition of genius itself. She seemed to float, a complete vision of peace and harmony, that very embodiment of the classical spirit that was her ideal.'[8] These are the words of one of the greatest of modern dancers, who knew what it was to be *trained*.

Fokine turned ballet into a resolutely modern art, and Tamara proved well suited to interpreting his ideas, although she found him 'extremely irritable' with 'no control of his temper.'[9] Only four years after Fokine's first full-length ballet was performed by students in 1905, he was chosen by Sergei Diaghilev to choreograph the first season of the Ballets Russes in Paris; Tamara was invited too, although she was not yet the prima ballerina of the Mariinsky Theatre. It so happened that Anna Pavlova, the star dancer a year or two ahead of Tamara, had taken a leave of absence to make an extended tour in the West, and Tamara was the next in line. She rose to the occasion and Paris fell in love with her. From then on, the Mariinsky Theatre, Diaghilev, and prestigious impresarios all over Europe competed to secure her presence on the stage.

Every artist wanted to make a portrait of her, 'in paint, in charcoal and in pencil; in marble, clay and bronze.'[10] Tamara became the most photographed ballerina of her time – not as we might understand it today, with admirers vying with paparazzi to snatch a candid shot of her in the street. Before the First World War, being photographed involved long hours in a studio, dressed in her performance costume, holding long poses that required the help of a supporting stand (which was edited out afterwards by the re-touchers). This accounts for the rigid stance and frozen smiles of so many early portrait photographs. What is striking about pictures of Tamara is the naturalness of her poses, the apparent spontaneity of her smiles, and the expressiveness of her eyes, adapted to the role she was playing: bold and challenging, imperially

Le Spectre de la Rose, a poster by Jean Cocteau for the third season of the Ballets Russes in Paris

haughty, soft and dreamy, and even mischievously twinkling. It is one thing to be 'in character' when performing on the stage; it is quite another to be able to re-create that character in a bare (and often chilly) studio, without movement or music, or the audience, and to hold the expression through a long exposure. Yet she achieved it so magnificently that it is hard to believe that some studio shots were not actually performance pictures. Right from the start, Tamara was a true professional – and a photographer's dream.

I mentioned her costumes: throw away all thought of a plain tutu. In her lead roles, Tamara wore flamboyant costumes designed by the most famous names of the day, most notably Leon Bakst. Yet none of this went to her head. She remained a modest young woman, with none of the egotism or tantrums that are popularly associated with prima donnas.

Only half of the photographs reproduced in her autobiography are of Tamara herself; many are of fellow artists; her best friends, Lydia Kyasht and Lydia Lopokova, are well represented, as are Anna Pavlova and Nijinsky. These three ballerinas all left St Petersburg before 1910, drawn by the much more generous conditions offered by western directors than by Russian ballet companies. (For example, Lydia Kyasht was earning £7 a month at the Imperial Russian Ballet in 1908 when an agent for the Empire Theatre in London offered her £40 a week. After one month, the Empire upped it to £75 a week; she accepted a second year at £100, and a third at £150 a week.[11]) Tamara provides affectionate glimpses of them all in their schooldays – with Pavlova her main rival for stardom, and Kyasht involving Tamara in her pranks and adventures. When Tamara was a senior dance student,

> one out of the group of the small pupils given now into my care was little Lopokova. The extreme emphasis she put into her movements was comic to watch in the tiny child with the face of an earnest cherub. Whether she danced or talked, her whole frame quivered with excitement; she bubbled all over. Her personality was manifest from the first, and very lovable....

When she came back [from America], there was a mastery in her technique which fully qualified her as a star; in some marvellous way, her spontaneity and unique blend of eagerness and naiveté... had remained unimpaired.[12]

These two ballerinas both married in England, and contributed to bringing Russian culture to Britain, but they are not included in this book, for lack of any involvement in the Revolution. Lydia Kyasht, for instance, was making one of her rare visits to St Petersburg when the March revolution broke out in 1917. She managed to leave before October, but the journey back to England took a whole month and left her 'in a state bordering on collapse.'[13]

Tamara in *Parade* depicted by Edmund Dulac.

Vaslav Nijinsky's rise to stardom was even more rapid than Tamara's. He graduated from the Theatre School in 1907 and joined her in the Ballets Russes in 1909. They were often partners and their performances of *Giselle*, *Petrouchka*, and *Le Spectre de la Rose* (to name but three of them) have gone down in history. (Arnold Haskell considered that 'no one has ever rendered [*Le Spectre*] so exquisitely as Karsavina. It remains hers for ever.') Tamara is perhaps most famous for creating the title role in the *Firebird* with Fokine. This part was originally offered to Anna Pavlova, but she could not work with Stravinsky's music, and preferred to leave the Ballets Russes and lead her own independent career. (Stravinsky, also from St Petersburg, was just three years older than Tamara. Coincidentally, he grew up in the apartment immediately above Tamara and Vasili's on Kryukov Canal.) Only once was Tamara prevented from dancing the *Firebird* during its first season. Unaware of Diaghilev's plans, she had accepted an offer to dance in London; her place was taken by Lydia Lopokova.

It was an extraordinary and well-filled life that Tamara was leading in those early years, yet no matter where she performed across Europe, she would ensure that she could fulfill her engagements at the Mariinsky Theatre and rest at home. In this she was unlike Anna Pavlova and Lydia Lopokova, who never returned to Russia for long. Tamara travelled outside Europe only once before 1918: a 1913 tour with the Ballets Russes took her to South America, where ballet was virtually unknown. Anything in the classical style went down very well there, and her dancing was much admired, but the revolutionary new styles of music and dance met with a cool reception. The well-bred young ladies of Argentina had to be protected from such sights as the explicit sensuality of *Schéhérazade*.

Back in St Petersburg, Tamara became a household name, lionized by every class of society. She was particularly admired by the artists, writers and poets of the time, as demonstrated by the now-famous evening in the ephemeral 'Wandering Dog' cabaret on 28 March 1914. This was a bohemian artists' club, in the cellar of a big house just behind the Mariinsky Theatre, frequented by all the leading names in the arts.[14] That evening, her admirers organized a tribute to celebrate her return from Paris; the cellar was specially decorated and the guests wore specially designed costumes. At the door, Tamara was lifted up into a chair and carried in at shoulder height; from this makeshift throne, she acknowledged their cheers and applause, not a little embarrassed by all this attention. Descending from her perch to the accompaniment of a harpsichord (her favourite musical instrument), she released Cupid (Natasha Danilova) from a cage of fresh roses set on a mirror-topped podium, placed not on the stage but in the centre of the cellar, amongst the audience. Then she danced for them, to the music of Couperin, on that same small podium, encircled by garlands of fresh flowers. Finally, she was presented with a *Bouquet* – not of flowers but a specially printed booklet with tributes to her by a host of famous writers, poets and artists, including Cocteau and Picasso.

It is a fascinating thought that, from 14 June 1913, Arthur

Ransome rented a flat in St Petersburg, in a house that overlooked the Mariinsky Square in front of the Theatre. Although their paths must have crossed numerous times in the course of the next five years, and they both left Russia at exactly the same time, each with a new partner, neither seems to have been aware of the proximity of the other.

Naturally, Tamara was often invited to grace receptions, dinners, parties, and private gatherings with her presence. For all his ignorance of Russian, the British Ambassador, Sir George Buchanan, was one of her admirers; in the autumn of 1913 he invited her to dine as the guest of honour with his family and a few friends on the occasion of his wedding anniversary, and she accepted. It was on this occasion that lightning struck. Opposite her at the table that evening was the Embassy's Head of Chancery; his work involved internal administration rather than diplomatic representation. As Tamara took her leave, he had the temerity to ask if he might call on her. And she said yes.

Henry James Bruce was youngest of four sons – the Benjamin, as they say; hence he was nicknamed Benjie by his family, and it stuck. His father was Sir Hervey Juckes Lloyd Bruce, 4th Baronet of Downhill, who had retired from the Coldstream Guards as a Lieutenant-Colonel around 1878, and his mother was born Ellen Maud Ricardo. Benjie's eldest brothers were twins, and they inherited titles and estates in England and Ireland. Third and fourth sons had to fend for themselves. After Eton, Benjie decided to earn his living in the Foreign Office, rather than join the armed forces, like his father, his maternal uncles, and his brothers. (Left to himself, he would have chosen to be head gardener, or possibly the manager, of a large estate like Clifton in Nottinghamshire which his father inherited in 1896, for Benjie was essentially a modest and unassertive young man, but his class and education debarred him from jobs like those.) His diplomatic career began with three years in Vienna; in 1908 he was transferred to Berlin; from there he was moved in 1913 to the Embassy in St Petersburg as Head of Chancery.

In those days, Whitehall employed young men to type out reports, or code and de-code messages, even though their education, training and experience made them suited for more elevated duties. When Bruce Lockhart first saw the Chancery at work in St Petersburg, his 'first impression was of a typing and telegraph bureau conducted by Old Etonians.' As their chief, Benjie 'could type as fast as any professional typist and cipher and decipher with astonishing speed.' Having real genius for organizing, he directed his staff with 'remarkable efficiency'.[15] He was also a striking figure – Lydia Kyasht claims that she first saw him when she 'was in the middle of practising a new dance … and the sight of such a handsome man so distracted me that my lesson was ruined.'[16] He was just thirty-three and still unattached when he met Tamara; she was twenty-eight and had been married for almost seven years. Never had there been the least whisper of scandal about her private life.

Tamara's impulsive admirer, having immediately realized the enormity of his spontaneous request, crawled to her door a few days later. His diplomatic training was useless on this occasion: self-consciousness made him clumsy to the point where, as he confessed in his autobiography, 'I gave what must have been a rich performance of a bumpkin in a boudoir. I think I did actually upset my teacup.' His hostess did not help by sitting bolt upright in her chair. Did she ever lean back, he wondered. 'I know now that she doesn't.' The dancer's discipline was second nature to Tamara; he called that posture 'ramrodding'.

Fortunately, Benjie could always laugh at himself:

I have since been told that I dropped my umbrella three times in the process of putting on my coat, shaking hands and backing out of the front door.…

The while, she observed me unblinkingly with those great solemn eyes. Were they really so solemn as they seemed, or was there, deep, deep down below the surface, some playful little imp of mischief sending bubbles of amusement to the top?

In truth,

Tamara in *The Awakening of Flora* in 1904

she has told me that she was enjoying my performance so much that she would not have spoiled it for the world.... What I [now] know ... is that nearest to her heart, of all theatrical performances, is the red-nosed circus clown, at whose antics she will rock in helpless laughter.... I have come to appreciate the iron restraint my hostess must have put upon herself to maintain even a semblance of solemnity in the face of a performance which, for sheer clownishness, she can seldom have seen equalled....

Yet my hostess's last words, spoken with apparent sincerity, were 'Please come again.'[17]

It was not just a repeat performance that she was looking forward to. She had divined the human qualities in the clown, the same integrity, sincerity and kindness that resided in her own heart. He came again, and again. Gradually Tamara drew him out, coached his taste, and discovered that he could draw rather well –

'Ramrodding' by Benjie

yet he was allowed to draw her once only, when she was sitting for a Russian friend of hers who had given Benjie drawing lessons. He sat 'well out of sight, behind the model's throne,' and thoroughly enjoyed trying to capture 'that well known, cushion-scorning pose.'[18]

She took him on expeditions to the street markets where she found, among other things, the beautiful pieces of china that she collected. 'There never was any snobbishness or class distinction about Karsavina's collecting. To charm the eye was all that ever mattered.... The china might be chipped or cracked. A figure might be armless. What did it matter if only the thing was good to look at?'[19]

He was present at that famous evening in 'The Wandering Dog', less than six months into their acquaintance. At that point he still had much to learn. She recalled:

To make this evening select, 'The Wandering Dog' had invited some distinguished guests, amongst them a great friend of mine, whose British dislike of the demonstrative kept him looking at his watch while my poets exerted themselves in recitations, and asking me how long I meant to stay with these microbes.[20]

Benjie may have observed that there was no snobbishness in Tamara's collecting; he had yet to overcome his own old-Etonian snobbishness.

He tells us that

neither teacher nor pupil was aware that these lessons were going on. Indeed, it was not for many years that I understood the compass of the lessons I was getting. They ranged from questions of artistic taste (mine at the beginning was abysmal) right into the field of ethics. In this latter field, I think there were two broad heads – kindliness in the judgment of one's fellows; simplicity, utter and unspoilt, in everything.[21]

Although neither of them mentions which language they spoke together, it was not English, for Tamara recorded that when Hugh Walpole returned to St Petersburg in February 1916 to set up a government-sponsored Anglo-Russian Propaganda Bureau, 'he had little Russian or French, and I absolutely no word of English.' With Benjie, she probably spoke a mixture of French and Russian, picking up a few words of English along the way. She tells us that, after she left Russia in 1918, Walpole

> was the first to educate me in my new language. He introduced me to English literature, and the very fact that I have been able to struggle through this book [her autobiography, *Theatre Street*] is due to him. He gave me a list of books and, just as I had begun my Russian reading with Pushkin, so now I began English with Lamb's *Essays*, Pepys, and the *Morte d'Arthur*.

What an extraordinary selection (even though I presume that the *Morte d'Arthur* was by Tennyson rather than Malory). No wonder she writes, 'As a result, my speech was a strange hash of archaisms and blunders which vastly amused my new family.' And she offers an example that she was never allowed to forget. 'In my enthusiasm for a new pig-skin bag, I exclaimed: "Look at new bag; why, it is real pork!"'[22]

It was not on her brief visits to England with the Ballets Russes that she was going to learn much English either, for the tours were intense and hectic, allowing no time for socializing. In July 1914, Benjie was given four months' furlough. As luck would have it, Tamara was dancing in London at the time, applauded more wildly than ever. But they had barely glimpsed each other when the war intervened. Benjie was recalled to his post on 31 July; Tamara made a late departure by train and was forced to turn back when she reached the Russian border. It took her weeks to get home.

Benjie and Tamara were both extremely discreet about the following years. Soon they were lovers, and they had a son, Nikita, who was born on 5 January 1916. Only after this did Tamara tell her husband Vasili that she loved another man and ask him to agree to a divorce. Having assumed that the child was his, and supposing that his wife was suffering from a passing infatuation, Vasili refused. Little did he realize that Tamara was determined to spend the rest of her life with Benjie. She was equally determined to be as kind as she could to her husband, which explains how he could be so blind to the reality of his situation. She hoped to persuade him to release her without having to tell him that the child was her lover's, fearing that the revelation might cause him to commit suicide. It took months for her to accept that Vasili would survive the shock, but in the end the deed was done. After two years, Vasili finally consented to divorce her, and he lived on into the 1940s.

Throughout this time, both Tamara and Benjie confided in the ballet critic Valerian Svetlov (1860–1934; his real name was Valerian Yakovlevich Ivchenko). He was a close associate of Diaghilev, and much despised by Nijinsky. Early in her career, when Tamara lacked confidence, she had been devastated by Svetlov's criticism of her dancing. Later she came to view his comments as simply his opinion and could respect them, without taking them personally. They got to know each other, and finally he became her 'staunch friend.' During the period of gradual separation from Vasili, when Tamara felt torn apart by her conflicting feelings and dread of what the future might bring, she was able to confide in him – although only by letter, since he was serving in the army – and he helped to wean Vasili off his dependence on Tamara through temporary separations. In this, they were aided by her professional engagements abroad. Benjie, who was all too aware of Tamara's suffering and was powerless to alleviate it, also corresponded with Svetlov, although they had never been formally introduced. His letters helped Svetlov to appreciate how deeply she cared for her husband's feelings, for all her determination to divorce him.

Tamara with Nikita, 1917

No wonder then that, in later years, they wrote nothing about this awful period. Not only were they anxious to conceal the fact that Nikita had been born to them while Tamara was still living with her husband (which in the eyes of British society, especially of Benjie's social class, was shockingly immoral), but they had no wish to relive the anxiety, pain and stress they had suffered. And there was more to come, all too soon.

Tamara, 1917

After Vasili agreed to live apart from Tamara, she remained in the flat on Kryukov Canal, surrounded by her familiar objects and conveniently close to the Theatre. (She and Benjie did not live together before they were actually married.) But when the revolution started in February 1917, Benjie judged her flat to be unsafe: it was opposite the old Lithuanian Castle (Litovsky Zamok) – 'a building which [Tamara] always liked for its beautiful proportions and the two kneeling angels over the gate.'[23] Because it served as a prison, it was burned down in the first days of the revolution. Then, shortly after the fire, Cromie, the Naval Attaché at the Embassy, 'spotted three Maxim machine-guns mounted on the roof of the Mariinsky Theatre.'[24] Tamara's walk home lay directly in their line of fire. So Benjie found another flat for her in Millionnaya Street, where most of the Embassy staff were accommodated. It was smaller; to move in she had to part with prized possessions. It was also right in the centre of St Petersburg, so she witnessed the Revolution from uncomfortably close quarters. On more than one occasion, when there were skirmishes and gunfights directly beneath her windows, she sought refuge in the neighbouring flat of Edward Cunard. (We met him previously as a guest at Moura's summer party in 1917.)

On the evening of 8 November 1917 (New Style), Tamara danced *Casse Noisette* in the Mariinsky Theatre, 'but the poor Mariinsky was the ghost of itself, the stage half empty,' wrote Benjie in his diary.

> After the ballet, T[amara], Madame B [i.e. Moura], C [Edward Cunard] and myself… walked down the Millionnaya…. Everything had been quiet in the rest of the town, so we were surprised to find the Lord's own holy racket going on round the Winter Palace, where the [Provisional] Government were putting up a last stand – field guns, machine guns, rifle fire, a destroyer from the river [that would be the *Aurora*, of course, which was actually a cruiser] *et tout le tremblement*. Never heard such a row. Altogether the walk [was] a very jumpy business. After supper, escorted Madame B home to a machine-gun obbligato and so to a very noisy bed.[25]

Tamara adds a poignant memory of that evening: as she was going to bed, she looked outside.

> From my window, I could see the barracks. A solitary figure in soldier's uniform crept from the shadow of the gate and started running towards Champ de Mars; a shot and the figure fell in the snow. I drew the curtain.[26]

In the Embassy the following morning, Benjie learned 'that Lenin was Prime Minister, Trotsky Foreign Minister.'[27] The Bolsheviks had stormed the Winter Palace and seized power that very night.

The Revolution turned society upside down. Every building had its *soviet* or house committee, and Tamara's servant presided over the *soviet* in her building. The Imperial Ballet became the State Ballet, stripped of its former glory; the eagles and royal crests were removed and the attendants wore old jackets in place of their smart uniforms. The artists elected Tamara to head their *soviet*, and she presided over meetings in her tarlatan so that she could practise during the breaks. The fearsome headmistress of the Theatre School now had to defer to Tamara, whose natural modesty made it hard for her to accept the reversal of roles. Stage performances continued, although ballerinas no longer 'owned' their roles, as they had before, and there was no money for new costumes, so old ones were brought out when ballets were revived. In this new working climate, Fokine began to collaborate with Tamara again.

It is not known exactly when her divorce was formalized. At any rate, she and Benjie did not manage to marry before the fateful day in February 1918 when the entire staff of the British Embassy was evacuated by train, along with about sixty members of the British colony in Moscow and St Petersburg. Of course Benjie swore he would return, but there was no knowing how long it would take him. Once back in London, he obtained leave to make a desperate bid to exfiltrate Tamara. He reached Moscow on 10 June, bringing news and instructions for Bruce Lockhart at the same time. Twelve hours later, he was off to St Petersburg, where Tamara was just taking leave of the State Ballet. They were married by the end of the month. With her on his passport, they could leave, but on 4 July, warned of the impending Allied – principally British – invasion, Trotsky published a decree forbidding any Englishman to leave the country; travel to Murmansk or Archangel was expressly forbidden. Yet that was precisely the direction which Benjie proposed to take.

It was a most dangerous route, through the much contested area of Karelia. In addition to fighting between the Red and White Armies – the latter supported with arms and ammunition by the Allies – the local population was fighting to affirm its Finnish identity. The diplomatic staff in Vologda made it safely – by the skin of their teeth. Denis Garstin, who was attached to the Embassy as member of the Anglo-Russian Commission, was ordered to join the British troops when they landed at Archangel; he managed to reach them by covering the last 400 kilometres (from Petrozavodsk to Kem, 250 miles) on foot, but he was shot by a Red sniper soon afterwards. Arthur Ransome opted to travel by ship directly to Sweden, rather than by the railway through Finland. Yet Benjie was desperate to go by this north-west route. 'I ran around like a rat in a trap, crazy to bite my way out somehow,' he recalled.

> It looked hopeless. But one evening my phone rang and a woman's voice asked if I would like two passes for a steamer leaving Liteiny Most, one of the St Petersburg bridges, the next morning at 8 and bound [north] through the great lakes, Ladoga and Onega. I accepted gladly. It seemed a start. All night we worked. At 8 we were on our river steamer.[28]

They never learned who provided those passes.

Being forbidden to leave, they had to avoid all authorities, especially the Cheka and the Red Guards. So they opted to travel as discreetly as possible, and left the boat at a tiny village, Povenets, at the northern end of Lake Onega, to continue their way by horse and cart along an old post road. After the agonies of choosing among her already reduced possessions when she packed to leave, Tamara found herself entrusting half her goods to the ship's purser, asking him to ensure that they were returned to the Embassy, there to join all her other abandoned possessions. (Everything disappeared – except for Tamara's favourite carpet, which she discovered by chance, and bought, in a London antique shop ten years later. As we have seen, the Bolsheviks used the empty Embassy as a storehouse for abandoned and confiscated goods. It was conveniently placed close to the port of St Petersburg, through which they could export them.) Surplus clothes for Nikita, now aged two-and-a-half, she gave to the peasants who gathered round to view this unique expedition.

In a train of five horse-drawn carts, they 'lumbered on through a nightmare country of devilish-looking trees, of foul marshes and clouds – dense clouds – of mosquitoes.... Hamlets ... were a whole day's drive apart. At each one, we changed horses, sleeping a few hours on the earthen floor of some poor hovel.'[29] One day, they arrived at a village where they were obliged to meet the local Commissar. 'I had expected to find a peasant,' writes Benjie; 'I found an educated man' – who asked to see Tamara's passport. He had recognized her name. Having spoken 'amiably but with reserve' with Tamara, the Commissar urged them, without offering a word

of explanation, to make all haste for a town called Sumski-Posad on
the banks of the White Sea.

At last we came in sight of Sumski itself. There was a barrier
across the road, guarded by two soldiers with fixed bayonets....
'Voui Angleechaneen?' – 'Yes,' I said I was English, and produced
my large Foreign Office passport with the big Royal Arms on top.
He almost danced with joy, shouted to our peasant driver to hurry
and ran along with us himself. We came to a wooden bridge over
a stream that flowed into the White Sea. On the bridge and
around it there was an operatic chorus of excited, gesticulating
peasants. Under it a small pinnace, chugging away and clearly
about to leave.... 'Quick, into the boat!' urged our soldier, and a
score of willing hands were at our service. Some helped us into the
boat. Others lifted the child gently down. Others again threw our
bundles down into the pinnace. All this time we were too dazed to
ask questions.... Only when we were well under way did we have
time to ask.... A British cruiser had been shelling Red troops just
up the coast, and the troops were retreating on Sumski.

The pinnace was the last to leave before the cruiser raised its anchor.
'We had made it, after three weeks' travel, by a bare five minutes.'[30]

The cruiser landed them at a town where they boarded a train for
Murmansk. On the way, they passed by Kadalashka, the nearest
town to the point from which, fourteen years later, the Tchernavins
were to make their risky escape, on foot, over the forested hills into
Finland. The railway line remained on lower ground. Tamara had
'never seen more desolate country.... Endless marshes and stones, a
few tortured dwarf trees, not a blade of grass anywhere; a God-
forsaken land. At one place we all alighted and walked over the
damaged track to the next formation of railway cars.'[31]

At Murmansk they found some of Benjie's Foreign Office colleagues who had been sent out from England, and they lived with
them for a while in disused railway carriages. Finally, berths were
found for them on a collier, which crawled its way across the
North Sea, narrowly escaping a torpedo. 'The night we arrived at

Middlesbrough, blast furnaces lit up the sky – these were the foot-lights of a new world.'[32] They had escaped by the skin of their teeth, and Tamara's Russian life was over. Yet just as she had made history with the Ballets Russes, so she made history in England.

Benjie was posted first to Tangiers and then to Sofia; from these foreign parts Tamara would be summoned by telegram from Diaghilev to dance in London, or Paris, or to go off on a tour. In the mid-20s, they decided to settle in London and Benjie resigned from the Diplomatic Service, but it proved impossible to find work. In his own words, they were 'Babes in the Wood', easy prey to every shark in London, spending money as fast as Tamara earned it. Only in the 1930s did Benjie secure a job as a consultant to the National Bank of Hungary, and for most of that decade they lived in Budapest. The Second World War brought an end to that life, and they settled in a modest flat high on Primrose Hill, in London, with Tamara in the role of British housewife, spending half her day in the kitchen. Love had put paid to her mother's determination that she should marry a man who could be counted on to assure her ease when she stopped dancing.

Tamara retired from the stage in March 1932, when she per-formed *Le Spectre de la Rose* one last time. More important – from a historical perspective – was her effect on the appreciation and practice of ballet, both classical and modern, in Britain, for she taught and coached and promoted the art of ballet for the rest of her life. At various points in their careers, dancers from Moira Shearer to Margot Fonteyn and Rudolf Nureyev benefitted from her coaching, and Sir Frederick Ashton learned the secrets of *La Fille Mal-Gardée* from her. She also taught him Petipa's original mimed dialogue for the celebrated 'When I'm Married' scene, and passed on his choreography for the *'Pas de Ruban'*; both passages are retained in the Ashton production. In 1920 she had co-founded the Association of Teachers of Operatic Dancing of Great Britain; following the grant of a royal charter in 1936, it became the Royal Academy of Dancing, of which she was vice-president from 1930 to

1955. The Karsavina syllabus, which she devised for the Royal Academy's teacher-training course in 1954, is still taught today. She also assisted in the establishment of The Royal Ballet.

In other words, by saving Tamara from the Revolution, Benjie brought Britain a gift of immense cultural value. She died in May 1978, almost exactly sixty years after their escape. Benjie predeceased her, in September 1951; Nikita lived on into his eighties.

☭

And what of Tamara's brother, Lev Karsavin? Two years older than her, he exhibited slightly different traits of character. She tells us that when they were children, one of their punishments was to stand with their noses in a corner of the room.

> Lev, my brother, usually shortened his penance by gently asking pardon. This, nothing would induce me to do on the spot; I only felt contrite when Father spoke to me kindly. He often took me by the hand and brought me to Mother to ask her pardon. Rebukes, even when deserved, wounded me deeply.[33]

Lev was very much an intellectual. Their mother Anna was a niece of Aleksei Khomiakov (1804–60), whose philosophy of religion had had a profound impact on the Russian Orthodox Church and on writers like Dostoevsky, Konstantin Pobedonostsev, and Vladimir Solovyov. Anna always hoped that Lev would follow in their footsteps.

He was certainly very talented as a student, winning prizes at every stage of his career as a medievalist; his *Essays on Religious Life in Italy in the 12–13th Centuries* (1912) was the best Russian work on medieval monasticism and it was widely read in Russia (and reissued in an anniversary edition in 2012). His erudition was widely recognized and he became a full professor at St Petersburg in 1918, much loved by his students. During the winter of 1919/20, when the university buildings were not heated, he gave his seminars in his home office. His colleague Count Zubov found him 'one of the most interesting and pleasant men I have ever met.'[34]

Lev was on Lenin's list of philosophers to expel. That he was the brother of a world-famous ballet dancer made no difference. But it did lead to a surreal discussion. On his arrest in August 1922, the Commissar read him a list of the charges against him. (The 'crimes' of the philosophers were all trifling matters, trumped-up charges; many were accused of mere association with fellow philosophers.)

'You write to and receive letters from people outside Russia. Who are your correspondents?'

'My sister.'

'You mean, you are the brother of Karsavina!'

The Commissar veered round in his revolving chair.

'*Giselle* is her best part, don't you think?'

'I can't agree with you,' said my brother. 'I consider the *Firebird* one of her finest achievements.'

'Oh, do you?' The conversation wandered onto the principles and aims of the art; the prosecution was forgotten.[35]

But not for long. It was typically Russian.

Lev had married in 1906. That his wife was the daughter of a trader from the Siberian city of Perm suggests that his mother may have nudged the union in the direction of money, as she had with Tamara. They had three daughters, the youngest of whom was born in 1920, at the height of Lev's love affair with one of his students, Yelena Skrzhinskaya (1897–1981). Apparently, they first met when she was still a pupil at the Bestuzhev Institute (a high school for girls), where he gave lectures, and it has been suggested that they also met during one of his trips to Italy (where she researched the Waldensians and Cathars). Be that as it may, she followed the courses for women in the Faculty of History and Philology at St Petersburg, and Lev was one of her professors there. If he had not met her before that, he could hardly have missed her then, for she was extremely talented. She was a medievalist and, in the course of her life, researched the ancient and medieval history of the Crimea (including the Genoese and Venetian colonies on its coast), the history of medieval Italy, and the development of crafts and mining in

Yelena Skrzhinskaya as a student

Europe. She published on the relations between medieval Russia and Europe, the ethnogenesis of the Cumans, the travels of Italians to Eastern Europe in the fourteenth century and, for her doctorate, she translated a Jordanian work 'On the origin and deeds of the Geths' (1960). (The Geths are a little-known people that settled in the Crimea in the third century.) In the course of all this, she learned Italian, Spanish, German, English, French, Czech, Latin, and Greek.

Lev fell passionately in love with her. Showing no more discretion than his father, he would ride her bicycle down the corridor of their university building; their affair lasted until Lenin exiled him in November 1922. Like Tamara, he knew that, were he to separate from his wife without her consent, his love would be poisoned by the suffering that it caused. As a philosopher of religion, he needed to reconcile his adultery with his faith, and he devoted a whole book called *Noctes Petropolitanae** to demonstrating how the 'lower love' (between mortals) was a pathway to the 'higher love' (divine love), taking Dostoevsky's Fyodor Karamazov as his prime example. He framed his love for Yelena Skrzhinskaya as a moment in the divine Love. Unfortunately, the book was not expressed in purely abstract terms: it was quite explicit as to the object of his love, and anticipated both the end of the affair and a break with his wife. It caused quite a scandal when it was published in 1922: the title may have been in Latin, but the text was in Russian that all could read. But his arrest came within weeks of publication, and he was expelled along with his colleagues Nikolai Lossky, Semyon Frank, and Sergei Bulgakov. Thus the lovers were separated.

Yelena scraped together the funds to visit him in Berlin, but found the situation unchanged: Lev would neither leave his wife nor renounce his love for Yelena. After three months, she returned to Soviet Russia. Lev spent the rest of his life with his wife and

---

* The Latin title (meaning 'Petersburg Nights') echoes Aulus Gellius's second-century *Noctes Atticae* (Attic Nights).

daughters, although he wrote many letters to Yelena, and met her just once more in St Petersburg in June 1947. It was a sad and painful occasion – precisely the outcome that Tamara had feared might result if Mukhin refused to divorce her. In Lev's case, his conscience held him painfully suspended between the two women, who suffered from his indecision for the rest of their lives. There are situations in which it can be cruel to be kind.

Lev's career continued in Berlin, where he published several books (some of which he had been working on when he was exiled). He moved on to Paris in 1926, where he published yet more books, and then – turning down an invitation to teach history at Oxford – he joined the University of Lithuania in Kaunas, which was renamed Vytautas Magnus University in 1932. His family saw this as an act of penance, in which he was sacrificing himself to Russian culture. Lev rapidly learned Lithuanian and began writing in that language – and Yelena quickly learned Lithuanian too so that she could read his publications.

She devoted her life to historical research, as an academic in Moscow and, mainly, St Petersburg. In the mid-1920s, she deciphered the Latin inscriptions left by the Genoese in the majestic fortresses at Sudak and Feodosia in the Crimea. They were published, with her comments (in French) in 1928. Her scholarship did not protect her from the Cheka: in 1930, she was suspended from the State Academy of the History of Material Culture in St Petersburg for corresponding with Lev (and attending church services); then in 1953, she was forcibly retired – but in 1956 she bounced back at the Institute of History of the Academy of Sciences, where she worked until 1970. Significantly, her most fruitful years were the ones that followed Lev's death in 1952.

A well-known and much liked figure in Lithuania, Lev suffered first the German and then the Soviet invasion of his new homeland – which Russia held on to after the war. He was arrested again in 1949 by the MGB (as the Soviet secret police was called at that point). He was sentenced to ten years, and sent to a camp at Abez in the Komi Republic, just south of the Arctic Circle, that was reserved for prisoners whose age or state of health rendered them unsuitable for work in coal mines. There he was treated as a sage by all who visited him. He died of tuberculosis in the camp hospital on 20 July 1952 and was buried in a grave in the polar tundra marked only 'P-11'.

The parallel between Tamara's love for Benjie and her brother's love for Yelena is quite striking; both were victims of passion, although hers was not made public at the time in the way that his was, and the outcome was very different – but it was a near thing. Lev and Tamara must have been much alike. When we remember that Benjie underlined how kindness was key to Tamara's character, it is striking to hear Lev's son-in-law describe him as 'the purest and kindest man I have ever met in my life.'[36]

Sources

Bainton, Roy. *Honoured By Strangers: Captain Cromie's Extraordinary First World War*. Little, Brown Book Group. Kindle Edition.

Bruce, H. J. *Silken Dalliance*. London: Constable, 1946.

——, *Thirty Dozen Moons*. London: Constable, 1949,

Karsavin, Lev. *Noctes Petropolitanae*. St Petersburg, 1922.

Karsavina, Tamara. *Theatre Street: the Reminiscences of Tamara Karsavina*. London: Heinemann, 1930.

Kyasht, Lydia. *Romantic Recollections*. London: Brentano, 1929. (Facsimile reprint by Noverre Press, 2010.)

'Lev Karsavin'. (In Polish) http://cz.psymethods.com/persons/259-leo_platonovich_karsavin.html?p=1

Lockhart, Robert Bruce. *Memoirs of a British Agent*. London: Putnam, 1932.

Rubin, Dominic. *The Life and Thought of Lev Karsavin: Strength Made Perfect in Weakness*. Amsterdam: Rodopi, 2013.

Rybakova, Alexandra. 'A Symphonic Personality' (in Russian). Originally published in the *Lithuanian Courier*, 19 April 2012. http://www.klaipeda1945.org/eto-interesno/simfonicheskaya-lich-nostj/

Skrzhinskaya, Marina. 'And Then I recited a Poem for Karsavin… Lev Platonovich Karsavin and Yelena Cheslavovna Skrzhinskaya.' (In Russian, by Yelena's daughter.) http://russophile.ru/2016/10/08/%d0%bc%d0%b0%d1%80%d0%b8%d0%bd%d0%b0-%d1%81%d0%ba%d1%80%d0%b6%d0%b8%d0%bd%d1%81%d0%ba%d0%b0%d1%8f-%d0%b8-%d1%82%d0%be%d0%b3%d0%b4%d0%b0-%d1%8f-%d0%bf%d1%80%d0%be%d1%87%d0%bb%d0%b0-%d0%ba%d0%b0/

Notes

1. Karsavina, p.37.
2. Karsavina, pp.21–22.
3. Kathrine Sorley Walker, 'Cyril W. Beaumont: Bookseller, Publisher, and Writer on Dance Part One.' *Dance Chronicle*, Vol. 25, issue 1 (2002), pp.51–94.
4. Much quoted, but original source unknown to me.
5. Karsavina, p.163.
6. Karsavina, p.176.
7. Karsavina, p.177.
8. Karsavina, pp.208–11.
9. Karsavina, p.212.
10. *Thirty Dozen Moons*, p.8.
11. Kyasht, p.152.
12. Karsavina, pp.123 and 267.
13. Kyasht, p.232.
14. A brief but detailed evocation of 'The Wandering Dog' at this time, titled 'Souvenir of a Petrograd Evening' by Alexandra Fredericks, appeared in *The Russian Review*, Vol. 9, No. 3 (July, 1950), pp.205–08.
15. Lockhart, Book iii, chapter 3.
16. Kyasht, p.86.
17. Bruce, *Thirty Dozen Moons*, pp.3–4.
18. Bruce, *Thirty Dozen Moons*, p.8.
19. Bruce, *Thirty Dozen Moons*, p.7.
20. Karsavina, p.314.
21. Bruce, *Thirty Dozen Moons*, p.9.

22 Karsavina, p.319.

23 Karsavina, p.321.

24 Bainton, Kindle Location 3320.

25 Bruce, *Silken Dalliance*, p.164.

26 Karsavina, p.327.

27 Bruce, *Silken Dalliance*, p.164.

28 Bruce, *Silken Dalliance*, p.137.

29 Bruce, *Silken Dalliance*, p.138.

30 Bruce, *Silken Dalliance*, pp.140–1.

31 Karsavina, p.340.

32 Karsavina, p.341.

33 Karsavina, p.7.

34 Chamberlain, p.119.

35 Karsavina, pp.266–7 (slightly edited).

36 Quoted in Rubin, p.129.

8 Ivy and Maxim

Few women living outside Russia can have had their lives quite so completely overthrown by the Bolshevik Revolution as Ivy Low's was. What is more, nothing prepared her better for her adult life than the death of her father, Walter Low, just before her fifth birthday. Walter was the son of Maximilian Humboldt Löwe, an Austrian supporter of the Hungarian revolution of 1848 who had followed his defeated leader to England. There he joined the thousands of Continental exiles, many of them Jews, who contributed to the rich cultural diversity of late-nineteenth-century London.

Maximilian had eleven children, five boys and six girls. By the time it came to educating the next-to-youngest son, Walter, the family finances were low, yet he was probably the cleverest of them all. On leaving school at sixteen, he took a job and began studying for himself in his spare time. By the time he was twenty, he had a BA (with honours) in French; this was followed three years later by an MA in French and German. After three more years of teaching in London (in two schools at the same time), he became a sizar (a subsidized student) at Cambridge where he completed the Medieval and Modern Languages Tripos. At the same time, he was working for William Briggs, whose booklets – called the University Correspondence Course – prepared university students for the questions that (on the basis of past years) they were very likely to encounter at their examinations. Walter helped assess the students' answers that came in by post, and also wrote twelve of the manuals (on English language, literature, and history, in particular) in

Briggs' Tutorial Series. These booklets long outlived their author: the fourteenth edition of *Matric English* was published in 1931.

Not content with French and German, Walter taught himself Norwegian and translated two of Bjørnstjerne Bjørnson's most important peasant novels. They sold well enough to bring in a small income, supplementing the £50 a year he earned by editing a periodical called the *Educational Times,* on which he collaborated with his good friend H. G. Wells. (Walter had helped Wells get started in journalism; following Walter's death in 1895, Wells dedicated his latest novel, *The Wonderful Visit,* to him.) By now, though, Walter desperately needed to earn more money: early in 1889, he had made a shotgun marriage to the youngest daughter of Lieutenant-Colonel Richard Aufrère Baker. The fruit of this unlikely union was Ivy, born in June that year. She was rapidly joined by two sisters, Letty and Olive.

At first they lived in Bloomsbury, close to the Foundling Hospital, to which Ivy's mother would threaten to send her daughter if she did not behave herself, for right from the start, little Ivy was self-willed, a trait that was enhanced by the early death of her father from a combination of pneumonia, influenza and – probably – overwork. At this point Ivy's mother was still only twenty-five; she had money from Walter's life insurance, and earned a tiny income by reviewing fiction for *Queen* and Frank Harris' *Saturday Review.* Selling the review copies afterwards brought in rather more than the reviews themselves. She easily found a second father for her three daughters. The man she chose was a lowly employee of the British Museum Library – but in Ivy's eyes no man could have supplanted her adored father who had taught her to read. She detested and scorned her stepfather from the word go, dismissing him as 'a mediocre intellectual with a safe job'.[1] Henceforth, Ivy was an exile in her own home.

She grew up rebellious and opinionated, outspoken and judgmental, especially of her elders. Boarding school helped little; it merely confirmed her feeling that she was not like other people.

She also learned to scorn her mother, whose trips to meet editors in town sometimes lasted until late the following morning, and who tried to instruct her daughter in the art of seducing men – for how else would she catch a husband? Anxious to get this obstreperous girl out of the house as soon as he could, her stepfather found a job for Ivy when she turned eighteen, as a clerk in the offices of the Prudential Assurance Company in Holborn, with lodgings of her own.

This freed her up to make new friends and acquaint herself with relations whom she had been discouraged from meeting before. Foremost among these was her uncle Dr David Eder; he had married her father's sister Edith. He too had an émigré background, and he became a medical practitioner in London, an active member of the Fabian Society, and a co-founder of the London Labour Party. Like her aunt Barbara, he was an early adept of psychoanalysis; he translated both Freud and Jung into English, founded and edited a journal called *School Hygiene,* and contributed to the radical *New Age.* In other words, he was just the kind of man that Ivy admired: intellectual and extremely hard-working. In her heart he stood in for the father she could now barely remember.

Ivy aspired to be a writer and wrote fan letters to authors whose works she appreciated. This led to a friendship with Viola Meynell, visits to the Meynells' house at Greatham, and to her own novel, *Growing Pains,* which came out in 1913. D. H. Lawrence's *Sons and Lovers* came out in the same year. She read it at once and recommended to all her friends, exclaiming, 'I've found a classic by a living author!' She started to correspond with Lawrence, who soon invited her to visit him. Off she hurried. He was living in Italy with Frieda, who was coldly suspicious of Ivy. After a month, he escorted her to the station, having found her (in her own words), 'fidgety, garrulous, clumsy and absurd.' A few weeks later, Lawrence and Frieda, now married, were back in England. Ivy met them when they were with their friend Katherine Mansfield, who found Ivy's behaviour unbearable. They allowed the acquaintance to lapse.

None the less, Ivy's enthusiasm for Lawrence's work was to have no small repercussions: she introduced her uncle Eder to *Sons and Lovers,* where he found confirmation of Freud's theories. She brought the two men together and Lawrence learned of Freud, which ultimately led to his own 1921 study, *Psychoanalysis and the Unconscious.* He also made Dr Eder a character in his Australian novel, *Kangaroo* (1923).

Through Eder, Ivy met many figures of the age, like George Bernard Shaw and H. G. Wells (who had not kept in contact with her family after her father's death), along with a wide variety of Zionists and political exiles. Among them was a Russian, Maxim Litvinov, whose gentlemanly behaviour – although he could be abrupt and short-tempered – revealed nothing of the exciting and eventful life that he had led.

He came from a prosperous Jewish family in Białystok, which is now in north-east Poland, close to the border with Belarus. Born in July 1876, which made him thirteen years older than Ivy, he joined the illegal Russian Social Democratic Labour Party (RSDLP) when he was twenty-two. Its members all took pseudonyms, calling themselves Lenin, Trotsky, Stalin, and so on; he used a great many different names, but 'Maxim Litvinov' was the one that he adopted durably. In 1901 he was arrested for his political activities. Eighteen months later he masterminded a daring escape for himself and ten other prisoners from the Lukyanivska Prison in Kiev, and took refuge in Switzerland. (Among the prisoners who escaped with him were Grigory Zinoviev and Lev Kamenev, both members of the first Politburo that was formed after the 1917 Revolution.) In Switzerland, Maxim edited a revolutionary newspaper, and then he returned to Russia, where he edited the RSDLP's first legal newspaper, *Novaya Zhizn* (*New Life*), which later became Gorky's political mouthpiece.

When the party split into Bolsheviks and Mensheviks at the 1903 Congress, Maxim sided with the former, becoming a trusted supporter of Lenin, travelling all over Russia to propagate his ideas and promote Party membership. After the revolution of 1905, in which he participated actively, he travelled throughout Europe, printing propaganda and buying rifles, smuggling them into Russia in preparation for the next revolution – always just one step ahead of the agents of the Okhrana, who were seeking to arrest him.

To finance these purchases – and the Party – the Bolsheviks resorted to robbing banks on a grand scale, which they called *expropriating,* or *liberating,* the sums involved. Litvinov, Stalin and Lenin were among the Bolshevik leaders who met in Berlin in April 1907 and planned to grab a major transfer of funds as it arrived at a bank in Tiflis (now Tbilisi), where Stalin was living with his wife and new-born son. The attack turned into a bloodbath, with around forty people killed and at least as many injured, but the Bolsheviks got away with an estimated 341,000 roubles, equivalent to something like six million US dollars today (with an even greater purchasing power).

Maxim masterminded the laundering operation. Unfortunately for him, much of the money was in brand new 500-rouble notes, whose serial numbers had been recorded. The State Bank rapidly circularized banks throughout Europe, asking them to arrest anyone who presented these notes. From Finland to France, and even in America, Bolsheviks, sympathizers, and a few people who had innocently accepted to exchange a note were apprehended. Maxim himself was caught with twelve of them as he was leaving Paris by train, en route for London. (Reporting his arrest on 2 February 1908, the *New York Times* described him as a student and 'a Nihilist of the most dangerous type.') Somehow, he managed to convince the French police that he could not possibly have been involved in the robbery, as he was in Paris at the time. To the intense annoyance of the Okhrana, which was rubbing its hands at the thought of getting hold of Litvinov at last, the French simply confiscated the banknotes and ordered him to leave the country; they even allowed him a couple of weeks in which to earn enough money to pay for the journey to London. He had already visited England on 1903 and in 1907 for the Marxist Congress, during which he and Stalin shared cheap lodgings among the poor émigrés in Stepney. (Lenin he had first met in the British Library Reading Room in 1903.) London was to be his base for the next ten years.

Maxim rapidly became a focal point for the Bolsheviks in England, in contact with other Bolshevik groups in Europe and America, corresponding with Lenin and, occasionally, Stalin. Producing a letter of introduction from Maxim Gorky, he found a job with Williams and Norgate, the publishers that specialized in non-English scientific literature. He did a great deal of reading for them, choosing titles suitable for publication in English translation, and was much appreciated for his competent reviews and good knowledge of foreign languages. He also gave private lessons in Russian, particularly to employees of Vickers, the shipbuilding and engineering firm that was looking to expand its business in Russia, but also to young men who were aspiring to enter the Foreign Office. One of them was Rex Leeper (later Sir Reginald Leeper), who went into the Intelligence Bureau of the Department of Information during the First World War. In 1939 Leeper became the head of Britain's Political Intelligence Department. When Bruce Lockhart accepted his mission to Moscow at the end of 1917, he wanted to take Leeper as his chief assistant, but at the last moment Leeper opted not to join him, feeling that he would be more useful on the home front, keeping an eye on Russian exiles like Maxim. So Lockhart took Captain Hicks instead.

Maxim's introduction to Vickers probably came through his friend Nikolai Klishko (or Klyshko), a fellow Bolshevik from Russia, resident in London since 1907. Klishko worked as a draughtsman and translator for Vickers, and partnered a beautiful English girl named Phyllis. Maxim regularly went round to their house in Hampstead High Street to talk with Klishko (in Russian, so as not to involve Phyllis in their politics).

In the summer of 1913, Maxim travelled to Geneva to attend a lecture by Lenin. Although he had seen the inside of prisons in

France, Germany and Russia, he made no attempt to disguise himself, apart from travelling under a false name. Tatiana Fyodorovna Lyudvinskaya, a Party member since 1903, recalled that 'Litvinov arrived in a Russian blouse with a belt and gave the impression of being a typical professional Bolshevik'.[2] After the lecture, he and Lenin had a long talk together. Lenin was forty-three by then, and Maxim thirty-seven, not a great difference in age, and they were of like mind, but Maxim was always most respectful of his elder.

Soon after his return to his shabby lodgings in Mornington Crescent, Maxim had a surprise visit from the Klishkos. Phyllis was shocked to see the conditions he was living in and at once invited him to join them in their house in Hampstead. Some weeks later, he moved in and informed Lenin of his new address. Lenin wrote back appointing him the official representative of the Russian SDLP in the International Socialist Bureau (ISB), and asking whether the mandate should be made out in the name of Litvinov or Harrison – one of Maxim's many aliases. It was a turning point in his life; thereafter he was an international political figure.

Following the International Socialist Congress of Paris of 1900, a permanent Socialist Bureau had been established which met periodically between congresses. Membership of the Bureau was fluid, each country sending one to three representatives at a time, with the result that many leading figures of the socialist movement, and several future heads of state or government were members at one time or another. For the fourteenth meeting in 1912, Lenin entrusted Maxim with arranging for the policies and decisions of the Central Committee of the RSDLP to be translated into English, French and German. The fifteenth meeting, held in London on 13 and 14 December 1913, was particularly important, being attended by all the leaders of the Second International and the Socialist parties of Europe – only Rosa Luxemburg failed to turn up – plus the principal Mensheviks, including those who had begun to campaign for the liquidation of the underground revolutionary party. Lenin, who had stayed back in Switzerland because of his wife's ill health, charged Maxim with confronting the Mensheviks' and Liquidators' attack on the Russian Social-Democratic movement.

On the morning when Lenin's letter of instructions arrived in Hampstead, Phyllis Klishko, who tended to mother Maxim, encouraging him to dress more warmly and to feed himself properly – neither of which he could afford – greeted him with, 'There's a letter here for you, Maxim, but it's not from a woman, judging by the envelope: it doesn't smell of scent'.[3] He took it and hurried out.

During the conference, Maxim wrote at least eight letters to Lenin; they are entertaining – 'The Liquidators ran around all day like poisoned mice, whispering to each other, putting their heads together, and writing, writing, writing. I could not make it out'[4] – and also illustrative of his calm pertinacity and steadfast Bolshevik position. Lenin was pleased with him, for he always kept his head and was perfectly organized.

A congress of the International Socialist Bureau was planned for mid-1914 in Vienna, and at Lenin's request Maxim began preparing to attend it. But just at this point Williams and Norgate gave up publishing translated books, and Maxim lost his job. 'Dear friend,' he wrote to Lenin, 'I'm afraid I shan't be able to go to Vienna. Can't take a vacation because my contract runs out in three weeks. I'll be free in June and July – free of all money, too. It follows that I cannot afford the trip'.[5] As it was, the opening of the First World War scuppered the plans for a congress in Vienna. It also brought a steady stream of political refugees to London.

Like all these exiles, Maxim lived from hand to mouth. He was honorary secretary of the Russian Herzen Circle in London, where in the evenings semi-starved emigrés were served coffee, buns and sandwiches prepared by Anna, the wife of Theodore Rothstein. Born to a family that sought refuge from persecution by moving to London in 1891, Rothstein was one of the founders of the British Communist Party; in 1921 he was appointed Soviet Ambassador to Iran, and made a member of the Collegium of the People's Commissariat for Foreign Affairs in 1922. Later he was director of the Institute of World Economy and Politics in Moscow and a member of the USSR Academy of Sciences. He survived the purges to die a natural death in Moscow in 1953.

In 1915 Maxim solicited donations to a fund in aid of his fellow émigrés. The list of contributions that was printed in *The Times* on 4 February 1915 makes for interesting reading and reveals his own limited resources. The Military Fund for Aid to Russians contributed £170, and the New York Aid Fund £20.10.8. Further down the list were contributions from private persons: the well-known actress Lydia Yavorskaya (Princess Baryatinskaya), who was stranded in London owing to the war, contributed the proceeds from her performances of *Anna Karenina* on her British tour, amounting to £430.11.4; Fanny Stepniak, the widow of the famous Russian revolutionary whom we met in chapter 2, gave £3.15; Nikolai Klishko £1.10; Mrs Rothstein gave 10 shillings; and, lastly, Litvinov 2 shillings.

Exceptional among these exiles was Georgy Chicherin (1872–1936), whom we have already seen as the second Bolshevik Commissar for Foreign Affairs. Maxim met him with increasing frequency, particularly at the Herzen Circle where they discussed world affairs; Maxim was pleased to observe how the erstwhile Menshevik was gravitating towards the Bolshevik point of view. They also met at the flat of a Russian émigré, Wolf Feitelson. On one occasion, when all the other guests were starting their meal, Chicherin, Maxim, and an Englishman named Simon were still vigorously setting the world to rights in the next room. Their hostess, Feitelson's wife Ida, also a Russian émigré, exclaimed in exasperation to her other guests, 'To listen to those young men, you would think they were foreign ministers!' All three did eventually become foreign ministers; the Englishman, as Sir John Simon, was British Foreign Secretary from 1931 to 1935. He became 1st Viscount Simon GCSI GCVO OBE PC when he was made Lord High Chancellor in 1940. Chicherin we already know. It remains to tell how Maxim became a minister too.

Ivy and Maxim in England, ca. 1916

With great difficulty he found work as a commercial traveller for a firm selling agricultural machinery. It was about this time that he met Ivy. They say that opposites attract; at any rate, this seems to have been true in their case. 'She was untidy, unpunctual, talkative, and defiant. He was exact, punctilious, disciplined, and taciturn,' writes John Carswell (whose mother was Ivy's best friend in England).[6] By this time she had had a second novel published, *The Questing Beast,* which W. H. Smith refused to handle because a

seduction scene in it was too explicit. She was dedicated to literature, and completely indifferent to politics. He was indifferent to
literature and dedicated to a secret political cause, to which he was
prepared to sacrifice everything, although he had not the words to
express his commitment. In fact, he seems to have told Ivy very
little about his past. It is possible that he did not even explain why
he was absent from her on Valentine's Day 1915, although they were
lovers by then: that was the day the conference of the Socialist
parties of the Entente countries opened in London.

In an attempt to gag the Russian internationalists, Mensheviks
and Socialist-Revolutionaries had been invited to represent Russia,
but not the Bolsheviks. Lenin asked Maxim to expose this
manoeuvre – but he had not been invited to attend. So Maxim did
what he was to do years later at the League of Nations and at international conferences, whenever it was vitally necessary to make the
Bolshevik standpoint known to the world at large: he turned up
without an invitation, requested the right to speak, and when this
was refused, simply walked onto the platform and began addressing the assembly. On this occasion, he was not allowed to finish,
but he sent Lenin a full report; a month later Lenin published in the
Sotsial-Demokrat the statement that Maxim had prepared to read.
During the following weeks, he toured all the groups of Russian
expatriates in Britain, speaking on behalf of Lenin. Absences like
these were something that Ivy had to get used to.

The activities of the revolutionaries among these Russian
émigrés, generally referred to as nihilists and notorious for their
illegal and often violent means of collecting funds, had long been a
headache for the Metropolitan police. The Siege of Sidney Street
was merely the worst of many similar incidents. In wartime Britain,
even though Russia was an ally, the police paid ever closer attention
to these exiles. In the summer of 1915, Phyllis Klishko was summoned to the local police station, where she was questioned at
length about Maxim – where he went, who he met, what he talked
about, and who came to see him. Phyllis could only say that he was

a fine man, very punctilious and polite, for she knew nothing of his political activities. She did not even know that her partner Nikolai was a Bolshevik, with a Party code name.

Then two CID men came and took Maxim to the police station, where he was questioned about Klishko. He could not help them. He was asked about his correspondence with Lenin and the activities of the Bolshevik group. He assured them that he was not violating any wartime regulations, and he was released. As a result of this intimidation, Maxim began to maintain an even lower profile.

It was in this climate that he and Ivy got married, on 22 February 1916. Neither of them was sure that they were doing the right thing. 'I nearly didn't marry him,' she recalled many years later. 'Don't you feel we've burned our sheeps?' he asked on the first evening of their married life. 'Boats,' corrected Ivy, without answering his question.[7] Neither was the kind of person who would go back on a commitment. She respected him and he admired her.

While correcting Maxim's English, and encouraging him to read English literature – the only use he saw in Trollope was the understanding of English society that it brought him – Ivy began learning Russian and complained when Maxim dragged her off to concerts in the evening. Beethoven and Mozart were his refuge; only much later in life did Ivy begin to appreciate music; she actually became a music teacher.

Less than a year into their marriage, their son Mikhail (known as Misha) was born; shortly after that came the news of the February revolution and the abdication of the Tsar. Maxim was so overjoyed that, as he reported in a journal he dictated to Ivy, in his excitement he tried to shave with the toothpaste and got into the bath without turning on the taps. Suddenly, he was found to be an expert on Russia; newspaper reporters came to their door to record his views on current events, and he advised them that Lenin was at that moment on his way to St Petersburg. Did he know Lenin, then? asked Ivy. She had no more idea of the correspondence between the two men than of the details of his past life.

Russian exiles flooded into London from the diaspora, all wanting to return to their homes; the only practicable route was to sail from Scotland and enter Russia through Sweden and Finland. Chicherin set up a Delegates Committee, and Maxim obtained funds from the old Russian Embassy. Between the two of them and a secretary, they prepared papers for hundreds of their compatriots, providing subsistence, hotel and travel allowances. Every day, groups of thirty to forty left by train for Aberdeen. Maxim would have loved to be among them, but Lenin thought he could be more useful if he remained in Britain, where he could both help the exiles and sway public opinion in favour of the Bolsheviks. This was a relief for Ivy, who had by now realized, with no small dismay, where her husband really wanted to be.

Unfortunately, Chicherin had not Maxim's caution; his adverse comments about Kerensky's government were reported and the British authorities took the opportunity to arrest him and hold him in Brixton prison without charge. Maxim worked tirelessly for his release, keeping Lenin abreast of the situation. In the end, the Sovnarcom (the Council of People's Commissars) informed the British government that no British subject, not even Ambassador Buchanan, would be allowed to leave Russia until Chicherin was freed. London capitulated: the exchange took place in January 1918, and Chicherin replaced Trotsky as Commissar for Foreign Affairs, a post he retained until 1930, when he retired and Maxim succeeded him. (Chicherin died a natural death in 1936, thereby escaping the purges that were just beginning.) Soon after Chicherin had left, Maxim, accompanied by Theodore Rothstein and Rex Leeper, met Bruce Lockhart in a Lyons Corner House and briefed him on his mission.

Meanwhile, in the summer of 1917, Ivy and Maxim had taken a walking tour in the Forest of Dean, with Misha in an improvised baby carrier on their backs. It was probably the only carefree holiday of their entire lives. They both enjoyed walking, although the part that Maxim seems to have loved best was planning their route.

They visited the Meynells at Greatham, where they learned a word game that was to remain with them for the rest of their lives. It was a form of anagramming, which they called 'words in a word': the aim was to see how many different words they could form by combining letters from a relatively long word (without recourse to a dictionary, of course). In later years, Maxim regularly played it during tedious meetings of the Soviet Supreme. Ivy became an expert, finding no less than seventy-one different words in 'pertinacious' when she was 87. She would have been a champion at Scrabble.

When news of the October Revolution and the triumph of the Bolsheviks reached London, Maxim immediately began writing – or rather, dictating to Ivy – *The Bolshevik Revolution: its rise and meaning*, which was published by the Socialist Party in March 1918. It's a valuable insider's account but, being written in London, it presents an idealist's view of what actually happened. It must have been an eye-opener for Ivy. The following year, there was an enlarged edition to which she contributed a chapter, updating the account to the end of 1918. The similarity of style suggests that Ivy revised her husband's text (unless of course she cleverly imitated his style in her addendum).

On 3 January 1918, their lives changed for ever: radio stations in St Petersburg announced that Maxim Litvinov had been appointed Russian Plenipotentiary (i.e. Ambassador) of the Russian Soviet Republic to Great Britain. The news was all over the evening papers in London. From his modest lodgings on Hillfield Road, Maxim wrote his first diplomatic note, informing the Foreign Secretary, Sir Arthur Balfour, of his appointment. Balfour, who did not wish to recognize Bolshevik Russia, declined to receive him and delegated liaison to Rex Leeper. The Russian Embassy, still imbued with an authority that had gone with the Tsar, would not allow Maxim to use its premises. Not to be outdone, he persuaded the bank that handled the Embassy's funding from St Petersburg to give him the money instead, and with that he rented a house in Victoria Street, part Embassy, part Consulate, and part home for his family.

In mid-January 1918, before they moved, the *Weekly Despatch* reported that

Life has completely changed in the Litvinov household, and all Hillfield Road is affected by the change. There are taxicabs and callers and Pressmen and messenger-boys all day and the neighbours are agog with excitement. Greatness has been thrust upon them also, and if you ring the Litvinovs' bell and nobody answers, some friendly neighbour can tell you just when they went out and when they are likely to return.

Ivy took all this in her stride; although she must have been immensely proud of her husband, becoming an ambassador's wife certainly did not go to her head. When the *Weekly Despatch* reporter rang at the door, she 'received [him] in the little room which is office, sitting-room, and the playroom of Misha Litvinov aged one year.' Described as 'tall and slender, with mobile features, dark eyes, and hair bobbed in the fashion which Chelsea borrowed from Russia some years ago,' Ivy protested gently:

We do not wish to be written up, and I absolutely will not discuss political questions or our plans with you, but I'll give you some tea and show you my son instead.

We are going to try to take a house with a little more room and a telephone, as that is necessary. In fact I never dreamed how necessary a telephone was till two weeks ago.

I cannot even say much about my husband because he would not like it. He simply wants to do his work and be undisturbed in that, but he cannot. This used to be a refuge for him, this little room, but it is not any more, for though he has an office in the City, people *will* come out here, and even my best efforts as a policewoman and guardian of the peace are not always effectual.

I am not really his secretary, though I do help him with his correspondence. He speaks and writes English splendidly, but he has so much to do, he cannot get through it all.

She closed the interview with a comment that showed where her interest really lay:

We are very ignorant about Russia, most of us here. Why, even Englishmen and Englishwomen who consider themselves well read will tell you they know nothing of Russian literature, one of the greatest, if not the greatest, literatures in the world. And how can you know the people if you know nothing of their literature?[8]

In August 1918, she had her second child, a daughter called Tatiana (Tania). At the same time, there occurred events that were to separate her from her husband for two full years. Britain sent troops to aid the White Army at Archangel, securing the arms and ammunition that had been supplied to Russia in support of its fight against Germany – in effect, rejecting the Bolsheviks and invading its erstwhile ally; thereupon the government's attitude towards Maxim changed overnight. Soon after, he found he could not enter the Russian Mission when he arrived there one morning; the owner of the building had decided that it was too dangerous to house such an institution and changed the lock on the door. When Maxim protested, he tore up the lease. Maxim took him to court.

> The court found that the owner of the house was, indeed, guilty of breach of contract. The owner argued that I, Litvinov, engaged in dangerous 'propaganda' against King and country. Thereupon, the court took the houseowner's side. It ruled that, though he had unilaterally breached the contract, my application should be turned down. It was useless to appeal to any higher instance. As a result, the Russian People's Embassy at 82 Victoria Street ceased to exist. I removed it to my own flat at 11 Bigwood Avenue, Golder's Green.[9]

Worse was to come. Following Fanny Kaplan's attempt to assassinate Lenin on 30 August, Bruce Lockhart was arrested in Moscow. Remembering how the Bolsheviks had reacted to the detention of Chicherin, the British government had Maxim arrested. His account continues,

> A few days after my arrest, Leeper came to see me in my cell. The reason for his visit was obvious. Before my arrest, the Foreign Office was able to contact the Soviet government through me.

There was no other way of communicating with Moscow (for Lockhart was in prison). The day I was arrested, this thread between London and Moscow was cut. Yet, owing to Lockhart's arrest, London was compelled to start some sort of negotiations with Moscow – if only to secure his release. But how? The Foreign Office sent Leeper to see me. He asked me to dispatch a coded message to Moscow with Britain's proposal for exchanging me for Lockhart. I told Leeper I would send no messages from a prison cell: either the British government considered me a plenipotentiary of the Soviet government, in which case I should have my freedom, or it considered me a convict, and should not ask me to send any coded messages. It would have to choose. Leeper went away empty-handed.

Finally, my words took effect. After ten days in the cell, I returned home; and with me, for I demanded it categorically, all the other people of my mission. True, after my release Scotland Yard agents were attached to me, and followed me day and night. But I was free, and now agreed to forward the Foreign Office proposal to the Soviet government.[10]

Moscow accepted the proposed swap, which took some weeks to arrange. Meanwhile, Maxim was watched, night and day. When he left the house, a policeman outside would say, 'Morning, Mr Litvinov.' Another would touch his helmet at the tube station. And it was like that throughout his day, ending with 'G'night, Mr Litvinov' as he walked home. In the end, it was really quite pleasant compared with what he had experienced in Russia – and continued to experience there for the rest of his life, when he never knew who was spying on him, or how, or when. Many years later, Ivy had one of their garden benches repaired. In a hollowed-out leg, a bugging device was discovered.

In 1918, women and diplomats' dependants were largely invisible: the Foreign Office had no thought for Ivy and her children. So it must have been with the heaviest of hearts that she said goodbye to Maxim at the beginning of October; she was not to see him for two years, or live with him again for another year after that. This was perhaps not such a bad thing, for Maxim was heading for a country in the grip of the Red Terror, during which the newly formed Cheka killed anything from 50,000 to 140,000, or even (for estimates vary greatly) more than one-and-a-half million Russians.

Leaving England, Maxim travelled to Oslo (which was still called Christiania at this point) and waited for news that Lockhart had crossed the border into Finland, whereupon he set out for St Petersburg, arriving there at the end of October, just in time for the first anniversary of the Revolution. The state of the country was far worse than anything he had imagined; the people were ragged and starving. Members of the Party were little better off. Yet when he met Lenin, who asked 'What about your family?' he answered confidently,

'My wife is most eager to come.'

'Your Englishwoman won't find it easy,' was Lenin's response. Here he was more considerate than the British had been.

Awaiting conditions suitable for Ivy and their two very young children, Maxim plunged into his career as a statesman and diplomat. He re-created the Foreign Office, the Narcomindel, and recruited its staff, becoming a key figure in shaping Soviet foreign policy right up until the mid-1940s. A superb administrator, he headed the People's Commissariat for State Control, setting up a Central Bureau of Complaints. Adopted by all Soviet Russia's central institutions, this agency played a big part in combating bureaucracy in the 1920s and 30s.

Back in England, Ivy was left in the most meaningless period of her life, a kind of limbo. Throughout this period she was supported by her closest friends, Catherine Carswell and, especially, the Meynells at Greatham. Thus she got to know Viola's brother Francis Meynell. For all his upper-class Anglo-Catholic background, he was a Socialist, working as an assistant editor on George Lansbury's *Daily Herald*. Both he and Lansbury went to Copenhagen in November 1919, joining up with the MP James O'Grady, who was negotiating with Maxim an exchange of British prisoners of war against Russian prisoners taken at Archangel. Francis brought Maxim news of Ivy and returned with news for her. He also had two strings of pearls, hidden in a jar of butter. They were intended to help fund the *Daily Herald,* which was in financial difficulties, but when the story was leaked in the conservative press, he was obliged to leave the newspaper.

A few months afterwards, Ivy herself managed to meet Maxim in Copenhagen, and this joyful reunion resulted in a third pregnancy. Then Maxim was appointed Soviet Ambassador to Latvia, Lithuania, Finland and Estonia, based in Tallinn, from 1921. Ivy sailed, with Misha and Tania (now aged three and two), to join him there, but the child she was carrying, a boy, was born during the journey and died soon after, overshadowing their reunion.

After a year in Estonia, during which they were visited by Isadora Duncan, they went to Moscow, so it was 1922 before Ivy started to live in Soviet Russia, where Maxim was always extremely busy. It was soon after their arrival that Arthur Ransome engineered the meeting between Maxim and Hodgson that resolved the 'Curzon ultimatum' (and saw Ransome play Nikolai Krylenko at chess). Unlike her husband, Ivy had few opportunities to meet foreign visitors at this time: in the 1920s, spouses were not invited to attend formal dinners. It was a lonely life – for them both.

As Max Eastman revealed in his autobiography, by 1924 Maxim 'was already disillusioned to the point of cynicism about the outcome of the Revolution.'[11] At that particular moment, he was objecting to the New Economic Policy, which he felt 'sold out' to capitalism and betrayed the ideals of the Revolution. But it was more than his life was worth to express his opinion. Rather than leave (for Maxim was not a quitter), he chose to remain and to quietly and discreetly work for the values he believed in.

The Bolshevik Commissars were provided with comfortable housing – compared with ordinary people – but they certainly did not live in style. For instance, the one thing for which ordinary women envied upper Party women, in the years immediately following the Revolution, was their access to good clothing. Admittedly, the clothes they had access to were rarely new, but they were of fine quality, being the clothes left behind by the bourgeois and aristocrats who had fled or been killed. That source of supply did not last long. Thereafter, they had to put up with the best that was available, while the rest of the population was obliged to dress in shoddy clothing. That Party members should enjoy privileges such as these was one of the complaints of the Kronstadt sailors, for they were an offence against the egalitarian ideal of communism that they had fought for in 1917. The Kronstadt revolt changed nothing; the practice continued and the privileges amplified – and continued after the collapse of the Soviet state at the end of the 1980s. President Putin may well be the richest man in the world; his net worth is estimated to be in excess of US$200 billion.

In the 1920s, Sovnarcom used Maxim as its roving ambassador, styled Deputy People's Commissar for Foreign Affairs, forever being sent abroad at a moment's notice to negotiate this or that, or speak for Russia at some international conference or another. For twenty years, his was the positive face that Russia showed the world, a friendly, teddy-bear figure, who believed that 'Soviet power and influence could best be promoted by cultivating areas of common interest by positive, albeit carefully circumscribed, collaboration with the West.'[12] A man of calm and conciliation, he became famous for firmly stating that 'peace is indivisible'. His international reputation was probably what preserved his life during the Great Purge of the 1930s, when Stalin wiped out all the Old Bolsheviks. Maxim's friend Klishko was executed, and his wife Phyllis, English though she was, spent almost thirty years in a Siberian gulag.

All this left Maxim little time for family life, which he clearly enjoyed, proving to be a loving and attentive father to Misha and Tania. When the children were older, Ivy was allowed to accompany him, sometimes as his official secretary, on journeys abroad, but she also remained alone with them for weeks at a time. Over the years, she came to meet a great many world figures and – Ivy being Ivy – she always belittled them when she described them to her English friends. 'She regarded men of power, authority and doctrine with a kind of withering cynicism which dwelt on the shape of their eyebrows, the cut of their suits, and the convincingness or otherwise of their false teeth.'[13] This attitude brought her few friends in Soviet Russia; Korney Chukovsky, the children's writer, was a notable exception. Her daughter Tania became a life-long friend of Chukovsky's daughter Lydia, a poet who was close to Anna Akhmatova. The woman to whom Ivy felt closest was Alexandra Kollontai (1872–1952). Like Ivy, Kollontai was an out-spoken and opinionated woman, a writer, and an early supporter of Lenin. She served as the Commissar for Social Welfare in the first Soviet government. She disagreed with Lenin from 1918 onwards, and was consequently sidelined, obliged to spend much of her life abroad, representing Soviet Russia in countries from Norway to Mexico. Ivy was full of admiration for her.

In Soviet Russia, everybody worked; Ivy was set to translating. I estimate that she translated into English some three dozen works by great Russian writers such as Pushkin, Turgenev, and Tolstoy. In this capacity she was in contact with Gorky, and surely met Moura in his entourage, although no record of this seems to have survived. When Tania grew up, she sometimes collaborated with her mother. Brought up and educated in Russia, both children were perfectly bilingual, whereas Ivy's Russian, although fluent, was not exactly idiomatic. So she translated into English and Tania mainly into Russian.

Having published two novels before she left England, Ivy always wanted to write more, but her life in Soviet Russia did not lend itself to inspiration or offer the free time required for extended composition. So she started to write short stories, and she was good at it. But she was very critical of her own work and few complete versions of her stories survived when finally she returned to England. She was in her eighties, then, when her best short stories were written, published, and collected as *She Knew She Was Right*, in 1971.

Even before Maxim was promoted to Commissar for Foreign Affairs in 1930, he regularly participated in the work of the League of Nations, and became well known and liked for his balanced views. In his *History of the League Nations*, Walters writes,

> Whatever may be thought of the quality and purpose of [Litvinov's] government, the long series of statements, the speeches in the Assembly and the Council, the Conferences, and the Committees of which he was a member between 1937 and 1939 can hardly be read without an astonished admiration. Nothing in the annals of the League can compare with them, in frankness, in debating power, in the acute diagnosis of each situation. No contemporary statesman can point to such a record of criticism justified, and prophecies fulfilled.[14]

Ivy's belief in him was wholly justified.

Meanwhile, she discovered C. K. Ogden's Basic English, and exchanged many letters with him about it. Thinking that his reduction of the vast vocabulary of English to a mere 850 words would help Russians learn the language, she began teaching it, using educational booklets that she wrote herself. In the mid-1930s, however, Maxim took a mistress, a young woman whom Ivy had invited to live with them out of pity for her situation. Ivy had always considered theirs an open marriage (although she took advantage of this only outside the USSR), but his flagrant infidelity was more than she could bear. From the autumn of 1936 onwards, she arranged to teach Basic English at a teacher-training college in Yekaterinburg (Sverdlovsk to the Soviets), where the Romanovs were assassinated, almost 1500 km east of Moscow. Years later, she would be recognized in the street by grateful ex-students, who embraced her with joy and disbelief at her survival. She enjoyed teaching, and quite liked the solitude, but sorely missed her children, although she was permitted to make phone calls to them, and they visited her several times.

The moment Maxim fell from grace in the summer of 1939, to be replaced by Vyacheslav Molotov (whom Maxim cordially despised), Tania called her mother, and Ivy came at once. Maxim's mistress took this opportunity to move on, for in Soviet Russia it was dangerous to associate with a man who had fallen out of favour. From then on, Ivy remained at his side.

Maxim's disgrace was not entirely due to his disagreement with Stalin's new foreign policy, which led to the pact of non-aggression with Nazi Germany. There was also 'his Jewishness, which made him totally unacceptable to the Nazis.'[15] And then, as Maxim and Ivy discovered later, Ivy herself had contributed to his fall. She had entrusted a letter, in which she had openly expressed her fears and feelings, to a visiting American couple. Her faith in them was misplaced, and the letter ended up on Stalin's desk. Confronting Maxim with it, Stalin observed, 'You have an extremely courageous and outspoken wife. You should tell her to calm herself. She is not threatened.'[16]

The implication that Maxim was threatened was of course not lost on him, or Ivy, and they supported each other in the face of imminent death. For years, Ivy had kept a packed suitcase under her bed in case she should be suddenly taken off to a gulag. Now Maxim played card games long into the night, determined not to be taken in his pyjamas, and slept with a loaded revolver under his pillow. They arranged that, should there be a knock on the door in the wee hours, Ivy would answer it; if it was indeed the secret police she would give a special knock on his bedroom door so that he should not be taken alive. A show trial was arranged – but not held. There was also a plan, never executed, to have him die in a road accident, run over by a truck, close to their dacha. (Revealed by Khrushchev in his memoirs, this gave rise to a widespread belief that it was actually the cause of his death.) They lived on, in fear and trembling, until November 1941, not knowing that Stalin had chosen to keep Maxim 'on ice' in case of need.

That moment came when the Nazis broke their pact of non-aggression (in which Maxim had never believed) and invaded Russia. He reacted at once by writing two letters, one to Molotov, the Commissar for Foreign Affairs, asking for a job, and the other to the local blood transfusion centre. Being now 65, he was turned down as a blood donor. Molotov summoned him to Moscow. Sheinis reports: 'His speech was dry and official. He asked what job Maxim expected. Maxim replied, "Your job, of course." That was the end of their conversation.' A few days later, it was Stalin who summoned him. I'll quote Zinovy Sheinis once again, for his biography supplies telling detail (the veracity of which I cannot vouch for, however; it sounds romanticized to me):

Stalin looked at Litvinov's clothes, and asked:

'Why not a black suit?'

Litvinov replied phlegmatically, 'It's moth-eaten.'[17]

On the following day, Maxim was re-enrolled in the People's Commissariat for Foreign Affairs.

Maxim's visit to the Kremlin did not go unnoticed, and there was speculation in the Allied press as to its significance; they had not forgotten him. Requests for articles and interviews started to come in and his writing appeared in British and American papers. Stalin seized the opportunity to ask Maxim to address the English-speaking world on the radio. On 8 July 1941, he told listeners as far away as Australia what he thought of the current situation, denouncing Hitler's bid to gain world supremacy. He ended with the words, 'The peoples of the Soviet Union ... have risen as one man to fight a patriotic war against Hitlerism, and will fight that war along with other freedom-loving peoples until fascist obscurantism and barbarity are wiped out.'[18] It was rousing stuff, and published in all the Soviet newspapers. So he was allowed to give more radio talks.

Ivy was evacuated, along with almost the entire staff of the Commissariat for Foreign Affairs, to Samara (called Kuibyshev by Soviet Russia from 1935 to 1991); it was considered a safe haven, theoretically out of range of Nazi bombers. On 15 August 1941, Maxim wrote to tell her that he had received a telegram from the editor of *Reynolds News,* asking for a contribution. I sent one, but had difficulties with the translation. I have neither a stenographer nor an English typist, and cannot write by hand. So I had the piece translated at the Informbureau, but the translation wasn't good enough. I had to make corrections, and there was no one to retype the copy, and I don't even have a typewriter.'[19]

Such were the conditions under which this favoured spokesman for Soviet Russia was obliged to work.

But then he overstepped an invisible line. Asked by foreign correspondents what he thought of the Soviet-German pact of non-aggression, he told them that the West

had done all it could to goad Hitler's Germany against the Soviet Union by secret deals and provocative moves. In the circumstances, the Soviet Union could either accept the German proposal for a non-aggression treaty and thus secure a period of peace in which to redouble preparations to repulse the aggressor, or turn down Germany's proposal and let the warmongers in the Western camp push the Soviet Union into an armed conflict with Germany in unfavourable circumstances and in a setting of complete isolation. In this situation, the Soviet government was compelled to make the difficult choice and conclude a non-aggression treaty with Germany.[20]

The interview was censored and Maxim was suspended for giving an unauthorised interview to foreign journalists.

As the Nazis advanced on the USSR, along a front that ran from the far north down to much of the Ukraine, Stalin realized that to defend the south, with its essential supplies of foodstuff and oil, he desperately needed Allied support, especially heavy weaponry and ammunition. So he chose to send Maxim's friendly face to the United States as the Soviet Ambassador – a mirror image of the events of 1917. This time, Ivy was to go with him – but not their children, who were now grown up, of course. They were to travel by air, but a series of missed connections (for which the Russians blamed the British) meant that instead of flying across the Atlantic, they were turned eastwards, across the Middle East, Asia, and the Pacific, a gruelling twenty-five-day journey in unpressurized aeroplanes (which caused Maxim considerable discomfort). On arrival in the United States, Maxim warned his hosts that the Japanese would soon attack. Unlike his remarkably prescient predictions in the late 1930s as to how Nazi Germany would behave, he probably benefited on this occasion from superior Russian intelligence. In the event, they arrived in Washington on 7 December 1941, the day the Japanese attacked Pearl Harbour; the US and Soviet Russia became instant allies.

The two years the Litvinovs spent in Washington were undoubtedly the happiest of their lives. They were made welcome everywhere, and it became a personal triumph for Ivy, 'whose wit and charm enliven the traditional dullness of Washington's social events.'[21] They each took the opportunity to write their memoirs, Ivy of the early years of her life and Maxim of his political career and ideas. He firmly believed that Moscow should maintain good relations with the West; he was disappointed – but not surprised – that his views were disregarded by Stalin. As his policies became increasingly at variance with his instructions, he was finally recalled 'for consultation'. At this point, both he and Ivy very seriously considered the possibility of not returning to Moscow, but they had left their family there, and knew how Stalin would punish them all. Maxim obeyed orders, and Ivy allowed herself six months more in America, using the time to research and write an autobiographical article, 'A Visit to D.H. Lawrence,' which was published in *Harper's Bazaar.*

When finally she left, she placed Maxim's heretical memoir and other papers in a security box in a New York bank, and left the key with a trusted friend, Joseph Freeman. (Freeman was the editor of the *New Masses,* a radical socialist journal which took its name from the periodical edited by Max Eastman in the nineteen teens.) Two years later, fearing what Stalin would do to them and their family if ever the memoir came into his hands, Ivy asked Freeman to destroy it, which he did, witnessed by a mutual friend appointed by Ivy. In his biography of Ivy, Carswell tells a slightly different story. According to him, in the mid-1950s, Ivy was summoned to the Lubianka and shown 'a sheaf of yellowed papers' and asked to confirm their authenticity, without being allowed 'to examine or even read them.'[22] Carswell claimed that the KGB had somehow managed to lay its hands on Maxim's memoir in the New York bank. However, Elena S. Danielson researched this matter six years after Carswell's book was published. On the basis of the documents that both Ivy and Joseph Freeman deposited in the Hoover Institution Archives, Danielson confirms that Freeman destroyed the memoir. This version is the more probable. As it was, after Ivy had admitted that the 'yellowed papers' (whatever they were) were genuine, so far as she could tell from a distance, the matter was dropped, and they have not resurfaced since then.

On his return to the USSR in August 1943, Maxim managed to express some of his unorthodox opinions in an article published in *Zvezda*, signed 'N. Malinin', proposing a new institution to replace the moribund League of Nations. Four weeks later, he admitted that he was the author of it. It re-appeared with official approval in August 1944 as part of the Soviet Memorandum for the Dumbarton Oaks conference which laid the foundations for the future United Nations.[23] He was also allowed the extraordinary freedom of expressing his own views in interviews with the Western press. In them he opined that the Yalta agreement, which Stalin saw as his greatest diplomatic victory, was in fact a disaster for the future of international relations. How right he was! So of course he was pensioned off, with a comfortable flat and a modest pension – and *no interviews*. He was invited back once to an official reception – probably by mistake – and was heard to complain to the correspondent of the *New Statesman* that Russia consistently 'refused to believe that goodwill could be the basis of any policy.' As usual, he was perfectly right: it is a failing that vitiated Soviet Russia's politics, both at home and abroad, from the start and continues to do so to this day. We have to understand that Russia, having a more Eastern mentality, views the West with mingled feelings of fear and admiration which are alien to Europeans.

Maxim lived out his final years in his official dacha, which had once belonged to Stalin's first wife Nadezhda Alliluyeva and would later be Khrushchev's. Ivy looked after him through to the end, keeping the lowest of profiles to ensure that she did not attract the attention of the secret police. For instance, when the British Embassy offered to send her books, she refused them, and begged that they should send her no visitors either. Maxim died of a heart attack on the last day of 1951, thereby escaping the purge of Russian Jews that was just being unleashed by Stalin, but not without gasping to Ivy, 'Englishwoman, go home.' It was the only occasion on which he ever referred to her in this way; he was surely recalling how Lenin had referred to her, back in 1918. Despite all the years of fear, she was without bitterness; on the contrary, she triumphed, 'they did not get him!' Stubborn and independent to the last, Ivy stayed for twenty more years in Russia before requesting permission to return to England.

During these years, Ivy occupied herself by translating Russian novels and short stories into English, acknowledging the help of Tatiana, who had a better grasp of Russian. A few years ago, Sarah Young attempted to trace them and posted a list of twenty-eight items on her website. Being published in Russia, they found few readers in the West.

Ivy was surely motivated to remain by her love, which Maxim had shared, for their grandchildren; there were four of them. Tania had two girls, Masha and Vera; Masha became a reporter and in 1983 married an Englishman, Robert Godfrey Phillimore, 3rd Baron Phillimore. Had she lived that long, Ivy would surely have been delighted. Misha had a son and a daughter; his son Pavel became a physics teacher at the Institute for Chemical Technology, where he discovered *samizdat* literature (that is, clandestine copies of censored and underground publications, duplicated by hand and circulated from reader to reader). When Alexander Ginzburg and Yuri Galanskov were tried for publishing *samizdat* in 1967, Pavel and Larisa Bogoraz released an 'Appeal to World Public Opinion', calling for international protest against the closed trial. The following year Pavel was one of the participants in the brief 1968 Red Square demonstration against the Soviet invasion of Czechoslovakia. The demonstrators were immediately arrested, brutally beaten, and tried in secret. Pavel was sentenced to five years in Siberia; on his release he managed to leave for the United States. In New York, he joined fellow émigré dissident Valery Chalidze in publishing *A Chronicle of Human Rights in the USSR*, which documented political repression.

After returning to England in 1973, Ivy was finally free to publish her writing (in the *New Yorker*, the *Manchester Guardian*, *Blackwood's Magazine*, *Vogue*). Friends and publishers begged her to write her memoirs, a 'Sorterbiography', as she called it, and she started on it. She had already written and published on her early years and her meeting with Maxim, in fictionalized form, but telling her story straight proved much harder to write. A fragmentary typescript, called 'Worlds Unrealized', exists, but it consists of notes rather than a continuous text. She died on 16 April 1977, in her 88th year, leaving her memoir unfinished.

After a lifetime of repressing her desire to express herself, knowing that no matter how hard she tried to hide her writing in Soviet Russia, every word that she put on paper would be read by the secret police, and could easily cost her her life, the vast openness of complete freedom disorientated her. Moreover, Ivy felt that her life was hers, and private. She belonged to a generation that had little in common with millennials, who want to share the least details of their lives, minute by minute, on social media. Discretion, especially after living in Soviet Russia, was the order of the day for her.

An anecdote from the time when she and Maxim were in America during the war may help to clarify this. Sitting in a motorcade, Ivy heard an admirer call out, 'For us, you are a symbol of the Russian people.' Without batting an eyelid, she called back: 'It's terrible being a symbol.'[24]

Once home in England, she loved seeing her family. Tania managed to come and live with her during her last year, and it was a joy to her that many of her grandchildren also found ways to come over to the West. They grew up as independent and strong-minded as herself, staunch defenders of the right to individual freedom of thought and expression. This, surely, is Ivy's legacy: throughout her fifty years in Russia, she remained a solitary representative of Western culture and Western values at the heart of Soviet Russia, a living symbol – terrible though that was – forever reminding Stalin and his ephemeral minions of what she stood for. Her spirit lives on in her grandchildren and their children.

Sources

Carswell, John. *The Exile: a Life of Ivy Litvinov.* Faber, 1983.

Danielson, Elena S. 'The Elusive Litvinov Memoirs.' *Slavic Review,* Vol. 48, No. 3 (Autumn, 1989), pp. 477–83.

Eastman, Max. *Love and Revolution. My Journey through an Epoch.* New York: Random House, 1964.

Holroyd-Doveton, John. *Maxim Litvinov. A Biography.* 2nd ed., New Generation Publishing, 2015.

Litvinov, Ivy. *She Knew She Was Right.* Gollancz, 1971.

Mastny, Vojtech. 'The Cassandra in the Foreign Commissariat: Maxim Litvinov and the Cold War.' *Foreign Affairs,* Vol. 54, No.2 (January 1976), pp. 366–76.

Sheinis, Zinovy. *Maxim Litvinov* (1988). Trans. Vic Schneierson, Moscow: Progress Publishers, 1990.

Young, Sarah J. http://sarahjyoung.com/site/

Notes

1   Carswell, p.31.

2   Sheinis, p.66.

3   Sheinis, p.69.

4   Sheinis, p.73

5   Sheinis, p.77.

6   Carswell, p.80.

7   Carswell, p.80.

8   Quoted in Sheinis, pp.105–6.

9   Sheinis, p.110.

10   Sheinis, pp.111–12.

11   Eastman, p.431.

12   Mastny, p.376.

13   Carswell, p.106.

14   Francis Paul Walters, *History of the League of Nations*, p.712, quoted by Holroyd-Doveton, p.286.

15   Mastny, p.367.

16   Carswell, p.146.

17   Sheinis, p.302.

18   Sheinis, p.303.

19   Sheinis, p.304.

20   Sheinis, p.304.

21   *Life* magazine, 12 October 1942, p.115, quoted by Holroyd-Doveton, p.438.

22   Danielson, p.482.

23   See Mastny, p.369.

24   Joseph Freeman Papers, Hoover Institution Archives, Box 174, folder 7.

9 Coda

ONE OF THE FASCINATING ASPECTS of these stories is how they turn out to be interconnected. I have already pointed to some links in the course of my narrative. Here are a few more that I left out.

When Constance Garnett first met the Ertel family in 1904, she was accompanied by her son David, who was always known as Bunny. He left us an autobiography full of memories of his early years; it includes a detailed account of the visit to Russia that he made with his mother when he was twelve. (I quoted from it in Chapter 3.) It obviously made a deep impression on him.

It cannot have been long afterwards that Bunny met H. G. Wells, for he says he was thirteen or fourteen when Sir Sydney Olivier, who lived close by with his wife and four daughters, brought Wells over several times to see the Garnetts.

> I can see him now as I first saw him, a small figure, bouncing along like a rubber ball between the tall figures of Edward [Garnett] and Sydney.... On another occasion, Wells was brought by the Olivier girls alone, and I walked back with them. H. G.'s liveliness and activity dominated all of us, and I remember his instant response to Brynhild's sparkling eyes and flashing smile.[1]

Wells was always susceptible to an attractive girl who smiled and made eyes at him.

The affairs he had with these girls were the inspiration for several of his novels, which caused great anxiety among the mothers of well-brought-up young ladies. Lady Olivier forbade her daughters to read Wells' 1902 fantasy, *The Sea Lady,* which daringly questioned Edwardian mores. When the scandal of *Ann Veronica* broke in 1909, the social outrage reached even Bunny's young ears. The problem was that Wells depicted his teenage heroine as taking the initiative in establishing a sexual relationship with an older man. 'My memory,' writes Bunny, 'is that the outraged parents of this young woman [Amber Reeves] attempted to destroy Wells, who became the target for a fantastic social persecution.'[2]

The Oliviers let their daughters, who were Bunny's childhood playmates, run wild in the woods and fields around their house. There was a line of beeches into which they liked to climb, having removed their skirts or dresses for greater freedom of movement. Bunny would join them, 'sometimes amusing ourselves by climbing from the top boughs of one tree into those of the next, and so on' down the line. 'In one or two places, this could only be done by a wild leap across an intervening chasm of two or three yards.... Some of our difficult traverses took place at a height of twenty-five feet.'[3] The father of these fearless young women – dubbed 'Neo-Pagans' by Virginia Woolf – feared that they could easily fall prey to fancy-free men, so he told Wells that he was not to seek their company.

Bunny tells us that one day, at the height of the *Ann Veronica* scandal, he and Brynhild, the second eldest 'pagan', were in a Bond Street gallery when 'she suddenly caught sight of H. G., hiding from us behind some pictures.... Brynhild called out to him in her clear voice and H. G. turned and fled like a rabbit.' They 'ran him to earth' and Brynhild's cheeks 'were scarlet as she said, "I won't let you cut me, Mr Wells, so don't ever try to do so again."

'I don't think I ever saw her look lovelier than she did at that moment,'[4] was Bunny's comment. He managed to resist the girls' increasing attractions.

In the summer of 1910, Ursula Cox and her best friend Lenochka Goncharova came over from Russia for a visit to England, staying at the Oliviers' house while the family was away. (Ursula's mother was Lady Olivier's sister-in-law, so Ursula was a cousin of the Olivier daughters, the same age as Daphne Olivier.) She and her mother had become close friends of the Ertel family: in 1911 they were sharing a large flat with them in Moscow.[5] Ursula also shared the Ertels' love of the theatre, getting to know both Konstantin Stanislavski and the second director of the Moscow Art Theatre, Vladimir Nemirovich-Danchenko. It was in this context that she left her mark.

To tell this story, we have to go back to Isadora Duncan – I warned you that she pops up in almost every one of my stories. Following up on her visit to Russia in 1904, during which she so impressed Tamara Karsavina, Duncan paid a second visit in 1906, accompanied by her lover Edward Gordon Craig (1872–1966), the son of the celebrated English actress Ellen Terry. On this occasion, she introduced Craig to Stanislavski. Craig had visionary ideas for staging plays, using simple, symbolistic designs. Stanislavski, on the other hand, had become the master of modern realism; he concentrated on the actor's state of mind, drawing on the budding science of psychology. His approach became known as 'method acting', and it is still taught today. (Marlon Brando and Dustin Hoffman come to mind as practitioners of the method.) So the respective aims and ambitions of the two men were quite different, yet after their meeting Stanislavski invited Craig to help put on *Hamlet* for the 1910 season of the Moscow Art Theatre. The production was severely delayed after Stanislavski contracted typhoid fever, so it finally opened only on 5 January 1912 (23 December 1911, Old Style). It attracted worldwide attention, and had repercussions on the staging of Shakespeare throughout the twentieth century, rather as Diaghilev's Ballets Russes revolutionized ballet and other arts at the same time.

There are few eye witness accounts – the best is in Japanese – and almost no photographs of this production. The one record of the discussions that Stanislavski and Craig had together was made in April 1908 by Ursula Cox and Mikhail Lykiardopoulos, who was the Secretary of the Moscow Art Theatre. As Craig spoke no Russian and Stanislavski knew little English, Ursula and Lyki (as everyone called him) were their interpreters, and on this occasion she made a precious transcript of their discussion.[6] (It is preserved in the French National Library, in Paris.)

Shortly after the play was put on, Lyki went to visit Arthur Ransome in London (thus creating yet another internal link between stories). He obtained the rights to Ransome's book on Oscar Wilde and translated it into Russian. It was in 1918 that Lyki became a close friend of Bruce Lockhart (see page 116).

It must have been during the preparations for his production of *Hamlet* that Craig met Elena Ertel. This should not surprise us: as already mentioned, her father was not only a patron of the Theatre but also a friend of Stanislavski's sister, Zinaida Sergeyevna Sokolova and her husband Konstantin. Twenty years later, as soon as Elena made it to England, Craig began writing to her. He remembered her fondly and hoped to involve her in one of his projects, but it failed to materialize for lack of funding. She put him in contact with her brother-in-law, Jack Duddington, in his capacity as Director of the Whitechapel Art Gallery. Jack offered to exhibit some of Craig's stage designs, to help 'educate the public.'[7] Craig declined the invitation, explaining that

> The *Daily Mail, Express, Post,* etc., are all educating the public, assisted by the Church, the shopkeepers, police, and the spirit of progress.
>
> These are going one way ... I am going the other; my way is down a small and utterly uninteresting little lane.
>
> If I could oppose anything effective against the modern notions of progress, I would.[8]

He wanted to see his ideas used in the theatre, not divorced from the stage in an art gallery. But play directors needed to see his designs before they dared ask him to produce a play; hence he was rarely invited.

After that visit in 1910, Ursula and Lenochka began to haunt Bunny's mind. During the following winter, he regularly exchanged letters with Ursula. In the spring, he decided that he wanted to tell her how much he loved her. His parents found the money for the journey to Moscow, and off he went. She welcomed him very happily, 'as merry and kind as always'.[9] When finally he summoned up the courage to tell her how he felt, she was tactful and patient as she made it clear that she did not feel the same about him. Instead, she introduced him to her Moscow friends and he had a memorable experience with one of them called Lidia: she asked him to demonstrate the judo moves that he had been learning. In 1911, judo was a sport unknown in Russia – in Britain it had been introduced in 1899 – so when Ursula's mother, alerted by thuds and bumps from the living room, came in to find Bunny and Lidia entangled on the floor, she could hardly believe her eyes.

Ursula and Lenochka took Bunny to the Moscow Art Theatre. He was impressed by the plain wood interior, 'without any gilding or paint', but he was disappointed by the girls' choice of play, Maeterlinck's *Blue Bird* (which had been launched in this theatre in 1908). He would rather have seen *Uncle Vanya*, but they thought that he would not have understood much of the Chekhov; for him, though, 'the consideration of those kind girls' had deprived him of 'an experience to set beside [his] memory of Eleonora Duse'.[10] He was just too early to see Craig's *Hamlet*.

When Ursula was back in England in the summer of 1912, she joined Bunny and two friends on a boating trip on the Severn, and they had a great time together – 'a week of unblemished happiness' for him. 'We laughed a lot. Ursula's dark eyes almost vanished when she went into a roar of laughter and afterwards she would chuckle merrily for a long time.'[11] Shortly after, the Ertels came and stayed with the Garnetts 'for a wet week', as Bunny put it. He felt embarrassed that neither his family's finances nor the English weather could afford the quality of hospitality that he felt the Ertels deserved. 'But for two people,' he continues, 'the weather did not greatly matter. Harold came over every day and was greatly attracted by Lola.' Harold Hobson was Bunny's lifelong friend, 'a very handsome little dare-devil',[12] whose parents lived close by, and 'Lola' was the familiar name for Natasha's sister Elena. 'When the time came for the Ertels to go back to Russia, Harold was invited to accompany them and went with them on the ship.'[13] He did not stay long in Moscow, and on his return journey he joined Bunny in Munich, where he had gone to attend some lectures in Botany.

Harold hankered after Elena for quite some time – on 25 March 1913, Frieda Lawrence exclaimed to Bunny, 'Harold and Lola!... I hope for both their sakes they will make a success of it, but Harold is an *enfant gâté* and, like in the 'Land of Cockayne', he expects the roast pigeons to fly into his mouth!'[14] However, Elena was not so attracted to him. Bunny wrote to Ursula Cox in Moscow to find out how things stood there. She answered that Elena

> has quite enough character to do a thing if she really wants to – the difficulty with her is that she never knows what she wants. I talked to her very seriously after getting your letter and all I could get out of her was that she wanted to be let alone and not to have to make up her mind about anything. When I asked her if she loved him she said that one day she loved him and the next felt absolutely indifferent to him. She is a typical Russian neurasthenic. I have never seen anyone more apathetic and indifferent to everything that seems to me personally to make life worth living. She has an absolute horror of any definite engagement and of the idea of being bound for the future. Only one thing I can say – she certainly loves Harold more than anybody else. She is fonder of him than I have ever known her of anyone....
>
> If Harold loves her enough to wait until he is able to get work out here, and then comes and settles out here, I think she will marry him in all probability, but it's not the least use his trying to rush her into anything....
>
> As for hope, there's as much hope as he likes if only he's got the patience of an angel and will wait an indefinite time.[15]

Harold did not persevere, so the affair fizzled out and, as we know, Elena married a Mr Tupikov.

But life had another adventure in store for Harold when he arrived in Germany on his way home from Moscow in 1912. Bunny had heard from his father Edward – who was D. H. Lawrence's editor – that Lawrence was staying at Icking in the Bavarian Alps. He made contact with Lawrence, who invited Bunny come and see him and Frieda in Mayrhofen in Zillerthal. Harold tagged along too. One afternoon, while Bunny and Lawrence went off in search of Alpine flowers, Frieda took the opportunity to make love with Harold. Shortly afterwards, it was Ivy Low's turn to come and visit Lawrence (see page 193). Frieda was not going to let him play the same trick as she had, and coolly ensured that Ivy was kept at a safe distance – which left Ivy feeling hurt and puzzled.

Four years later, Ivy had a husband of her own, Maxim Litvinov. His pre-eminence among London's Russian exiles ensured that he knew Yakov Peters, who just escaped being cornered with his fellow 'anarchists' in the Siege of Sidney Street. When Peters returned to Russia after the Revolution, he was Robert Bruce Lockhart's friendly jailor, lending him a book by H. G. Wells.

That was in September 1918, the moment when Tamara Karsavina turned up unannounced in London, having escaped from Bolshevik Russia. Diaghilev was delighted to have her available again for the Ballets Russes. She had after all created most of the ballets he was putting on, and he much preferred her to Tamara's young friend, Lydia Lopokova, whom he had been employing *faute de mieux*. Quite understandably, Lydia rather resented losing the prima ballerina's limelight, but her compensation came in 1925 when she married one of Bunny Garnett's friends, the economist John Maynard Keynes.

These young people were fortunate to be in England at the time of the Revolution. Ursula Cox's mother had to be evacuated from Russia in 1919, having lost everything to the Bolsheviks, whereas Ursula had left before the First World War. She studied medicine in London and served as Birmingham's deputy medical officer for maternity and child welfare for thirty years.

Sources

Craig, Edward Gordon. Unpublished letters in a private collection.

Garnett, David. *The Golden Echo*. New York: Harcourt, Brace, 1954.

Garnett Papers in the Charles Deering McCormick Library of Special Collections & University Archives at Northwestern University, Illinois.

Lawrence, D. H. *The Letters of D. H. Lawrence*. Ed. James T. Boulton, and Lindeth Vasey. Cambridge: CUP, 2003.

Osanai, Kaoru. 'Gordon Craig's Production of *Hamlet* at the Moscow Art Theatre.' Trans. Andrew T. Tsubaki. *Educational Theatre Journal*, Vol.20, No 4, December 1968, pp.586–93.

Senelik, Laurence. *Gordon Craig's Moscow Hamlet: A Reconstruction*. Westport, Conn: Greenwood Press, 1982.

Notes

1   Garnett, p.163.
2   Garnett, p.164.
3   Garnett, p.262.
4   Garnett, pp.164–5.
5   Garnett, p.212.
6   See Senelik, p.62–71.
7   Undated letter 1 from Craig to Jack Duddington, winter 1927/28.
8   Undated letter 2 from Craig to Jack Duddington, winter 1927/28.
9   Garnett, p.213.
10 Garnett, pp.217–18.
11 Garnett, p.239.
12 Garnett, p.45.
13 Garnett, p.240.
14 Lawrence, p.533.
15 Unpublished letter from the Garnett Papers at Northwestern.